Costs and revenues

Tutorial

David Cox

osborne
BOOKS

Published by Osborne Books Limited
Unit 1B Everoak Estate
Bromyard Road
Worcester WR2 5HP
Tel 01905 748071
Email books@osbornebooks.co.uk
Website www.osbornebooks.co.uk

Design by Laura Ingham
Cover and page design image © Istockphoto.com/Petrovich9

Printed and bound by CPI Group (UK) Ltd, Croydon, CR0 4YY

British Library Cataloguing in Publication Data
A catalogue record for this book is available from the British Library

ISBN 978 1905777 310

Contents

Acknowledgements

The publisher wishes to thank the following for their help with the reading and production of the book: Jean Cox, Mike Gilbert and Claire McCarthy. Thanks are also due to Roger Petheram for his technical editorial work and to Laura Ingham for her designs for this series.

The publisher is indebted to the Association of Accounting Technicians for its help and advice to our authors and editors during the preparation of this text.

Author

David Cox has more than twenty years' experience teaching accountancy students over a wide range of levels. Formerly with the Management and Professional Studies Department at Worcester College of Technology, he now lectures on a freelance basis and carries out educational consultancy work in accountancy studies. He is author and joint author of a number of textbooks in the areas of accounting, finance and banking.

Introduction

what this book covers

This book has been written specifically to cover Learning Area 'Costs and Revenues' which combines two QCF Units in the AAT Level 3 Diploma in Accounting:

- Principles of costing
- Providing cost and revenue information

The book contains a clear text with worked examples and case studies, chapter summaries and key terms to help with revision. Each chapter has a wide range of activities, many in the style of the computer-based assessments used by AAT.

This book covers the recording and analysis of direct and indirect costs, including the allocation, apportionment and absorption of overhead costs. Methods of costing – including the use of marginal and absorption costing – are fully explained. An important aspect is the use of costing information to help with decision-making – in the short-term and long-term.

Downloadable blank documents for use with this text are available in the Resources section of www.osbornebooks.co.uk

Osborne Workbooks

Osborne Wookbooks contain practice material which helps students achieve success in their assessments. 'Costs and Revenues Workbook' contains a number of paper-based 'fill in' practice exams in the style of the computer-based assessment. Please telephone the Osborne Books Sales Office on 01905 748071 for details of mail ordering, or visit the 24-hour online shop at www.osbornebooks.co.uk

International Accounting Standards (IAS) terminology

In this book the following IAS terminology is used (UK terms shown here in brackets):

trade receivables or receivables (debtors)
trade payables or payables (creditors)
inventory (stock)
non-current assets (fixed assets)
revenue or sales revenue (sales)
income statement (profit and loss account)
statement of financial position (balance sheet)

1 An introduction to cost accounting

this chapter covers...

- This first chapter examines the purpose of cost accounting and its role in providing information to the managers of a business or organisation. In particular we see how the role of cost accounting provides information to assist them with:
  - decision-making
  - planning for the future
  - control of expenditure

  These themes will be developed in later chapters.

- We then identify cost units and see how responsibility centres, cost centres, profit centres and investment centres are used to monitor the performance of sections of a business.

- The identification and coding of costs and revenues is an important step towards providing correct information to the managers of a business.

- We then see how costs can be grouped together or classified in different ways:
  - by element
  - by nature
  - by function
  - by behaviour

  Each of these ways enables us to see the same business from a different viewpoint, which will help managers to run the business better.

- The total cost statement shows how the cost of goods and services is calculated.

- After studying this chapter you should have a clear idea of the role of costing and appreciate some of the ideas that it uses.

PURPOSE OF COST ACCOUNTING

Cost accounting, as its name implies, enables the managers of a business to know the cost of the firm's output – whether a product or a service – and the revenues from sales. Once costing information is available, managers can use it to assist with

- decision-making
- planning for the future
- control of expenditure

Cost accounting (which is also often referred to as management accounting) is widely used by all types of businesses and organisations – the cost of a hospital operation, the cost of building a new hospital ward, the cost of tuition to a student, the cost of a swim at a sports centre, the cost of a passenger's bus journey, the cost of a new road are all just as important as the cost of making a product. A business or organisation – whether it provides a service or makes a product – needs to keep its costs under review; in order to do this it needs accurate cost information. Thus a cost accounting system will provide answers to questions such as:

What does it cost us to provide a student with a day's accountancy course?

What does it cost us to carry out a hip replacement operation?

What does it cost us to make a pair of trainers?

What does it cost us to serve a cheeseburger and fries?

What does it cost us to provide a week's holiday in the Canaries?

The cost accounting system helps managers with production planning and decision-making, such as:

- short-term decisions, eg "how many do we need to make and sell in order to break-even?"; "shall we increase production of Aye or Bee, bearing in mind that shortages of skilled labour mean that we can't do both?"
- long-term decisions, eg "we need to buy a new machine for the factory – shall we buy Machine Exe or Machine Wye?"

The Case Study that follows shows how cost accounting enables the managers of a business to have better information about its activities.

Case Study

S & T MANUFACTURING COMPANY

situation

The following information is given for S & T Manufacturing Company, a two-product (S and T) company, for last year:

			£	£
Revenue (sales):	S			100,000
	T			200,000
				300,000
Less:	Cost of materials	S	50,000	
		T	95,000	
	Labour costs	S	40,000	
		T	50,000	
	*Cost of overheads	S	20,000	
		T	30,000	
				285,000
Profit				15,000

* Overheads include factory rent, depreciation of machinery, and other production costs.

How would you present this information in a way which will be of more use to the management of the business? What conclusions do you draw for this business?

solution

The information is best presented in a way which analyses the cost and profit of each product:

	S	T	Total
	£	£	£
Cost of materials	50,000	95,000	145,000
Labour costs	40,000	50,000	90,000
Cost of overheads	20,000	30,000	50,000
Total cost	110,000	175,000	285,000
Revenue (sales)	100,000	200,000	300,000
Less Total cost	110,000	175,000	285,000
Profit/(loss)	(10,000)	25,000	15,000

On the basis of this information, product S should be discontinued because it is making a loss. However, there may be other factors which will have to be considered, eg sales of product T may be linked to sales of S; the overheads of T are likely to increase if S is discontinued because of the way in which the cost of overheads has been split between the two products.

This Case Study emphasises two important functions of cost accounting:

- to find out the costs (in this case for each product)

- to give responsibility to someone for those costs (here for the manager of product S to investigate the reasons for the loss of £10,000)

COST ACCOUNTING AND FINANCIAL ACCOUNTING

The Case Study of S & T Manufacturing Company, above, illustrates some of the differences between cost accounting and financial accounting. These two types of accounting, although they produce different reports and statements, obtain their data from the same set of transactions carried out by the business or organisation over a given period. This is illustrated in the diagram below.

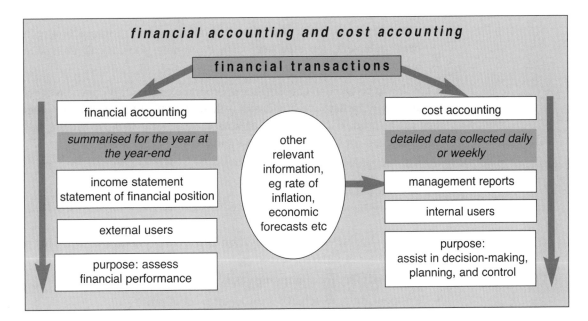

Financial accounting uses the financial data relating to transactions carried out over a period of time. The information is processed through the accounting records and extracted in the form of financial statements – income statement and statement of financial position. The statements are often required to be produced by law, eg the Companies Act, and are available to external users such as shareholders, suppliers, bank, HM Revenue and Customs, Companies House.

Cost accounting uses the same data to produce reports containing financial information on the recent past and projections for the future. The reports are available to internal users only, such as managers, directors, and owners (but not to shareholders generally). There is no legal requirement to produce this information and the content of the report and the principles used can be suited to the activities of the business or organisation and the requirements of its managers. The information is prepared as frequently as it is required, and speed is often vital as the information may go out-of-date very quickly.

COST UNITS

Before we begin our study of costing we need to understand the term cost units.

Cost units are units of output to which costs can be charged.

A cost unit can be:

- a unit of production from a factory such as a car, a television, an item of furniture
- a unit of service, such as a passenger-mile on a bus, a transaction on a bank statement, an attendance at a swimming pool, a call unit on a telephone

Care should be taken in choosing the appropriate cost unit. Within a business – particularly in the service industry – there may well be several cost units that can be used. For example, in an hotel the cost units in the restaurant will be meals, and for the rooms, the cost units will be guest nights.

RESPONSIBILITY CENTRES

Within a business or organisation different managers will have responsibilities at different levels, eg

- a responsibility for controlling costs
- a responsibility to achieve a particular level of profit
- a responsibility to achieve a particular return on money invested

Responsibility centres are sections of a business or organisation for which a manager is accountable.

Examples of responsibility centres are:

- cost centres
- profit centres
- investment centres

COST CENTRES

As well as charging costs to cost units they also need to be charged to a specific part of a business – a **cost centre.**

Cost centres are sections of a business or organisation to which costs can be charged.

A cost centre in a manufacturing business, for example, is a department of a factory, a particular stage in the production process, or even a whole factory. In a college, examples of cost centres are the teaching departments, or particular sections of departments such as the college's administrative office. In a hospital, examples of cost centres are the hospital wards, operating theatres, specialist sections such as the X-ray department, pathology department.

Collecting costs together in cost centres assists with control of the business or organisation. The manager of a cost centre can be held responsible for its costs – budgeted costs can be compared with actual costs.

PROFIT CENTRES

For some sections of businesses the cost centre approach of analysing costs is taken to a further level by also analysing sales revenue to centres. As revenue less costs equals profit, such centres are called profit centres. Note that the source of information on sales revenue comes from sales orders and sales invoices.

Profit centres are sections of a business or organisation to which costs can be charged, revenue can be identified, and profit can be calculated.

From the definition we can see that profit centres have both costs and revenue. It follows, therefore, that profit centres will be based on sections of the business that make products or services (incur costs) and sell them to customers (receive revenue). For example, a garden centre has conservatory plants as a profit centre as shown in the following diagram:

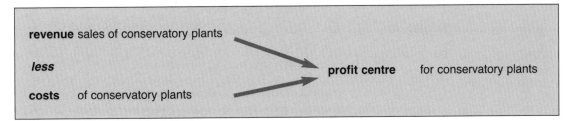

Note that many cost centres provide support services within a business or organisation and, so, cannot become profit centres because they do not have any significant revenue. For example, the administration department of a business is a cost centre to which costs can be charged, but it does not have any revenue. As we have seen profit centres both incur costs and generate revenue.

Managers of profit centres will be seeking information from the accounting system about the costs incurred and the revenue generated by their centre. By deducting costs from revenue they can quantify the profit made and can make comparisons with previous periods (eg last month, last quarter, last year, etc), with profit targets set for the current period (eg 'our profit is 10 per cent above target'), and also with other profit centres (eg 'our profit last month was higher than the other profit centres').

INVESTMENT CENTRES

A further development of profit centres is to consider profit in relation to the amount of money invested in the centre. For **investment centres** the profit of the centre is compared with how much money the business has put in to earn that profit.

Investment centres are sections of a business or organisation where profit can be compared with the amount of money invested in the centre.

Profit is compared with money invested by means of a percentage as shown in the following diagram for a garden centre's conservatory plants investment centre.

Managers of investment centres will wish to make comparisons of the return on investment for the current period with that of previous periods (eg 'have we done better than last year?') against targets set for the current period (eg 'are we on target for the current period?'), and also with the other investment centres of the business (eg 'how do we compare with the other investment centres?').

Case Study

PROVIDING INFORMATION FOR MANAGEMENT

situation

You are an accounts assistant at Severnvale Garden Centre.

The managing director, Charlie Rimmack, has asked you for accounting information that is needed for this afternoon. Apparently the managers of two sections of the garden centre – the manager for conservatory plants and the manager for shrubs – have been arguing about which one is doing better. Charlie wants information in order to resolve the dispute; she requests details for each section of costs and revenue for last year, and the amount of money invested in each section at the end of the year. (She says that all figures can be to the nearest £000.)

solution

You go to accounts which have been set up to show costs, revenue and money invested for each section, and extract the following information for last year:

		Conservatory plants	Shrubs
		£000	£000
Costs:	materials	137	151
	labour	93	134
	expenses	45	70
Revenue		425	555
Money invested		300	400

In order to help the managing director you decide to present the management information for each section in the following way:

	Conservatory plants	Shrubs
	£000	£000
Cost Centre		
Materials	137	151
Labour	93	134
Expenses	45	70
Total	275	355

Here the cost centre for conservatory plants has the lower costs.

	Conservatory plants	Shrubs
Profit Centre		
Revenue	425	555
less		
Costs (see above)	275	355
Profit	150	200

These figures show that shrubs is the better profit centre.

Investment Centre

Profit (see above)	150	200
Investment	300	400
Expressed as a percentage (multiplied by 100)	50%	50%

Based on last year's figures both sections of the business, as investment centres, are performing as well as each other.

Conclusion

- The accounting information provided is based on figures taken from the *financial accounting* records. It is taken from the accounts which record the transactions that have happened already.

- The managing director and the managers of the sections will also be interested in using *management accounting* to provide them with information to help with decision-making, planning and control.

IDENTIFICATION AND CODING OF COSTS AND REVENUES

The objective of coding costs and revenues is to provide correct analysis so as to give information from the costing system to managers. By analysing costs and revenue to cost/revenue centres we can answer questions such as 'how much was basic pay in the sales department last month?'; 'how much was factory overtime last week?'; 'what sales did the Birmingham office make of product Exe last month?'

coding of costs

Both cost units and cost centres have costs charged to them. This process is carried out in two steps:

- *identification* of the cost unit or cost centre to which the cost is to be charged

- *coding* the cost so that it is charged to the correct cost unit or cost centre

Code numbers are used in cost accounting because:

- they are easier to process than a description of a cost

- once coded there is no doubt as to which cost unit or cost centre the item relates

- they are easily input into a computer accounting system

Various systems are used to code costs. It is for a business to use the system that meets its needs – a smaller business will use a less sophisticated system than does a larger business. Most codes incorporate two sets of numbers that indicate:

- which cost centre or cost unit incurred the cost
- what cost has been used, eg wages, materials

For example, a business uses the following codes:

- code for administration office, 500
- code for sales department, 550
- code for salaries, 200

Thus the cost code for administration salaries is:

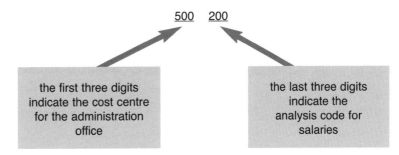

Using the same principles, the cost code for sales department salaries is 550200. By using coding in this way, the correct cost centre is charged with the cost.

coding of revenues

In a similar way to coding of costs, revenue needs to be coded so that information is available to management on:

- which product has been sold
- which department, or salesperson, made the sale

For example, a restaurant uses the following codes:

- code for revenue from meals, 700
- code for revenue from the bar, 800
- code for Jason, a waiter, 082

Thus the revenue code for meals sold by Jason is:

082 700

the first three digits
indicate the analysis
code for Jason,
the waiter

the last three digits
indicate the
revenue code for meals

Using the same principles, the revenue code for bar sales made by Jason is 082800.

You can often see the use of revenue codes in use in a shop, or a bar, or a restaurant – the salesperson first keys in his or her personal code number on the till and then records the items sold by either scanning them through a bar code reader, or by pressing the appropriate keys. The information on sales revenue is then available to the managers of the business.

CLASSIFICATION OF COSTS

Within any business or organisation, whether it manufactures a product or provides a service, there are certain costs involved at various stages to produce the units of output. The diagram on the next page shows the costs of a manufacturing business which are incurred by the three main sections or 'areas' of a manufacturing business.

These three separate sections are:

- **factory** – where production takes place and the product is 'finished' and made ready for selling

- **warehouse** – where finished goods are stored and from where they are despatched when they are sold

- **office** – where the support functions take place – marketing, sales, administration, finance and so on

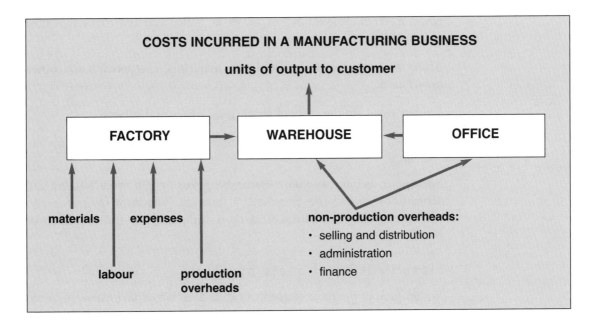

Note that while the diagram above shows the costs of a manufacturing business, it can be adapted easily to fit non-manufacturing organisations, such as a shop, a hospital, a school or college, a church, a club. While the units of output of these organisations differ from those of a manufacturer, nevertheless they still incur costs at various stages of the 'production' process.

In order to prepare information for the managers of a business, costs must be classified, ie organised into sets in a way which the managers will find useful.

This can be done in four ways:

- by element
- by nature
- by function
- by behaviour

classification of costs by element

Businesses and organisations incur many different kinds of cost in the production of goods or 'output', including costs of the warehouse and the office. The most basic way of splitting up costs is according to the type of expenditure under the headings:

- materials, eg the components to make a car
- labour, eg wages of an employee
- expenses, eg rent and rates, telephone charges, insurance

Note: material, labour, and expenses are often referred to as the three elements of cost.

Materials costs are the costs of raw materials, components and other goods used.

Labour costs are the costs of employees' wages and salaries.

Expenses are other costs, which cannot be included in 'materials' or 'labour'.

Splitting costs into these three elements applies to both manufacturing and service businesses. The classification provides important information to managers as they can see the breakdown of the total into different kinds of cost.

classification of costs by nature

Within each of the three elements of materials, labour and expenses, some costs can be identified directly with each unit of output. For example:

- the cost of components used in making cars
- the wages of workers on a production line in a factory

These are termed **direct costs**. In manufacturing, the total of all the direct costs is called the **prime cost** of the output.

A direct cost is a cost that can be identified directly with each unit of output.

Prime cost is the total of all direct costs.

Costs which cannot be identified directly with each unit of output are **indirect costs** or overheads.

Indirect costs (overheads) are all costs, other than those identified as 'direct costs', and they cannot be identified directly with each unit of output.

There are many examples of overheads, including:

- telephone charges
- insurance premiums
- cost of wages of non-production staff, such as managers, secretaries, cost accountants and so on
- running costs of delivery vehicles
- depreciation charge for non-current assets

Note particularly the last two examples. In cost accounting, as in financial accounting, we distinguish between capital and revenue expenditure. In our analysis of costs we are referring to revenue expenditure, and therefore include the running costs and depreciation of non-current assets, rather than the capital cost of their purchase.

We now have six possible classifications for costs, each of the three elements of materials, labour and expenses being split by their nature into direct and indirect costs. These are illustrated for a manufacturing business in the table below, while the Case Study on page 18 is for a service business.

Classification of costs by element and by nature		
nature element	DIRECT COSTS	INDIRECT COSTS
MATERIALS	The cost of raw materials from which the finished product is made.	The cost of all other materials, eg grease for machines, cleaning materials.
LABOUR	Wages paid to those who work the machinery on the production line or who are involved in assembly or finishing of the product.	Wages and salaries paid to all other employees, eg managers and supervisors, maintenance staff, administration staff.
EXPENSES	Any expenses which can be identified with particular units of output, eg royalties payable to the designer of a product, fees linked directly to specific output and paid to people who are not employees.	All other expenses, eg rent, rates, telephone, lighting and heating costs, depreciation of non-current assets, insurance, advertising, etc. These are costs which cannot be identified directly with units of output.
TOTAL	**TOTAL DIRECT COST** **= PRIME COST**	**TOTAL INDIRECT COST** **= TOTAL OVERHEADS**

classification of costs by function

Another method of classifying costs is to look at the costs incurred in different sections of the organisation, according to their 'function', or the kind of work being done.

In manufacturing, the main function is production of the goods. The business could not be run, however, without administrators, accountants, sales and delivery staff and so on – these are examples of non-production costs.

When costs are classified by function, the main headings generally used are:

production

administration

selling and distribution 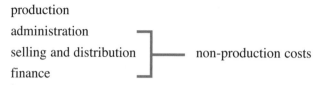 non-production costs

finance

Other functions can be added to suit the needs of a particular business. For example, a 'Research and Development' heading could be used if a company spent large sums of money in researching and developing new products.

Non-manufacturing organisations – such as a hospital or a college – may use other 'function' headings, according to the kind of work each section of the organisation carries out.

Please note that, in classifying costs by their function, we are looking at the same set of costs for the organisation as before. We are simply presenting them in different groupings.

It is an important function of accounting that information should be presented in the form most suitable for the purpose for which it is required. For some management purposes, classification of costs by function provides better information.

classification of costs by behaviour

In cost accounting, it is important to appreciate the behaviour of costs – in particular to understand that not all costs increase or decrease directly in line with increases or decreases in output. By behaviour, costs in the short-term are:

• fixed, or

• semi-variable, or

• variable

The diagram below shows the differences between these.

It is important to know the behaviour of costs and how they are affected by changes in the level of output. For example, a business decides to increase its output by 25% – will all costs increase by 25%? Fixed costs, such as rent and rates, are likely to remain unchanged, provided that there is capacity for the increased output within the existing building. Variable costs, such as direct materials and direct labour, are likely to increase by 25% as they generally vary directly with output (unless any economies of scale can be achieved). Semi-variable costs, such as the telephone bill, will increase as the extra business generates more 'phone calls; however, the increase should certainly be much less than 25%.

Whilst we can classify costs in the short-term as fixed, or variable, or semi-variable, in the long-term all costs are variable. For example, the fixed cost of rent will increase when output increases beyond the capacity of the premises and additional premises have to be rented.

REASONS FOR CLASSIFYING COSTS

The question might be asked, "Why classify costs in four ways?" The answer is that we can see the same business from four different viewpoints – this will help managers to run the business better:

- **by element**

  looking for the high cost elements in order to make savings, eg labour might be identified as being too high

- **by nature**

  looking at the direct and indirect costs to see where savings could be made – eg the business might be able to reduce the cost of direct labour

- **by function**

  looking at the different departments to see which are the high-spending departments – perhaps savings can be made

- **by behaviour**

  identifying the costs as being fixed, semi-variable, or variable – the business might be able to make savings by altering the balance between fixed and variable costs

Thus classifying costs helps management with:

- decision-making, when implementing changes
- planning, when preparing forecasts and budgets
- control, when checking results against what was planned

The two Case Studies which follow illustrate the classification of costs by element and by nature (Albion Restaurant), and by function (Thyme plc). The behaviour of costs – fixed, semi-variable, and variable will be considered in more detail later in the book (Chapters 4 and 9).

Case Study

1.850

1.600

ALBION RESTAURANT:
COST CLASSIFICATION BY ELEMENT AND BY NATURE

situation

Albion Restaurant is a large restaurant. Some of the costs incurred by Albion Restaurant are listed below:

(a)   wages of the cleaner

(b)   cost of heating the restaurant

(c)   wages of the chefs

(d)   telephone charges

(e)   paper table covers and napkins

(f)   cost of ingredients for meals

(g)   cleaning materials

(h)   advertising costs

(i)   maintenance contract for ovens

(j)   wages of waiters and waitresses

As an accounts assistant at Albion Restaurant, you are to:

• suggest a suitable cost unit for a restaurant.

• classify the costs by element and by nature into the six categories shown in the table below; give your answer by entering the costs into the table:

nature element	DIRECT COSTS	INDIRECT COSTS
MATERIALS		
LABOUR		
EXPENSES		

solution

An appropriate cost unit for a restaurant would be one meal.

nature / element	DIRECT COSTS	INDIRECT COSTS
MATERIALS	(f) cost of ingredients for meals	(e) paper table covers and napkins (g) cleaning materials
LABOUR	(c) wages of the chefs (j) wages of waiters and waitresses*	(a) wages of the cleaner
EXPENSES		(b) cost of heating the restaurant (d) telephone charges (h) advertising costs (i) maintenance contract for ovens

* You may have classified (j) 'wages of waiters and waitresses' as 'indirect wages'. This is an equally valid answer. A cost accounting system is designed to suit a particular organisation. There are some costs that may be treated as either direct or indirect costs, depending on the particular situation and the information required from the system. Costs which could be linked directly to cost units may be treated as overheads if this is easier and saves time without losing any useful information. Whichever treatment is used, it is important to be consistent so that, next time the cost is incurred, it is dealt with in the same way.

Case Study

THYME PLC:
COST CLASSIFICATION BY FUNCTION

situation

Thyme plc is a manufacturer of TV sets.

Some of the indirect costs incurred by Thyme plc are listed below:

(a) depreciation charge for delivery vehicles

(b) salary of the human resources manager

(c) materials used for maintaining factory machinery

(d) cost of paper for office printer

(e) interest payable on a bank overdraft

(f) salary of the sales manager

(g) cost of power used for running factory machinery

(h) maintenance contract for office photocopier

As an accounts assistant at Thyme, you are to classify the costs by function and give your answer by entering the costs into a table.

solution

PRODUCTION COSTS	(c) materials used for maintaining factory machinery
	(g) cost of power used for running factory machinery
SELLING AND DISTRIBUTION COSTS	(a) depreciation charge for delivery vehicles
	(f) salary of the sales manager
ADMINISTRATION COSTS	(b) salary of the human resources manager
	(d) cost of paper for office printer
	(h) maintenance contract for office photocopier
FINANCE COSTS	(e) interest payable on a bank overdraft

CALCULATING THE COST OF GOODS AND SERVICES

Using the principles of costing will help to calculate the cost of a product – whether goods or services. Only when the cost of producing each unit of output is known, can a business make decisions about the selling price.

The steps towards calculating the cost of goods and services are:

identify the unit of output

The cost units for a particular business or organisation must be identified. As we have seen earlier, these are the units of output to which costs can be charged. Only by recovering costs through the sales of output can a business make a profit.

calculate the number of units of output for a particular time period

Once the unit of output is identified, the business is then able to calculate how many units can be produced or provided in a given time period, such as a day, week, month, quarter or year. For example, a garage will work out how many hours of mechanics' time are available, or a car manufacturer will calculate how many cars it can produce in a year.

calculate the direct costs for a particular time period

Having established the number of units of output for a particular time period, the next task is to calculate the direct costs, or prime cost, for that time period. As we have seen earlier in this chapter, the direct costs comprise:

direct materials   identifiable with the product

direct labour   the wages paid to those who make the product

direct expenses   identifiable with the product

The amounts of the direct costs are added together to give the total direct costs (prime cost) of the output for the time period.

calculate the indirect costs for a particular time period

The indirect costs, or overheads, of the production or service must be calculated for the particular time period. Indirect costs comprise:

indirect materials   materials used that are not identified directly with production

indirect labour   wages and salaries paid to those who are not directly involved in production

indirect expenses   expenses of the business not identified directly with production

Once the indirect costs have been calculated, we must then ensure that their total cost is charged to the cost units for a particular time period. Only by including indirect costs in the total cost of the output can a business recover their cost from the sales made.

The amounts of the indirect costs are added together to give the total indirect costs (overheads) for the time period.

calculate the total cost of a unit of output

Once the direct and indirect costs for a time period are known, the total cost of a unit of output can be calculated, as follows:

$$\frac{direct\ costs\ +\ indirect\ costs}{number\ of\ units\ of\ output} = total\ cost\ of\ a\ unit\ of\ output$$

The total cost is also known as the absorption cost – because it absorbs (includes) both the direct costs and the indirect costs. Once total cost is known, the business can use the information to help it make pricing and other decisions. Note that, for inventory (stock) valuation purposes, only those indirect costs which relate to production are to be included in total cost (see page 57).

calculating the cost – a summary

The process of calculating the cost of output is illustrated in the diagram shown below.

costs for a service business

While the units of 'output' of businesses or organisations that produce a service are not manufactured products, they still incur the costs of:

- materials
- labour
- expenses

Some of the costs of a service business can be linked directly to the 'output' or the cost units of the organisation, but others are classified as overheads.

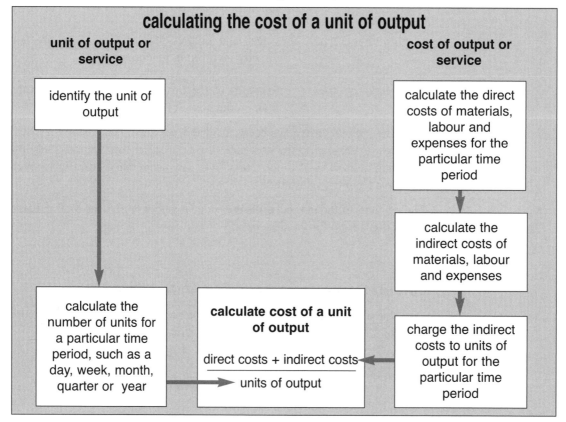

TOTAL COST STATEMENT

The total cost statement brings together all the costs involved in producing the output of a business. It can be prepared on the basis of:

- a single cost unit, eg the cost of making one car in a car factory
- a batch, eg the cost of making 1,000 'special edition' cars
- the whole factory, eg the cost of all the car factory's output for a given time period

The total cost statement is prepared using the following layout:

	TOTAL COST STATEMENT	£
	Direct materials	x
add	Direct labour	x
add	Direct expenses	x
equals	PRIME COST	x
add	Production overheads	x
equals	PRODUCTION COST	x
add	Selling and distribution costs ┐	x
add	Administration costs ─────┼─ non-production overheads	x
add	Finance costs ──────────┘	x
equals	TOTAL COST	x

Note that:

- *prime cost* is the direct cost of manufacturing products, before the addition of production overheads
- *production cost* is the factory cost of manufacturing the products, ie prime cost plus production (factory) overheads
- *total cost* is production cost plus non-production overheads

The cost structure above is especially appropriate for a manufacturing business; indeed a separate *manufacturing account* – which shows costs through to production cost – is prepared prior to the income statement (profit and loss account). Manufacturing accounts are covered in more detail in Chapter 7.

By taking total cost away from revenue we can create an income statement. This shows the profitability of the business after all costs have been taken into account. The income statement is:

	INCOME STATEMENT	
		£
	Revenue	x
less	Total cost	x
equals	PROFIT	x

SOURCES OF DATA FOR COSTING

In order to code, analyse and classify costs and revenues we need to obtain the information from a data source. There will be many of these within a business or organisation – potential sources include:

- materials
  - purchase orders
  - goods received notes
  - returns notes
  - invoices received
  - materials requisitions
  - inventory records
  - job sheets
  - ledgers
- labour
  - clock and time cards
  - payroll analysis sheets
  - income tax and National Insurance Contributions
  - job sheets
  - ledgers
- expenses
  - invoices received
  - receipts
  - cash book
  - petty cash book
  - cheque counterfoils
  - bank transfers made
  - bank statements
  - ledgers

- revenue   – invoices issued
  - cash receipts issued
  - bank paying-in book
  - bank transfers received
  - bank statements
  - ledgers

Note: at this stage in your studies you may not be familiar with all these sources of data – specialist terms will be explained in subsequent chapters.

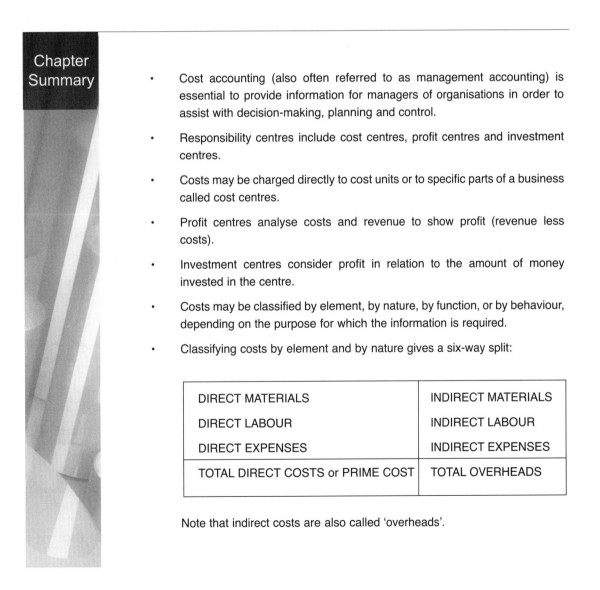

Chapter Summary

- Cost accounting (also often referred to as management accounting) is essential to provide information for managers of organisations in order to assist with decision-making, planning and control.

- Responsibility centres include cost centres, profit centres and investment centres.

- Costs may be charged directly to cost units or to specific parts of a business called cost centres.

- Profit centres analyse costs and revenue to show profit (revenue less costs).

- Investment centres consider profit in relation to the amount of money invested in the centre.

- Costs may be classified by element, by nature, by function, or by behaviour, depending on the purpose for which the information is required.

- Classifying costs by element and by nature gives a six-way split:

DIRECT MATERIALS	INDIRECT MATERIALS
DIRECT LABOUR	INDIRECT LABOUR
DIRECT EXPENSES	INDIRECT EXPENSES
TOTAL DIRECT COSTS or PRIME COST	TOTAL OVERHEADS

Note that indirect costs are also called 'overheads'.

- Overheads may be classified by dividing them amongst the functions or sections of the business:
  - – factory (or production)
  - – selling and distribution
  - – administration
  - – finance
  - – other section headings as appropriate to the organisation
- By behaviour, costs are fixed, or semi-variable, or variable.
- Total cost of producing a unit of output $=\dfrac{\text{direct costs + indirect costs}}{\text{number of units of output}}$
- A total cost statement lists the total of the direct costs and the overheads. An income statement shows revenue minus total cost equals profit.

Key Terms

cost unit	unit of output to which costs can be charged
responsibility centre	section of a business or organisation for which a manager is accountable
cost centre	specific part of a business or organisation to which costs can be charged
profit centre	section of a business or organisation to which costs can be charged, revenue can be identified, and profit can be calculated
investment centre	section of a business or organisation where profit can be compared with the amount of money invested in the centre
materials costs	the costs of raw materials, components and other goods used
labour costs	the costs of employees' wages and salaries
expenses	other costs, which cannot be included in 'materials' or 'labour'
direct cost	a cost that can be identified directly with each unit of output

indirect cost (overhead)	a cost that cannot be identified directly with each unit of output
prime cost	the total of all direct costs
fixed costs	costs which remain fixed over a range of output levels
semi-variable costs	costs which combine a fixed and variable element
variable costs	costs which vary directly with output
total cost statement	list of the total of the direct costs and the overheads

Activities

1.1 Select an organisation – either where you work, or one with which you are familiar.

    (a) Prepare a diagram, similar to that shown on page 13, identifying the main functions of the organisation and the costs incurred by each section.

    (b) Describe the cost units and cost centres used by the organisation.

    (c)   • Explain responsibility centres
        • Identify the responsibility centres used by the organisation

1.2   (a) Explain the difference between
        • cost centre
        • profit centre
        • investment centre

    (b) Suggest likely cost centres for
        • a school or a college
        • a manufacturing business which makes two product lines

1.3 You work as an accounts assistant at City News and Books, a company which owns a group of shops selling newspapers and magazines, books and stationery. The accounting system has been set up to show costs, revenue and money invested for each of these three sections of the business: newspapers and magazines, books, stationery.

The finance director has requested details for each section of costs and revenue for last year, and the amount of money invested in each section at the end of the year. (She says that all figures can be to the nearest £000.)

The accounts supervisor asks you to deal with this request and you go to the accounts and extract the following information for last year:

	Newspapers and magazines	Books	Stationery
	£000	£000	£000
Costs: materials	155	246	122
labour	65	93	58
expenses	27	35	25
Revenue	352	544	230
Money invested	420	850	250

The accounts supervisor asks you to present the information for the finance director in the form of a report which shows the costs, profit, and return on investment (to the nearest percentage point) for each section of the business.

1.4 (a) Why is it important to analyse costs in different ways, eg by element, by nature, by function and by behaviour?

(b) Classify each of the following costs by behaviour (ie fixed, or semi-variable, or variable):

• raw materials

• factory rent

• telephone

• direct labour, eg production workers paid on the basis of work done

• indirect labour, eg supervisors' salaries

• commission paid to sales staff

Taking the costs in turn, explain to a friend, who is about to set up a furniture manufacturing business, why you have classified each as fixed, or semi-variable, or variable. Answer the comment, 'What difference does it make anyway, they are all costs that have to be paid.'

1.5   Severn Manufacturing Limited makes chairs for school and college use. The chairs have plastic seats, and tubular steel legs. You are to classify the company's costs into:

- direct materials

- indirect materials

- direct labour

- indirect labour

- direct expenses

- indirect expenses

The cost items to be classified are:

COST ITEM	CLASSIFICATION (write your answer)
Tubular steel	
Factory supervisor's salary	
Wages of employee operating the moulding machine which produces the chair seats	
Works canteen assistant's wages	
Rates of factory	
Power to operate machines	
Factory heating and lighting	
Plastic for making chair seats	
Hire of special machinery for one particular order	
Cost of grease for the moulding machine	
Depreciation of factory machinery	
Depreciation of office equipment	

If you believe alternative classifications exist, argue the case and state if you need further information from the company.

1.6 Betterwell NHS Trust is a large hospital with many departments. Costs of the general operating theatre have been identified and you are to classify them into:

- direct materials
- indirect materials
- direct labour
- indirect labour
- direct expenses
- indirect expenses

The cost items to be classified are:

COST ITEM	CLASSIFICATION (write your answer)
Dressings	
Disposable scalpels	
Surgeon's salary	
Floor cleaning materials	
Laundry	
Depreciation of staff drinks machine	
Theatre heat and light	
Porter's wages	
Anaesthetic gas	
Depreciation of theatre equipment	
Maintenance of theatre equipment	
Cost of CDs for music in theatre	
Anaesthetist's salary	

If you believe alternative classifications exist, argue the case and state if you need further information.

1.7   Wyvern Water Limited bottles natural spring water at its plant at Walcoll at the base of the Wyvern Hills. The natural spring is on land owned by a local farmer to whom a royalty is paid for each bottle of water produced.

You are working in the costing section of Wyvern Water and are asked to analyse the following cost items into the appropriate columns and to agree the totals:

Cost item	Total cost	Prime cost	Production overheads	Admin-istration costs	Selling and distribution costs
	£	£	£	£	£
Wages of employees working on the bottling line	6,025				
Wages of employees in the stores department	2,750				
Cost of bottles	4,050				
Safety goggles for bottling line employees	240				
Advertisement for new employees	125				
Depreciation of bottling machinery	500				
Depreciation of sales staff's cars	1,000				
Royalty paid to local farmer	750				
Cost of trade exhibition	1,500				
Computer stationery	210				
Sales staff salaries	4,095				
TOTALS	21,245				

1.8 The following figures relate to the accounts of Hughes Limited, a manufacturing business, for the year ended 31 December 20-4:

	£
Raw materials used in the factory	118,830
Rent and rates of factory	16,460
Factory wages	117,315
Factory power	3,825
Factory heat and light	1,185
Factory expenses and maintenance	4,095
Salaries of office staff	69,350
Advertising	11,085
Office expenses	3,930
Depreciation of factory plant and machinery	3,725
Revenue	426,350

You are to:

(a) Prepare a total cost statement for the year which shows:

- prime cost
- production cost
- total cost

Discuss any assumptions that you make and state if you need further information from the company.

(b) Prepare an income statement for the year (on the assumption that all the goods manufactured have been sold).

1.9 Which one of the following is normally classed as a fixed cost for a manufacturing business?

(a) raw materials to make the product

(b) salaries of maintenance staff

(c) production workers paid on the basis of work done

(d) royalties paid to the designer of the product

Answer (a) or (b) or (c) or (d)

1.10 Which one of the following is normally classed as a variable cost for a 'high street' printing shop?

(a) supervisor's salary

(b) rent of shop

(c) electricity used

(d) cost of paper

Answer (a) or (b) or (c) or (d)

1.11 The following figures relate to the accounts of Manley Manufacturing Limited for the year ended 31 December 20-8:

	£
Raw materials used in factory	75,280
Wages of production workers	69,180
Salaries of maintenance staff	30,950
Royalties paid to designer of product	15,110
Depreciation of factory plant and machinery	5,000
Electricity	4,160
Rent and rates	10,290
Salaries of office staff	38,450
Depreciation of office equipment	2,400
Factory expenses	3,020
Office expenses	1,590
Revenue	315,840

You are to:

(a) Prepare a total cost statement for the year which shows:

- prime cost
- production cost
- total cost

Discuss any assumptions that you make and state if you need further information from the company.

(b) Prepare an income statement for the year (on the assumption that all the goods manufactured have been sold).

2 Materials costs

In Chapter 1 we saw how costs can be classified by element as materials, labour and expenses. In this chapter we focus on materials – or inventory – costs. Inventory is the word used for stock.

Businesses and other organisations hold materials inventory in the form of raw materials and components, products bought for resale, and service items. Often the value of such materials is high, representing a considerable investment of money. In this chapter we explain:

- purchasing and control of materials
- re-ordering procedures
- records that are kept for materials
- purposes of the inventory take and inventory reconciliation
- valuation of inventory
- use of inventory records
- book-keeping entries for materials costs

TYPES OF MATERIALS INVENTORY

Materials inventory is the cost of:

- raw materials and components bought for use by a manufacturing business
- products bought for resale by a shop or a wholesaler
- service items, such as stationery, bought for use within a business or organisation

In costing we need to distinguish between direct materials and indirect materials. Thus a manufacturer classifies the cost of materials from which the finished product is made as direct materials; other materials used – grease for machines, cleaning materials, etc – are classified as indirect materials, and form part of the overheads of the business.

The buying of materials is normally undertaken by a firm's Purchasing Department, although in smaller businesses the responsibility will be carried out by an individual or the owner. The job of the buyer(s) is to ensure that the purchases made by the business are bought at the lowest possible cost, consistent with quality and quantity.

At any time, most businesses will hold materials ready to use or for resale. The diagram shown on the next page examines the materials held by three types of business: a manufacturing business which makes products, a trading business such as a shop, which buys and sells goods, and a service business or organisation, which holds consumable materials.

PLANNING OF PURCHASES AND CONTROL OF MATERIALS

Planning for the purchase of materials and the control of materials inventory is critical to the efficiency of a business. However, holding materials is expensive:

- they have to be financed, possibly by using borrowed money (on which interest is payable)
- there are storage costs, including rent and rates, security, insurance

Within an organisation there are conflicting demands on its policy for materials. On the one hand, the finance department will want to minimise materials inventory levels to keep costs as low as possible; on the other hand, production and marketing departments will be anxious to keep materials inventory high so that output can be maintained and new orders satisfied speedily before customers decide to buy elsewhere.

MATERIALS HELD BY BUSINESSES

Manufacturing Business	Trading Business	Service Business
raw materials and components	**goods for sale**	**consumable materials**
These inventories are held by a manufacturer to reduce the risk of production delays if a supplier fails to deliver on time. A vehicle manufacturer may hold plastic bumpers ready to use, for example.	These are items the retailer or wholesaler has bought in (eg from the manufacturer) and has available for sale to the customer. For example: ■ *retailers* a supermarket will have cans of orange drink ready for sale ■ *wholesalers* a timber merchant will have quantities of wood for sale to customers	These are materials that are either for use in the organisation or for sale to the customer as part of the service provided. For example: ■ *for use in the organisation* in a college there will be paper ready for use in the photocopiers ■ *items for sale* an optician will sell reading glasses as part of the service provided
work-in-progress		
These are part-finished goods on the production line. In a car factory these would be cars partly assembled, for example.		
finished goods		
These are goods that have been completed and are ready for sale to customers. A vehicle manufacturer would have completed cars ready for sale, for example.		

There are a number of methods of planning purchases and of inventory control. Which is adopted will depend on the size and sophistication of the organisation. It is important that an organisation knows how much inventory it has at any time – either by making a physical inventory count, or by keeping computer records (which need physical verification at regular intervals) – and it must know when it will have to re-order more inventory. The organisation then needs to know the quantity that needs to be re-ordered. The methods used include:

estimation   Some small businesses do not keep much inventory, and the owner may estimate the quantity and timing of materials purchases. This is not a recommended method for a well-managed business or organisation.

'two bin' system	The principle here is to keep two 'bins' for each item of inventory. When the first bin has run out, the item is re-ordered to be delivered before the second 'bin' runs out. The term 'bin' is used loosely, and can apply to any measure of inventory. This is a very basic principle, but it works well in many situations.
perpetual inventory	This system records receipt and issue of inventory as the items pass in and out of the organisation, and re-orders are made accordingly. Inventory records are kept manually, or more commonly now on computer file activated by reading of bar codes. Many supermarkets and manufacturing businesses work on this basis.
formulas	Organisations need to calculate when to order inventory, and how much to order; formulas can be used to help with this. These are explained in the sections which follow.

MATERIALS PURCHASES: LEVEL METHOD OF RE-ORDERING

This method orders materials in fixed quantities, eg 750 reams of photocopying paper (a ream is 500 sheets). For such a system to operate, the organisation should know:

- the *lead time*, ie how long it takes for new inventory to be delivered after being ordered
- the appropriate *re-order quantity*
- the *minimum inventory level,* ie the lowest level that inventory should fall to before the new order from the supplier is delivered (the minimum inventory level is also known as the *inventory buffer* to meet unexpected emergencies)
- the *maximum inventory level* that can be held – this can be calculated (see below) but may well be determined by the amount of storage space available in the warehouse, shop or office stationery 'cupboard'
- the *re-order level*, ie the point at which a new order is to be placed – this is often the most critical factor to determine

Many organisations use manual or computer inventory control systems to keep a running record of the amount of each material held, the lead time for re-ordering, and the minimum inventory level. The level method of re-ordering is illustrated as follows:

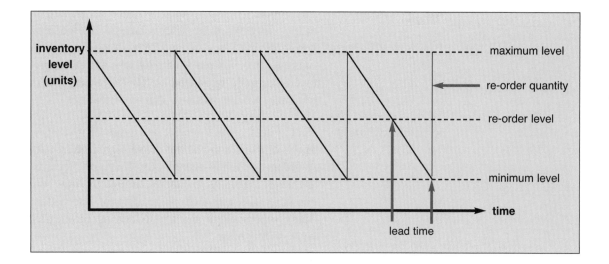

re-order level

The re-order level is calculated so that replacement materials will be delivered just as the inventory level reaches the minimum level. The calculation of re-order level is:

(maximum usage per day/week/month x maximum lead time) + minimum inventory level

re-order quantity

At the re-order level, a purchase order for new inventory is forwarded to the supplier. The quantity to be purchased is the re-order quantity; which is calculated as:

maximum inventory level – minimum inventory level

maximum and minimum inventory levels

By the time new inventory is delivered, the remaining inventory should have fallen to the minimum level, so that the new inventory restores the level to the maximum.

The maximum and minimum inventory levels can be set as follows:

- *maximum inventory level = minimum inventory level + re-order quantity*
- *minimum inventory level = re-order level – (average usage x average lead time)*

However, maximum inventory may be determined by other factors, eg the amount of storage space available, a policy decision not to hold usage of more than a certain number of days/weeks/months.

---

example

A4, white photocopying paper

daily usage	30 reams (a ream is 500 sheets)
lead time	5 days
re-order quantity	750 reams*
minimum inventory level	150 reams**
maximum inventory level	900 reams***

Re-order level = (30 daily usage x 5 days' lead time)
+ 150 minimum inventory

= (30 x 5) + 150

= 150 + 150

= 300 reams (re-order level)

When the balance of inventory falls to 300 reams, a purchase order for 750 reams is forwarded to the supplier of the paper.

* re-order quantity
  = maximum inventory level – minimum inventory level
  = 900 – 150
  = 750 reams

** minimum inventory level
  = re-order level – (average usage x average lead time)
  = 300 – (30 x 5 days)
  = 150 reams

*** maximum inventory level
  = minimum inventory level + re-order quantity
  = 150 + 750
  = 900 reams

It is important not to treat inventory calculations in isolation – there does need to be consideration of wider issues which may affect the business or organisation. Such issues include:

- needs of the business – for example, if an inventory item is being used less frequently than before, the calculations will need to be revised to suit current and future needs

- obsolescence of inventory – for example, if spare parts are kept for a particular make and model of vehicle, inventory levels will need to be run down when the vehicles are being replaced by those of a different make and model

- seasonal variations affecting usage and inventory levels – for example, a business using oil for heating may be offered a cheaper price when usage is low in the summer which may make it worthwhile to buy; by contrast, when usage is high in the winter, the supplier's price and lead times may increase

MATERIALS PURCHASES: ECONOMIC ORDER QUANTITY (EOQ)

It is clear that the re-order quantity is critical to the efficiency of inventory holding:

- if re-order amounts are *too large*, too much inventory will be held, which will be an expense to the business
- if re-order amounts are *too small*, the expense of constantly re-ordering will outweigh any cost savings of lower inventory levels, and there will be the danger that the item might 'run out'

The most economic re-order quantity – **the economic order quantity (EOQ)** – can be calculated by a mathematical formula which involves a number of different costs and other figures:

- *ordering cost* – the administration cost of placing each order, eg stationery, postage, wages, telephone
- *inventory holding cost* – the cost of keeping the inventory on the shelves expressed as the cost of holding one unit of inventory per year; examples of inventory holding costs include rent and rates, insurance, wages, deterioration, obsolescence, security
- *annual usage* – the number of inventory units used per year

The formula is:

$$\textit{Economic Order Quantity (EOQ)} = \sqrt{\frac{2 \times \text{annual usage} \times \text{ordering cost}}{\text{inventory holding cost}}}$$

On a calculator with a square root function, this formula can be worked out easily. Calculate the figures in the formula first, and then press the square root button ($\sqrt{}$).

For example, for a particular inventory item, the ordering cost of each order is £30, the inventory holding cost is £2 per unit per year, and annual usage is 2,000 units. The EOQ formula is applied as follows:

$$\textit{Economic Order Quantity (EOQ)} = \sqrt{\frac{2 \times 2{,}000 \times £30}{£2}}$$

$$= \sqrt{\frac{120{,}000}{2}}$$

$$= \sqrt{60,000}$$

$$= \underline{245 \text{ units}}$$

As a result of using EOQ, a balance is struck between the cost of placing an order and the cost of holding inventory; EOQ represents the most efficient level of order to place because it minimises the total cost of ordering and storage.

Once the EOQ has been calculated, it is used as the quantity of inventory to be ordered each time an order is placed. This principle is illustrated in the Case Study on page 53.

INVENTORY RECORDS

Most organisations will have records of their inventories. Such records may be kept either by using a computer inventory control system, or manually on individual inventory records. Under both methods – computer and manual – a separate record is maintained for each type of inventory. The system is used whether the materials are held for resale by a retailer, or for use in production by a manufacturer. When supplies of the material are received they are entered in the inventory record, and when items are sold (or issued to production) they are shown as issues on the inventory record.

A typical inventory record is shown below. Note that:

- a separate inventory record is used for each type of inventory
- the 'quantity' column can be expressed in units, kg, litres, metres, etc – whatever is suitable for the inventory item
- the 'cost per unit' and 'total cost' columns are always the cost price of the inventory

INVENTORY RECORD

Date	Receipts			Issues			Balance		
	Quantity (units)	Cost per unit	Total Cost	Quantity (units)	Cost per unit	Total Cost	Quantity (units)	Cost per unit	Total Cost
		£	£		£	£		£	£

The layout of the inventory record may vary slightly from one business to another.

The way in which inventory records are used is shown in the Case Study on page 46.

INVENTORY TAKE AND INVENTORY RECONCILIATION

inventory take

A business or organisation will check regularly that the quantity of inventory held is the same as the number recorded on the inventory records. This is done by means of an inventory take – counting the physical inventory held to check against the balance shown by the records, and to identify any theft or deterioration.

An inventory take is carried out on either a periodic basis or continuously.

A *periodic basis* involves carrying out an inventory take of all items held at regular intervals (often twice a year).

Continuous inventory taking is a constant process where selected inventory items are counted on a rotating basis, with all being checked at least once a year (expensive, desirable or high-turnover inventory will need to be checked more frequently).

The number of units of each item actually held is recorded on an inventory list by the person doing the inventory take. An extract from an inventory list is shown below – the list will, of course, contain several inventory items when the inventory take has been completed.

inventory list as at 9 April 20-6		**checker** H Ramsay				
product code	item description	unit size	units counted	inventory record balance	discrepancy	checker's initials
P1026	A4 white photocopying paper	ream	895	895	nil	HR
checker's signature H Ramsay			**Authorised for write-off**			

inventory reconciliation

The object of the inventory take is to see if the inventory records represent accurately the level of inventory held. The two columns on the inventory list – 'units counted' and 'inventory record balance' – enable this comparison to be carried out; the process is known as *inventory reconciliation*. It is an important process because

- an accurate figure can then be used to value the inventory
- it will highlight any discrepancies which can then be investigated

Discrepancies and queries should be noted on the inventory list and referred to the supervisor and any other people who may need to know, eg the storekeeper, or the firm's auditors who are organising the inventory take. If the discrepancy is small it will be authorised for write-off. Larger discrepancies will need to be investigated, as they could have been caused by:

- an error on the inventory record, such as a failure to record an inventory movement or an error in calculating the inventory balance
- theft of inventory
- damaged inventory being disposed of without any record having been made

inventory queries

Inevitably, even in the best-run system, queries will arise about inventory. These queries may come from within the organisation, eg the Production Department, or externally, eg suppliers.

It is important that such queries are resolved swiftly and efficiently by referring directly to the correct department, as indicated in the following diagram:

QUERY	DEPARTMENT or SECTION
inventory levels	stores
materials usage	production, purchasing, goods inwards, auditors
materials prices	purchasing, accounts
quality and rejects	quality control, stores (scrap)
inventory returns	purchasing, accounts

VALUATION OF INVENTORY

The amount of materials inventory held by a business or organisation invariably has considerable value and ties up a lot of money. At the end of the financial year, it is essential to value the inventory for use in the calculation of profit in the financial statements. As we have just seen, a process of inventory taking is used to make a physical check of the inventory held, which is then compared with the inventory records. The inventory held is then valued as follows:

number of items held x cost per item = inventory value at cost

The auditors may make random checks to ensure that the inventory value is correct.

The general rule is that inventory can be valued at *either*:

- what it cost the business to buy (including additional costs to bring the product or service to its present location or condition, such as delivery charges), *or*

- the net realisable value – which is the actual or estimated selling price (less any extra costs, such as selling and distribution) – ie what you would get for it

Inventory valuation is normally made at the *lower of cost and net realisable value*. This valuation is taken from International Accounting Standard (IAS) No 2, entitled *Inventories*. This method of valuation applies the 'prudence' concept of accounting. It is illustrated as follows:

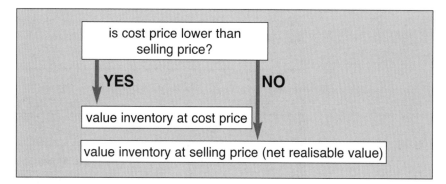

The difficulty with inventory valuation is in finding out the cost price of inventory – this is not easy when quantities of a particular item are continually being bought in – often at different prices – and then sold. Some organisations have inventory in a number of different forms, eg manufacturing businesses have raw materials, work-in-progress and finished goods.

METHODS OF INVENTORY VALUATION

issuing of materials and goods

The costing process requires that a value is given to raw materials (for a manufacturer) and goods (for a shop) when they are 'issued'. This means the point at which they are handed over to the production line or placed on the shop shelves. Traditionally the materials and goods were issued from 'stores' – a storage area – where they had been kept by the business since delivery from the supplier. The phrase 'issued from stores' is still used, although nowadays materials and goods are often delivered just before they are needed – this saves on storage and finance costs.

The cost of the materials or goods at the time of issue is normally the purchase cost – ie the price the business paid the supplier. But purchase costs do vary – so which cost do you take and what valuation do you give the materials or goods?

The two most commonly used methods for deciding which 'cost' to use for raw materials used in the production process or sold from shop shelves are either FIFO (first in, first out) or AVCO (weighted average cost). A third method, LIFO (last in, first out), is sometimes used for cost accounting purposes but is not permitted by IAS 2 for financial accounting. The methods work as follows:

FIFO (First In, First Out)

In this method, the first (oldest) cost prices are used first when goods are issued from stores. This means that the remaining inventory is valued at the most recent cost prices.

AVCO (Weighted Average Cost)

In this method, a weighted average cost is calculated for the inventory held at a given time, using the formula:

$$\textbf{weighted average cost} \quad = \quad \frac{\textbf{total cost of inventory held}}{\textbf{number of items held}}$$

The weighted average cost is then used to attach a value to issues from stores. A new weighted average must be calculated each time that further purchases are made.

LIFO (Last In, First Out)

In this method, the most recent (last) cost prices are used first when goods are issued from stores. This means that the remaining inventory is valued at older cost prices.

The use of a particular method of inventory valuation does not necessarily correspond with the method of physical distribution adopted in a firm's stores. For example, in a car factory one car battery of type X is the same as another, and no-one will be concerned if the issue is one from the last batch received, even if the FIFO system has been adopted. However, perishable goods are always physically handled on the basis of first in, first out, even if the accounting inventory records use another method.

Having chosen a suitable inventory valuation method, a business will continue to use that method unless there are good reasons for making the change. This is in line with the 'consistency' concept of accounting.

Case Study

H RASHID COMPUTER SUPPLIES: INVENTORY RECORDS

situation

H Rashid runs a computer supplies company. One of the items he sells is the 'Zap' data disk.

To show how the inventory records would appear under FIFO, LIFO and AVCO, and the closing inventory valuation at 31 May 20-4, the following data is used for each method:

January	Opening inventory of 40 units at a cost of £3.00 each
February	Bought 20 units at a cost of £3.60 each
March	Sold 36 units for £6 each
April	Bought 20 units at a cost of £3.75 each
May	Sold 25 units for £6 each

What will be the profit for the period using each inventory valuation method?

> Tutorial notes:
>
> • This Case Study shows the inventory records using the three methods: FIFO, LIFO and AVCO. AAT Assessments will usually ask for either FIFO or AVCO – this is because LIFO is not permitted under IAS 2 and, therefore, is not used for financial accounting purposes. For assessments you need to be able to identify and explain the principles behind all three methods.
>
> • The inventory records in this Case Study include, under the 'balance' heading, a column for 'cost per unit'. This column is not always given in AAT Assessments (see Case Study on page 53) but is included here to show the workings clearly.

solution

Note: In the first two methods – FIFO and LIFO – units issued at the same time may be valued at different costs. This is because the quantities received, with their costs, are listed separately and used in a specific order. There may be insufficient units at one cost, eg see the May issue using both FIFO and LIFO methods.

FIFO

INVENTORY RECORD

Date	Receipts			Issues			Balance		
	Quantity (units)	Cost per unit	Total Cost	Quantity (units)	Cost per unit	Total Cost	Quantity (units)	Cost per unit	Total Cost
20-4 Jan	Balance	£	£		£	£	40	£ 3.00	£ 120.00
Feb	20	3.60	72.00				40 20 60	3.00 3.60	120.00 72.00 192.00
March				36	3.00	108.00	4 20 24	3.00 3.60	12.00 72.00 84.00
April	20	3.75	75.00				4 20 20 44	3.00 3.60 3.75	12.00 72.00 75.00 159.00
May				4 20 1 25	3.00 3.60 3.75	12.00 72.00 3.75 87.75	19	3.75	71.25

Note: In the 'Balance' columns, a new list of inventory quantities and costs is started after each receipt or issue. When inventory is issued, costs are used from the **top** of the list downwards.

LIFO

INVENTORY RECORD

Date	Receipts			Issues			Balance		
	Quantity (units)	Cost per unit	Total Cost	Quantity (units)	Cost per unit	Total Cost	Quantity (units)	Cost per unit	Total Cost
20-4 Jan	Balance	£	£		£	£	40	£ 3.00	£ 120.00
Feb	20	3.60	72.00				40	3.00	120.00
							20	3.60	72.00
							60		192.00
March				20	3.60	72.00			
				16	3.00	48.00			
				36		120.00	24	3.00	72.00
April	20	3.75	75.00				24	3.00	72.00
							20	3.75	75.00
							44		147.00
May				20	3.75	75.00			
				5	3.00	15.00			
				25		90.00	19	3.00	57.00

Note: In the 'Balance' columns, a new list of inventory quantities and costs is started after each receipt or issue. When inventory is issued, costs are used from the **bottom** of the list upwards. However, the new balance list each time must be kept in date order.

AVCO

In this method, each quantity issued is valued at the weighted average cost per unit, and so is the balance of inventory. The complete list of different costs does not have to be re-written each time.

INVENTORY RECORD

Date	Receipts			Issues			Balance		
	Quantity (units)	Cost per unit	Total Cost	Quantity (units)	Cost per unit	Total Cost	Quantity (units)	Cost per unit	Total Cost
20-4 Jan	Balance	£	£		£	£	40	£ 3.00	£ 120.00
Feb	20	3.60	72.00				40	3.00	120.00
							20	3.60	72.00
							60	3.20	192.00
March				36	3.20	115.20	24	3.20	76.80
April	20	3.75	75.00				24	3.20	76.80
							20	3.75	75.00
							44	3.45	151.80
May				25	3.45	86.25	19	3.45	65.55

Note: Weighted average cost is calculated by dividing the quantity of inventory held into the value of the inventory. For example, at the end of February, the weighted average cost is £192 ÷ 60 units = £3.20, and at the end of April it is £151.80 ÷ 44 = £3.45.

The closing inventory valuations at the end of May 20-4 under each method show total cost prices of:

FIFO	£71.25
LIFO	£57.00
AVCO	£65.55

There is quite a difference, and this has come about because different inventory valuation methods have been used.

effect on profit

In the example above, the selling price was £6 per unit. The effect on gross profit of using different inventory valuations is shown below.

	FIFO	LIFO	AVCO
	£	£	£
Revenue: 61 units at £6	366.00	366.00	366.00
Opening inventory: 40 units at £3	120.00	120.00	120.00
Purchases: 20 units at £3.60 and 20 units at £3.75	147.00	147.00	147.00
	267.00	267.00	267.00
Less Closing inventory: 19 units	71.25	57.00	65.55
Cost of sales	195.75	210.00	201.45
Gross profit = Revenue − Cost of sales	170.25	156.00	164.55

Notice that the cost of sales figure in each case is also obtainable by adding up the values in the 'Issues' column. You can also check in each case that, both in Units and in Values:

opening inventory + receipts − issues = closing inventory

The Case Study shows that in times of rising prices, FIFO produces the highest reported profit, LIFO the lowest, and AVCO between the other two. However, over the life of a business, total profit is the same in total, whichever method is chosen: the profit is allocated to different years depending on which method is used.

The choice of method depends on which method is considered to give the most useful information for management purposes.

ADVANTAGES AND DISADVANTAGES OF FIFO, LIFO AND AVCO

FIFO (first in, first out)

advantages

- it is realistic, ie it assumes that goods are issued in order of receipt
- it is easy to calculate
- inventory valuation comprises actual costs at which items have been bought
- the closing inventory valuation is close to the most recent costs
- permitted under IAS 2, *Inventories*

disadvantages

- costs at which goods are issued are not necessarily the latest prices
- in times of rising prices, profits will be higher than with other methods (resulting in more tax to pay)
- the method is cumbersome as the list of different costs must be maintained

LIFO (last in, first out)

advantages

- goods are issued at the latest costs
- it is easy to calculate
- in manufacturing, materials are issued at more up-to-date costs, giving a more realistic production cost

disadvantages

- illogical, ie it assumes goods are issued in reverse order from that in which they are received
- the closing inventory valuation is not usually at most recent costs
- when inventories are being run down, issues will 'dip into' old inventory at out-of-date costs
- may not be acceptable for taxation purposes as the method overstates cost of sales and understates profit
- the method is cumbersome as the list of different costs must be maintained
- not permitted under IAS 2, *Inventories*

AVCO (weighted average cost)

advantages

- over a number of accounting periods reported profits are smoothed, ie both high and low profits are avoided
- fluctuations in purchase costs are evened out so that issues do not vary greatly
- logical, ie it assumes that identical units, even when purchased at different times, have the same value
- closing inventory valuation is close to current market values (in times of rising prices, it will be below current market values)
- the calculations can be computerised more easily than the other methods
- permitted under IAS 2, *Inventories*

disadvantages

- a new weighted average has to be calculated after each receipt, and calculations may be to several decimal places
- issues and inventory valuation are usually at costs which never existed
- issues may not be at current costs and, in times of rising prices, will be below current costs

The important point to remember is that a business must adopt a consistent inventory valuation policy, ie it should choose one method of finding the cost price, and not change it without good reason. FIFO and AVCO are more commonly used than LIFO; in particular, LIFO usually results in an inventory valuation for the final accounts which bears little relationship to recent costs – for this reason it is not permitted by IAS 2. However, LIFO has the advantage that it gives a more realistic production cost – this is because materials are issued at more up-to-date prices. It is also appropriate to apply LIFO principles when costing materials in a quotation to be given to a potential customer: in times of rising prices you wouldn't want to quote old prices – for example, under FIFO – and then, when the quotation is accepted, find that there is no more of the older-priced materials left.

Now study the table on the next page to consolidate what you have learnt so far.

a comparison of the methods of inventory valuation

	FIFO	LIFO	AVCO
method	The costs used for goods sold or issued follow the order in which the goods were received.	The costs used for goods sold or issued are opposite to the order in which the goods were received.	Does not relate issues to any particular batch of goods received, but uses a weighted average cost.
calculation	It is easy to calculate costs because they relate to specific receipts of materials or goods.	It is easy to calculate costs because they relate to specific receipts of materials or goods.	More complex because of the need to calculate weighted average costs.
inventory valuation	Inventory valuations are based on the most recent costs of materials or goods received.	Inventory valuations are based on older costs of materials or goods received.	Weighted average costs are used to value closing inventory.
profits and taxation	In times of rising prices this method will result in higher reported profits than the other methods, resulting in more tax being payable. This method is acceptable for tax purposes and is permitted under IAS 2, *Inventories*.	In times of rising prices this method will result in lower reported profits than the other methods. This is not usually acceptable for tax purposes and is not permitted under IAS 2, *Inventories*.	The weighted average method will smooth out some of the peaks and troughs of profit and loss. This method is acceptable for tax purposes and is permitted under IAS 2, *Inventories*.
administration	Use of this method will mean keeping track of each receipt until the goods are issued or sold.	Use of this method will mean keeping track of each receipt until the goods are issued or sold.	There is no need to track each receipt as a weighted average cost is used. This also means it is easier to computerise the inventory records.
cost of sales	In a time of rising prices this method will use older, out of date prices for cost of sales or goods issued.	In a time of rising prices this method will use more up-to-date prices for cost of sales or goods issued.	This method will give an average price for the cost of sales.

| Case Study | USING ECONOMIC ORDER QUANTITY AND INVENTORY RECORDS |

1.850

1.600

Tutorial note: This Case Study is based on AAT Assessments – note that the inventory record does not give a 'cost per unit' under the 'balance' heading.

situation

You are an accounts assistant at Stoke Park Limited and have been asked to help with the inventory records.
The cost accountant has given you the following information for metal grade FE4.

- Annual demand – 28,125 kilograms

- Annual holding cost per kilogram – £0.50

- Fixed ordering cost – £20

(a) **You are to calculate the Economic Order Quantity (EOQ) for FE4.**

The inventory record shown on the next page for metal grade FE4 for the month of September has only been fully completed for the first three weeks of the month.

(b) **You are to complete the entries in the inventory record for the two receipts on 25 and 29 September that were ordered using the EOQ method.**

(c) **You are to complete all entries in the inventory record for the two issues in the month and for the closing balance at the end of September using the FIFO method of issuing inventory.**

Inventory record for metal grade FE4

Date	Receipts			Issues			Balance	
	Quantity (kg)	Cost per kg	Total Cost	Quantity (kg)	Cost per kg	Total Cost	Quantity (kg)	Total Cost
		£	£		£	£		£
Balance as at 23 September							740	814
25 September		1.20						
27 September				850				
29 September		1.25						
30 September				1,630				

solution

(a) Economic Order Quantity (EOQ) $= \sqrt{\dfrac{2 \times 28{,}125 \text{ kg} \times £20}{£0.50}}$

$= \sqrt{\dfrac{1{,}125{,}000}{0.50}}$

$= \sqrt{2{,}250{,}000}$

$= \underline{1{,}500 \text{ kg}}$

(b) and (c)

Inventory record for metal grade FE4

Date	Receipts			Issues			Balance	
	Quantity (kg)	Cost per kg	Total Cost	Quantity (kg)	Cost per kg	Total Cost	Quantity (kg)	Total Cost
		£	£		£	£		£
Balance as at 23 September							740	814
25 September	1,500	1.20	1,800				740 1,500 2,240	814 1,800 2,614
27 September				740 110 850	1.10 1.20	814 132 946	1,390	1,668
29 September	1,500	1.25	1,875				1,390 1,500 2,890	1,668 1,875 3,543
30 September				1,390 240 1,630	1.20 1.25	1,668 300 1,968	1,260	1,575

Tutorial notes:

- This Case Study uses the FIFO method of issuing inventory – AAT Assessments will usually ask for either FIFO or AVCO. As LIFO is not permitted under IAS 2 it is, therefore, not used for financial accounting purposes – nevertheless, you should be able to identify and explain the principles behind the three methods.

- With the FIFO method you will note that issues may be valued at different costs – as here on 27 and 30 September. This is because the quantities received, with their costs are listed separately and used in a specific order.

CATEGORIES OF INVENTORY

International Accounting Standard No 2, *Inventories*, requires that, in calculating the lower of cost and net realisable value, note should be taken of:

- separate items of inventory, or
- groups of similar items

This means that the inventory valuation 'rule' must be applied to each separate item of inventory, or each group or category of similar inventory. The total cost cannot be compared with the total net realisable value, as is shown by the Case Study which follows.

Case
Study

1.850

1.600

PAINT AND WALLPAPER SUPPLIES: INVENTORY VALUATION

situation

The year-end valuations for the two main groups of inventory held by the business Paint and Wallpaper Supplies are found to be:

	Cost	Net realisable value
	£	£
Paints	2,500	2,300
Wallpapers	5,000	7,500
	7,500	9,800

Which one of the following inventory valuations do you think is correct?

(a)   £7,500

(b)   £9,800

(c)   £7,300

(d)   £10,000

solution

Inventory valuation (c) is correct, because it has taken the 'lower of cost and net realisable value' for each group of inventory, ie

	£
Paints (at net realisable value)	2,300
Wallpapers (at cost)	5,000
	7,300

You will also note that this valuation is the lowest of the four choices, indicating that inventory valuation follows the *prudence concept* of accounting.

INVENTORY VALUATION FOR MANUFACTURING BUSINESSES

We saw earlier that, under IAS 2, inventory is normally valued at the lower of cost and net realisable value. This principle applies to a manufacturer for the three types of inventory that may be held at the year-end:

- raw materials
- part-finished goods or work-in-progress
- finished goods

For raw materials, the comparison is made between cost (which can be found using techniques such as FIFO, LIFO, or AVCO) and net realisable value.

For part-finished and finished goods, IAS 2 requires that the cost valuation includes expenditure not only on direct materials but also on direct labour, direct expenses and production overheads. Thus for part-finished and finished goods, 'cost' means 'production cost', ie the total of:

- direct materials
- direct labour
- direct expenses
- production overheads (to bring the product to its present location or condition)

Such 'cost' is then compared with net realisable value – less any further costs necessary to complete the item or get it in a condition to be sold – and the lower figure is taken as the inventory valuation. (Remember that different items or groups of inventory are compared separately).

Case Study

ABC MANUFACTURING: INVENTORIES VALUATION

situation

ABC Manufacturing started in business on 1 July 20-3 producing security devices for doors and windows. During the first year 2,000 units were sold and, at the end of the year, on 30 June 20-4, there were 200 units which were finished and 20 units which were exactly half-finished as regards direct materials, direct labour and production overheads.

Costs for the first year were:

	£
Direct materials used	18,785
Direct labour	13,260
Production overheads	8,840
Non-production overheads	4,420
Total cost for year	45,305

At 30 June 20-4 it was estimated that the net realisable value of each completed security device was £35. At the same date, the company holds raw materials as follows:

	cost	net realisable value
	£	£
Material A	1,400	1,480
Material B	400	360
Material C	260	280

Calculate the inventories valuation at 30 June 20-4 for:

- raw materials
- work-in-progress
- finished goods

solution

RAW MATERIALS

Using the IAS 2 rule of the 'lower of cost and net realisable value' the total value is:

	£	
Material A	1,400	(cost)
Material B	360	(net realisable value)
Material C	260	(cost)
	2,020	

WORK-IN-PROGRESS

To calculate the value of both work-in-progress and finished goods we need to know the production cost, ie direct materials, direct labour and production overheads. This is:

	£
Direct materials used	18,785
Direct labour	13,260
Production overheads	8,840
Production cost for year	**40,885**

All these costs are included because they have been incurred in bringing the product to its present location or condition. Non-production overheads are not included because they are not directly related to production.

Thus, a production cost of £40,885 has produced:

Units sold	2,000
Closing inventory of completed units	200
Closing inventory of work-in-progress –	
20 units exactly half-finished equals	
10 completed units	10
Production for year	**2,210**

The **cost per unit** is:

$$\frac{£40,885}{2,210} = \textbf{£18.50 per unit}$$

The 20 half-finished units have a cost of $(20 \div 2) \times £18.50 = \textbf{£185}$.
They have a net realisable value of $(20 \div 2) \times £35 = £350$.
The value of work-in-progress will, therefore, be shown in the financial statements as £185, which is the lower of cost and net realisable value.

FINISHED GOODS
The completed units held at the end of the year have a production cost of $200 \times £18.50 = £3,700$, compared with a net realisable value of $200 \times £35 = £7,000$. Applying the rule of lower of cost and net realisable value, finished goods inventory will be valued at the cost price, **£3,700**.

BOOK-KEEPING FOR MATERIALS COSTS

In this section we look at the cost book-keeping entries to record inventory transactions – the purchase of materials either on credit from suppliers or on cash terms, and the issue or return of inventory to production. These entries form part of the book-keeping system for costing.

When making cost book-keeping entries, remember to use the principles of double-entry book-keeping:

- a debit entry records a gain in value, an asset or an expense
- a credit entry records the giving of value, a liability or an income item

With materials, the general ledger entries are:

- **purchase of materials on credit from a supplier**
    - debit inventory (asset gained)
    - credit trade payables (creditors) control (liability incurred)

- **purchase of materials on cash terms** (ie immediate payment from bank)
    - debit inventory (asset gained)
    - credit bank (value given by bank)

- **issue of materials to production**
    - debit production (asset of materials gained)
    - credit inventory (value of materials given to production)

- **return of materials from production to inventory**
    - debit inventory (asset gained)
    - credit production (value given by production)

Four accounts are involved in these transactions
    - inventory account
    - production account
    - trade payables control account
    - bank account

The cost book-keeping entries are shown diagrammatically as follows:

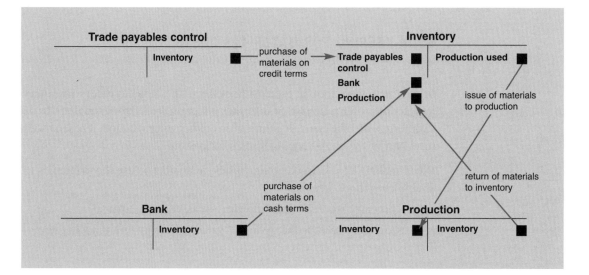

Case Study

1.850

BLUE JEANS LIMITED:
BOOK-KEEPING FOR MATERIALS COSTS

situation

Blue Jeans Limited manufactures and sells denim jeans and jackets. The company uses the first in, first out (FIFO) method for valuing issues of materials to production and for valuing inventory.

The company has been very busy in recent weeks and, as a consequence, some of the accounting records are not up-to-date. The following inventory record has not been completed:

INVENTORY RECORD

Product: **Blue denim**

Date	Receipts			Issues			Balance	
	Quantity (metres)	Cost per metre	Total Cost	Quantity (metres)	Cost per metre	Total Cost	Quantity (metres)	Total Cost
20-4		£	£		£	£		£
Balance at 1 Oct							20,000	10,000
11 Oct	10,000	0.60	6,000				30,000	16,000
14 Oct				25,000				
19 Oct	20,000	0.70	14,000					
25 Oct				20,000				

All issues of blue denim are for the manufacture of blue jeans. The following cost accounting codes are used to record material costs:

code number	description
2000	inventory – blue denim
2200	production – blue jeans
4000	trade payables control

As an accounts assistant at Blue Jeans Limited, you are asked to complete the inventory record and to fill in the table below to record the journal entries for the two purchases and two issues of blue denim in the cost accounting records.

20-4	Code number	Debit £	Credit £
11 October	2000		
11 October	4000		
14 October	2000		
14 October	2200		
19 October	2000		
19 October	4000		
25 October	2000		
25 October	2200		

solution

The inventory record is completed as shown on the next page.

Note that there may be a need to calculate the balance from more than one receipt cost. For example, on 11 October, the balance is made up of:

			£
20,000	metres at £0.50 per metre	=	10,000
10,000	metres at £0.60 per metre	=	6,000
30,000	metres	=	16,000

Similarly, on 19 October, the balance is made up of:

			£
5,000	metres at £0.60 per metre	=	3,000
20,000	metres at £0.70 per metre	=	14,000
25,000		=	17,000

INVENTORY RECORD

Product: **Blue denim**

Date	Receipts			Issues			Balance	
	Quantity (metres)	Cost per metre	Total Cost	Quantity (metres)	Cost per metre	Total Cost	Quantity (metres)	Total Cost
20-4		£	£		£	£		£
Balance at 1 Oct							20,000	10,000
11 Oct	10,000	0.60	6,000				20,000 10,000 30,000	10,000 6,000 16,000
14 Oct				20,000 5,000 25,000	0.50 0.60	10,000 3,000 13,000	5,000	3,000
19 Oct	20,000	0.70	14,000				5,000 20,000 25,000	3,000 14,000 17,000
25 Oct				5,000 15,000 20,000	0.60 0.70	3,000 10,500 13,500	5,000	3,500

The cost book-keeping entries are:

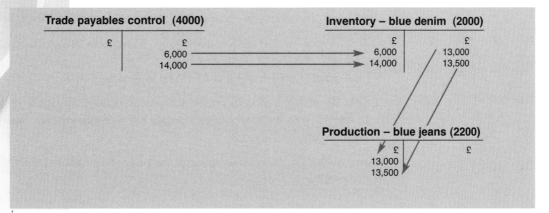

The cost book-keeping transactions are recorded as journal entries in the following way:

20-4	Code number	Debit £	Credit £
11 October	2000	£6,000	
11 October	4000		£6,000
14 October	2000		£13,000
14 October	2200	£13,000	
19 October	2000	£14,000	
19 October	4000		£14,000
25 October	2000		£13,500
25 October	2200	£13,500	

Chapter Summary

- Businesses and other organisations hold materials inventory in the form of raw materials and components bought for production, products bought for resale, and service items bought for use within the business.

- Two important inventory costs are the ordering cost and the inventory holding cost.

- Materials purchases can be made using:
  - the level method of re-ordering
  - Economic Order Quantity (EOQ)

- The level of inventory is recorded on an inventory record, which also indicates
  - the level at which inventory should be ordered
  - the quantity of inventory that should be re-ordered

- Levels of materials inventory are monitored regularly by means of an inventory take; inventory reconciliation notes any discrepancies and reports them for further investigation.

- Inventory valuation is normally made *at the lower of cost and net realisable value* (IAS 2).

- Inventory valuation methods include:
  - FIFO (first in, first out)
  - LIFO (last in, first out)
  - AVCO (weighted average cost)

  LIFO is not permitted under IAS 2 and is, therefore not used for financial accounting purposes

- For a manufacturer, cost comprises the direct manufacturing costs of materials, labour and expenses, together with the production overheads which bring the product to its present location or condition.

- Cost book-keeping entries are made to record inventory transactions such as:
  - purchase of materials on credit from suppliers or on cash terms
  - issue of materials to production
  - return of materials from production to inventory

Key Terms

materials	the cost of: - raw materials and components used in production - products bought for resale - service items bought for use within the business
level method of re-ordering	the re-ordering of materials in fixed quantities
Economic Order Quantity (EOQ)	a method of minimising ordering costs and inventory holding costs; calculated by the formula: $$\sqrt{\frac{2 \times \text{annual usage} \times \text{ordering cost}}{\text{inventory holding cost}}}$$
inventory record	record held for each inventory item which shows receipts of supplies and sales (or issues to production)
inventory take	the process of counting the physical inventory held
inventory reconciliation	comparison of the physical inventory held with the inventory record balance and identification of the reason(s) for discrepancies

inventory value	number of items held x inventory valuation per item
cost	the amount it cost to buy the inventory (including additional costs to bring the product to its present location or condition)
net realisable value	selling price (less any extra costs, such as selling and distribution)
FIFO	'First in, first out' method of attaching a value to each issue of materials or goods from stores, using the oldest cost prices first
LIFO	'Last in, first out' method of attaching a value to each issue of materials or goods from stores, using most recent cost prices first
AVCO	'Average cost' method of attaching a value to each issue of materials or goods from stores, using a weighted average of the cost prices of all items in inventory at the date of issue
inventory record	method of recording inventory data in order to ascertain the cost at which materials are issued, and to ascertain a valuation of closing inventory
cost book-keeping	double-entry system to record costing transactions; uses the principles of double-entry book-keeping

Activities

2.1 Calculate, for inventory items D and E, the re-order inventory level and the re-order quantity to replenish inventory levels to the maximum level, from the following information:
- daily usage of D = 3 units, of E = 4 units
- total inventory should never exceed 95 days' usage
- 10 days' inventory should always be held
- there is space available in the store for 350 units of each item of inventory
- lead time is 7 days

2.2 The following information is available for material XX5:
- annual demand – 56,250 kilograms
- annual holding cost per kilogram – £2
- fixed ordering cost – £10

You are to calculate the Economic Order Quantity (EOQ) for material XX5.

2.3   Complete the following sentences:

(a)   Inventory levels and movements are recorded on an ....

(b)   A person carrying out an inventory check will record the inventory on an ....

....

(c)   The process of comparing inventory on the shelves with inventory in the records is known

as ....

(d)   The usual basis for inventory valuation is at the lower of .... and ....

....

2.4   From the following information prepare inventory records for product X using:

(a) FIFO

(b) LIFO

(c) AVCO

•   20 units of the product are bought in January 20-4 at a cost of £3 each

•   10 units are bought in February at a cost of £3.60 each

•   8 units are sold in March

•   10 units are bought in April at a cost of £4.00 each

•   16 units are sold in May

Notes:

•   a blank inventory record, which may be photocopied, is provided in the Appendix

•   where appropriate, work to the nearest penny

2.5   XY Limited is formed on 1 January 20-4 and, at the end of its first half-year of trading, the inventory records show the following:

20-4	TYPE X		TYPE Y	
	Receipts (units)	**Issues (units)**	**Receipts (units)**	**Issues (units)**
January	100 at £4.00		200 at £10.00	
February		80	100 at £9.50	
March	140 at £4.20			240
April	100 at £3.80		100 at £10.50	
May		140	140 at £10.00	
June	80 at £4.50			100

At 30 June 20-4, the net realisable value of each type of inventory is:

type X	£1,750
type Y	£1,950
	£3,700

You are to:

- Complete inventory records for products X and Y using (a) FIFO, (b) LIFO, (c) AVCO.

- The business has decided to use the FIFO method. Show the amount at which its inventory should be valued on 30 June 20-4 in order to comply with international accounting standards.

Note: a blank inventory record, which may be photocopied, is provided in the Appendix

2.6 Breeden Bakery Limited makes 'homestyle' cakes which are sold to supermarket chains.

The company uses the first in, first out (FIFO) method of issuing inventory.

As an accounts assistant at Breeden Bakery you have been given the following tasks.

Task 1

Complete the following inventory record for wholewheat flour for May 20-4:

INVENTORY RECORD

Product: Wholewheat flour

Date	Receipts			Issues			Balance	
	Quantity (kgs)	Cost per kg	Total Cost	Quantity (kgs)	Cost per kg	Total Cost	Quantity (kgs)	Total Cost
20-4 Balance at 1 May		£	£		£	£		£
							10,000	2,500
6 May	20,000	0.30	6,000				30,000	8,500
10 May				20,000				
17 May	10,000	0.35	3,500					
20 May				15,000				

Task 2

All issues of wholewheat flour are for the manufacture of fruit cakes. The following cost accounting codes are used to record materials costs:

code number	description
3000	inventory – wholewheat flour
3300	production – fruit cakes
5000	trade payables control

Complete the table below to record the journal entries for the two purchases and two issues of wholewheat flour in the cost accounting records.

20-4	Code number	Debit £	Credit £
6 May	3000		
6 May	5000		
10 May	3000		
10 May	3300		
17 May	3000		
17 May	5000		
20 May	3000		
20 May	3300		

2.7 The following information is available for plastic grade P5:

- Annual demand – 57,600 kilograms
- Annual holding cost per kilogram – £2
- Fixed ordering cost – £25

(a) You are to calculate the Economic Order Quantity (EOQ) for P5.

EOQ = ...kg

The inventory record shown below for plastic grade P5 for the month of June has only been fully completed for the first three weeks of the month.

(b) Complete the entries in the inventory record for the two receipts on 23 and 26 June that were ordered using the EOQ method.

(c) Complete ALL entries in the inventory record for the two issues in the month and for the closing balance at the end of June using the AVCO method of issuing inventory.

Show the costs per kilogram (kg) in £ to 3 decimal places, and the total costs in whole £.

Inventory record for plastic grade P5

Date	Receipts			Issues			Balance	
	Quantity (kg)	Cost per kg £	Total Cost £	Quantity (kg)	Cost per kg £	Total Cost £	Quantity (kg)	Total Cost £
Balance as at 22 June							4,400	10,560
23 June		2.634						
25 June				1,000				
26 June		2.745						
29 June				1,500				

2.8 Crossways Limited uses the following accounts to record inventory transactions in its cost book-keeping system:

- inventory account

- trade payables control account

- bank account

- production account

For each of the four transactions in the following table show the account which will be debited and the account which will be credited.

Transaction	Account debited	Account credited
1. Receipt of materials into inventory, paying on credit		
2. Issue of materials from inventory to production		
3. Receipt of materials into inventory, paying immediately by BACS		
4. Return of materials from production to inventory		

3 Labour costs

In Chapter 1 we saw how costs can be classified by element as materials, labour and expenses. In this chapter we focus on labour costs and explain:

- the factors that affect labour costs
- the methods by which the direct labour employees of a business or organisation can be paid
- how payroll information is gathered
- the advantages and disadvantages of different labour payment methods
- overtime and idle time
- the use of a time sheet to calculate gross wages
- the book-keeping entries for labour costs

ACCOUNTING FOR LABOUR COSTS

Labour cost is one of the elements of costs – all businesses incur labour costs which are the costs of wages and salaries of all their employees.

factors that affect labour costs

There are many factors that need to be considered by a business when deciding how much to pay employees. The starting point will always be the amount that is paid by other businesses in the area for similar grades of employees but, at the same time, the wider economic implications of supply and demand will affect wage rates.

The factors to consider include:

- wage rates paid by other local businesses

- comparisons with national average wage rates

- the national minimum wage rate imposed by government

- any government incentives to take on additional employees, such as young people or the long-term unemployed

- local employment conditions – high unemployment in the area will drive down wage rates; conversely low unemployment, and especially a shortage of skilled labour, will increase wage rates

- housing and transport costs in the locality

- the impact of interest rate changes, and exchange rates (eg against the euro) on business confidence

- for a new business, it might be prudent to choose to locate in an area of high unemployment – in addition to lower wage rates, there may be government incentives in the form of reduced rents and rates, training and other grants

Before taking on labour, a business must decide how to calculate gross pay for its employees. Labour payment methods are looked at in detail on the next page. Wages are usually calculated according to time worked or work done, or a combination of both.

LABOUR PAYMENT METHODS

Direct labour cost is the wages paid to those who work on a production line, are involved in assembly, or are involved in the output of a service business.

The three main payment methods for direct labour are:

time rate   Time rate, or basic pay, is where the employee is paid on the basis of time spent at work. Overtime is often paid for hours worked beyond a standard number of hours, or for work carried out on days which are not part of the working week, eg Saturdays or Sundays. Overtime is often paid at rates such as 'time-and-a-quarter', 'time-and-a-half', or 'double-time'. 'Time-and-a-half', for example, means that 1.5 times the basic hourly rate is paid.

Time rate is often referred to as a 'day rate'.

piecework rate   The employee is paid an agreed sum for each task carried out or for each unit of output completed.

In some cases, employees may have a guaranteed minimum wage.

bonus system   The employee is paid a time rate and then receives a bonus if output is better than expected when comparing the time allowed with the time taken. The bonus is calculated as an agreed percentage of the time saved multiplied by the time rate.

Bonus systems base employees' earnings on a combination of time taken and work done.

Most other employees, eg factory supervisors, sales staff, office staff, are usually paid on a weekly or monthly basis. Such wages and salaries – classed as indirect labour costs – may be increased by bonus payments; for example, a production bonus for factory supervisors, commissions for sales staff, a profit-sharing scheme for all employees.

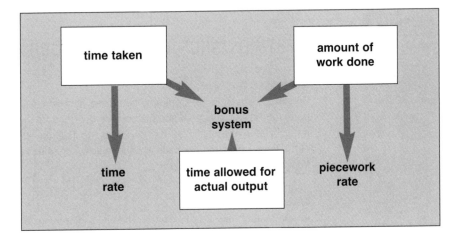

There are many variations on the three methods outlined above and, indeed, changing patterns of employment create different payment methods from those that would have been the norm just a few years ago. For example, the contracting out of many business support services – such as cleaning, security, computers – means that the costing of such services by the provider may incorporate time rates and bonus systems whereas previously the employees would have been paid on a weekly or monthly basis.

In order to calculate gross wages, information about hours worked and/or work done must be recorded. The documents used include:

- *time sheets,* where employees record the hours they have worked (see page 83)

- *clock cards,* where employees 'clock in' at the start of work, and 'clock out' at the end – these are often computerised

- *piecework tickets,* completed by employees who work on a batch of output

- *job cards,* where each employee records the amount of time spent on each job

- *route cards* – which are used to follow a product through the production process – on which employees record the amount of time they spend working on the product

- *computer cards* – 'swipe' cards which link direct into the computerised payroll are increasingly being used by employers to record attendance

WESTMID MANUFACTURING: LABOUR PAYMENT

situation

Westmid Manufacturing Company has three factories in the West Midlands making parts for the car industry. Each factory was bought from the previous owners and, as a result, each has a different method for paying its direct labour workforce. The details of the labour payment methods in each factory, together with data on two employees from each factory, are as follows:

WALSALL FACTORY

In this factory, which is involved in heavy engineering, employees are paid on the basis of a time rate. Employees are required to 'clock in' and 'clock out' each day.

John Brown is a machine operator and his clock card for last week shows that he worked 39 hours; his basic pay is £10 per hour.

Stefan Wozniak is a skilled lathe operator and his clock card shows that he worked 42 hours; his basic pay is £12 per hour, with overtime for hours worked beyond 37 hours at 'time-and-a-half'.

DUDLEY FACTORY

This factory operates a number of light engineering production lines making car components such as windscreen wiper blades, headlamp surrounds, interior mirrors etc. The production line employees are all paid on a piecework basis; however, each employee receives a guaranteed time rate which is paid if the piecework earnings are less than the time rate. This may happen if, for example, there are machine breakdowns and the production line has to be halted.

Tracey Johnson works on the line making headlamp surrounds. For each one that passes through her part of the process, she is paid 40p; her guaranteed time rate is 35 hours each week at £10 per hour. Last week's production records show that she processed 910 units.

Pete Bronyah is on the line which makes interior mirrors. For his part of the process he receives £1.00 for each one, with a guaranteed time rate of 35 hours at £10 per hour. Last week there was a machine failure and he was only able to process 250 units.

WOLVERHAMPTON FACTORY

In this factory a number of engineering production lines are operated. The direct labour force is paid on a time rate basis, but a bonus is paid if work can be completed faster than the time allowed. The bonus is for the savings achieved to be shared equally between employer and employee. Wages are, therefore, paid on the following basis: time rate + 50% of (time saved x time rate). If no bonus is due, then the time rate applies.

Martin Lee worked a 38 hour work last week; his time rate is £10 per hour. He is allowed a time of 30 minutes to carry out his work on each unit of production; last week he completed 71 units.

Sara King has a time rate of £11 per hour; last week she worked 40 hours. She is allowed a time of 15 minutes to carry out her work on each unit of production; last week she completed 184 units.

What were the gross earnings of each employee?

solution

WALSALL FACTORY

John Brown	39 hours x £10.00 per hour	=	£390.00
Stefan Wozniak	37 hours x £12.00 per hour = £444		
	5 hours x £18.00 per hour = £90	=	£534.00

DUDLEY FACTORY

Tracey Johnson	Piecework rate, 910 units x 40p per unit	=	£364.00
	Guaranteed time rate, 35 hours x £10.00 per hour =		£350.00
	Therefore piecework rate of £364.00 is paid.		

Pete Bronyah	Piecework rate, 250 units x £1.00 per unit	=	£250.00
	Guaranteed time rate, 35 hours x £10.00 per hour =		£350.00
	Therefore guaranteed time rate of £350.00 is paid.		

WOLVERHAMPTON FACTORY

Martin Lee	Time rate, 38 hours x £10.00 per hour	=	£380.00
	Bonus, time allowed 71 units x 30 minutes each = 35 hours 30 minutes		
	Therefore no time saved, so no bonus payable.		
	Time rate of £380 paid.		

Sara King	Time rate, 40 hours x £11.00 per hour	=	£440.00
	Bonus, time allowed 184 x 15 minutes each = 46 hours		
	Therefore time saved is 6 hours		
	Bonus is 50% of (6 hours x £11.00)	=	£33.00
	Therefore wages are £440.00 + £33.00	=	£473.00

The Case Study illustrates some of the direct labour payment methods in use, however it should be appreciated that there are many variations on these to be found.

DIRECT LABOUR PAYMENT METHODS: ADVANTAGES AND DISADVANTAGES

time rate

Time rate is often used where it is difficult to measure output, and where quality is more important than quantity. Variations include a high time rate, used to motivate employees where a higher standard of work is required.

advantages:
- easy to understand and to calculate
- no requirement to establish time allowances and piecework rates
- the employee receives a regular wage, unaffected by fluctuations in output
- the employer pays a regular amount, making planning for cash flows easier
- can be used for all direct labour employees
- quality of the finished product does not suffer as a result of hurried work

disadvantages:
- both efficient and inefficient employees receive the same wage
- no incentive is given to employees to work harder
- slower working will not affect basic wage, but may lead to overtime
- more supervisors are needed to ensure that output is maintained

piecework rate

Piecework rate is used where the quantity of output is important, and there is less emphasis on quality. Variations include:

- piecework with guaranteed time rate, which ensures that employees are paid if production is stopped through no fault of their own, eg machine breakdown, or shortage of materials

- differential piecework system, where a higher rate is paid for all output beyond a certain level, eg 50p per unit for the first 100 units each day, then 60p per unit thereafter; used to motivate employees to produce more than a basic level of output

- attendance allowances, paid to encourage employees on piecework to attend each day, thus ensuring that the production-line can be staffed and operated every working day *advantages:*

- payment of wages is linked directly to output
- more efficient workers earn more than those who are less efficient
- work is done quicker and less time is wasted

disadvantages:

- not suitable for all direct labour employees
- pay is reduced if there are production problems, eg machine breakdown or shortage of materials
- quality of the finished product may be low, so not suitable where quality is more important than quantity
- more inspections may be needed
- control systems needed to check the amount produced by each worker
- more complex pay calculations
- may be difficulty in agreeing piecework rates with employees
- the employer cannot plan ahead for wages costs so easily, as they may be irregular amounts

bonus systems

Bonus systems are used to encourage employees to be more efficient in an environment where the work is not so repetitive. Variations include an accelerating premium bonus – which is an increased bonus paid for higher levels of output, and group bonuses paid to groups of employees who achieve increased output – the group could be as large as the entire workforce of a large company, or as small as a work team of two or three people.

advantages:

- wages linked to output, but minimum wage is guaranteed each week
- work is done quicker and less time is wasted
- more efficient workers earn more
- a bonus system can often be applied to the entire workforce

disadvantages:

- bonus is not paid if circumstances beyond employee's control prevent work, eg machine breakdown or shortage of materials
- quality of finished product may be low
- more inspections may be needed and additional control procedures
- pay calculations may be more complex

- there may be difficulty in agreeing bonus rates with employees

- group bonus schemes may cause conflict within the group, if some workers consider that others are working too slowly

qualities of a good labour payment method

These include:

- reward should be related to effort and fair to all staff

- the method should be easy to manage and administer, and cheap and efficient to run

- it should be easy for employees to understand how pay is calculated

- payment should be made at regular intervals and soon after the event, eg employees on piecework should be paid in the week after the production has been achieved

- the principles of the scheme should remain constant, but there should be flexibility to deal with changes in production techniques

summary

The three main labour payment methods, together with some alternative systems, are summarised in the table on the next page.

As an accounts assistant, always remember that payroll information is confidential and any queries should be referred to the appropriate person – for example, the payroll manager, or the accounts supervisor.

OVERTIME AND IDLE TIME

In Chapter 1 we divided labour costs between:

- **direct costs,** labour costs of production-line employees
- **indirect costs,** labour costs of other employees, such as supervisors, office staff, etc

Whilst this distinction appears clear enough, there are times when a proportion of the labour costs of production-line employees is classed as an indirect cost (rather than a direct cost) and is included amongst the overheads of the business. This is done if part of the cost of wages of the direct workers cannot be linked to specific work.

continued on page 82

labour payment methods – a summary

	TIME RATE	PIECEWORK RATE	BONUS SYSTEM
situation	This method is used where it is difficult to measure the quantity of output and where quality is more important than volume of output.	This method is used where the work is repetitive and quantity of output is more important than quality.	This method is used to motivate employees, where the work is not so repetitive as in piecework but is measurable.
gross pay calculation	*Hours worked x rate per hour = basic pay.* This is easy to calculate and understand. Overtime often paid for extra hours worked	*Number of items produced x rate per item.* This is easy to calculate and understand.	*Basic pay + proportion of the time saved.* Time saved is the difference between time allowed and time taken to do a task. More complex to calculate and understand.
motivation	Pay is not linked to output and therefore there is no incentive to work hard. Slower workers may get paid overtime at higher rates.	Pay is related directly to output. There is a direct incentive to work as the amount of output determines the amount paid.	There is some incentive to work in order to earn a bonus as well as basic pay.
quality of output	There is no pressure on time and so quality should be maintained.	The fact that pay is related to output means it is important that quality standards of output are met.	The link between pay and output means that the quality of output needs to be checked.
control	It is important that the volume and quality of output is maintained.	It is important that the volume and quality of output is maintained.	It is important that the volume and quality of output is maintained.
administration	There is no need to set time allowances for output.	There is a need to set time allowances for work done and to keep these up to date.	There is a need to set time allowances for work done and to keep these up to date.
payment to employees	A regular amount is earned by the employee.	The amount earned by the employee varies with the output the employee produces.	There is some regular income but pay can be increased by additional effort.
ALTERNATIVE SYSTEMS	**High day rate** – employees are paid a higher than average rate per hour but agree to produce a given amount of output at a given quality.	**Attendance allowance** – to ensure employees turn up. **Guaranteed day rate** – to give employees a minimum payment. **Differential piecework** – to pay efficient workers more for output beyond a given level of output, ie an extra amount per unit.	**Group bonus schemes** – used where employees work as a group. This can include all workers, eg cleaners. This may create problems as the most efficient workers may be held back by the less efficient workers.

overtime payments

When production-line employees work overtime they are usually paid at a rate above the time rate. For example, overtime might be paid at 'time-and-a-half'; thus an employee with a time rate of £12 an hour will be paid overtime at £18 an hour. The additional £6 per hour is called **overtime premium**. For normal cost accounting purposes, any overtime worked is charged at £12 an hour to direct labour, and £6 an hour to indirect labour.

Example:

A group of employees on a production line have a working week consisting of 35 hours each. Anything over that time is paid at time-and-a-half. One employee has worked 40 hours during the week at a normal rate of £10.

• Direct wages cost is 40 hours at £10 = £400

• Overtime premium is 5 hours at £5 (half of £10) = £25, which is charged to indirect labour

In this way, the cost of overtime is spread across all output and is not charged solely to the output being worked on during the overtime period. As another issue, management will wish to know why there was the need to work overtime, and will seek to control such an increase in labour costs.

However, where a customer requests overtime to be worked to get a rush job completed, then the full overtime rate (£15 an hour in the above example) is charged as direct labour, and passed on as a cost to the customer.

Other additional payments made to employees – such as a bonus – will be treated in a similar way to overtime and will normally be treated as an indirect labour cost.

idle time

Idle time occurs when production is stopped through no fault of the production-line employees – for example, a machine breakdown, or a shortage of materials. Employees paid under a piecework or a bonus system will receive time rate for the period of the stoppage. Such wages costs are normally charged to overheads as indirect labour.

Similarly, time spent by direct workers on non-productive work – eg attendance on a training course – would also usually be treated as an overhead.

USING A TIME SHEET

In order to calculate gross wages, as noted earlier (page 75), a business or organisation must obtain information about hours worked and/or work done.

A time sheet is used for each employee to record:

– hours worked each day, split between production and indirect work

– amount of basic pay each day (using the hourly rate paid to the employee)

– amount of overtime premium each day (using the hourly rate)

– total pay each day

– total hours worked for the week

– total basic pay, overtime premium and pay for the week

A time sheet is shown in the Case Study which follows:

Case Study

CALCULATING THE PAY

situation

You are an accounts assistant at Onslow Limited and have been asked to help with calculating labour costs.

The cost accountant has given you the following time sheet for one of Onslow Limited's employees, P Cusack, who is paid as follows:

• For a basic seven-hour shift every day from Monday to Friday – basic pay at £12.00 per hour

• For any overtime in excess of the basic seven hours on any day from Monday to Friday – the extra hours are paid at time-and-a-half (basic pay plus an overtime premium equal to half of basic pay)

• For any hours worked on a Saturday or Sunday – double-time (basic pay plus an overtime premium equal to basic pay)

You are to complete the time sheet columns headed basic pay, overtime premium and total pay (enter a zero figure, '0', in the columns where nothing is to be paid).

The employee's weekly time sheet for week ending 14 June 20-2 is shown on the next page.

	Hours spent on production	Hours worked on indirect work	Notes	Basic pay £	Overtime premium £	Total pay £
Employee: P Cusack			Profit Centre: Metal cutting			
Employee number: 260			Basic pay per hour: £12.00			
Monday	7	0				
Tuesday	5	2	2pm-4 pm first aid course			
Wednesday	7	0				
Thursday	6	1	8 am-9 am cleaning			
Friday	8	0				
Saturday	3	0				
Sunday	0	0				
Total	36	3				

solution

P Cusack's time sheet is completed as follows:

	Hours spent on production	Hours worked on indirect work	Notes	Basic pay £	Overtime premium £	Total pay £
Employee: P Cusack			Profit Centre: Metal cutting			
Employee number: 260			Basic pay per hour: £12.00			
Monday	7	0		84	0	84
Tuesday	5	2	2pm-4 pm first aid course	84	0	84
Wednesday	7	0		84	0	84
Thursday	6	1	8 am-9 am cleaning	84	0	84
Friday	8	0		96	6	102
Saturday	3	0		36	36	72
Sunday	0	0		0	0	0
Total	36	3		468	42	510

BOOK-KEEPING FOR LABOUR COSTS

In this section we look at the cost book-keeping entries to record labour costs – the transfer of labour costs to production and to overheads. These entries form part of the book-keeping system for costing.

A **wages control account** – which may also include salaries – links to the payroll accounting system. It is used to charge labour costs to the various cost, profit, or investment centres of a business or organisation. In this way:

- direct labour costs are charged to production

- indirect labour costs are charged to production overheads

- administration labour costs are charged to non-production overheads

The cost book-keeping entries are:

- **transfer of direct labour costs to production**

    - debit production

    - credit wages control

- **transfer of indirect labour costs to production overheads**

    - debit production overheads

    - credit wages control

- **transfer of administration labour costs to non-production overheads**

    - debit non-production overheads, eg administration

    - credit wages control

The cost book-keeping entries are shown diagrammatically as follows:

Note: Here all of the labour costs have been transferred to production and overheads. From time-to-time, however, some part of labour costs may relate to capital expenditure (see page 98) – for example, own workforce used to build an extension to the premises; here the book-keeping entries for the relevant labour costs are:

– debit premises account (or relevant capital expenditure account)
– credit wages control account

Case Study

1.850

1.600

BLUE JEANS LIMITED: BOOK-KEEPING FOR LABOUR COSTS

situation

Blue Jeans Limited manufactures and sells denim jeans and jackets. The payroll for the week ended 21 May 20-4 has been completed with the following amounts to pay:

• net wages to be paid to employees	£5,000
• Income Tax and National Insurance Contributions (NIC) to HMRC	£1,000
• pension contributions to be paid to the pension fund	£500
Total	£6,500

The payroll for the week has been analysed as:

• direct labour costs	£3,500
• indirect labour costs	£2,000
• administration labour costs	£1,000
Total	£6,500

All of the direct labour costs are for the manufacture of blue jeans. The following cost accounting codes are in use to record labour costs:

code number	description
2200	production – blue jeans
2400	production overheads
2600	non-production overheads – administration
4200	wages control

As an accounts assistant at Blue Jeans Limited, you are asked to prepare the wages control account and to fill in the table below to record the journal entries which show how the total cost of the payroll is split between the various cost centres of the business.

20-4	Code number	Debit £	Credit £
21 May	2200		
21 May	4200		
21 May	2400		
21 May	4200		
21 May	2600		
21 May	4200		

solution

Wages control account is prepared as follows:

Dr		**Wages Control Account**		Cr
	£			£
Cash/bank (net wages)	5,000	Production (direct labour)		3,500
HM Revenue & Customs		Production overheads		
(income tax and NIC)	1,000	(indirect labour)		2,000
Pension contributions	500	Non-production overheads		
		(administration)		1,000
	6,500			6,500

The cost book-keeping entries are:

The cost book-keeping transactions are recorded as journal entries in the following way:

20-4	Code number	Debit £	Credit £
21 May	2200	£3,500	
21 May	4200		£3,500
21 May	2400	£2,000	
21 May	4200		£2,000
21 May	2600	£1,000	
21 May	4200		£1,000

In this way, the total cost of the payroll is split between the various cost centres of the business.

Chapter Summary

- Labour costs – the costs of wages and salaries – are incurred in every kind of business.

- Levels of wage rates paid to employees are influenced by a number of factors including the rates paid by similar local businesses, compulsory minimum rates and national averages.

- The main labour payment methods are based either on time or amounts of work done or on a combination of both.

- Different labour payment methods have advantages and disadvantages for the employer and the employee. The employer needs to control the cost of wages, but also to motivate employees to produce work of suitable quality within a reasonable time.

- A good labour payment method should be fair, easy to understand and efficiently managed.

- Certain wages costs of the direct workers may be classed as indirect labour costs: these include overtime premium and payment for idle or non-productive time.

- Cost book-keeping entries are made to charge labour costs to the various cost centres of a business or organisation.

Key Terms	**time rate**	labour payment method based on the time worked by an employee, giving the formula: hours worked x rate per hour
	piecework rate	labour payment method based on the work done by an employee, giving the formula: units produced x rate per unit
	bonus system	labour payment method in which an employee is paid a time rate and then receives a bonus if output is better than expected when comparing the time allowed with the time taken – the bonus is calculated as an agreed percentage of the time saved multiplied by the time rate
	time sheet	method by which employees record the hours they have worked
	clock card	where employees 'clock in' at the start of work, and 'clock out' at the end
	piecework ticket	documentation completed by employees who work on a batch of output
	job card	documentation completed by employees which records the amount of time spent on each job
	route card	documentation which follows a product through the production process – employees record the amount of time they spend working on the product
	overtime premium	the additional pay above normal rates which is paid to employees working overtime, for example, the premium part of 'time-and-a-half' is the extra 'half' of the hourly rate
	idle time	time during which work is stopped, due to reasons such as machine breakdown or shortage of materials; employees usually receive time rate for idle time, and the cost is normally classified as an indirect cost
	wages control account	used to charge labour costs to the various cost, profit or investment centres: – direct labour to production – indirect labour to production overheads – administration labour to non-production overhead

Activities

3.1 A manufacturing business pays its production workers on a time rate basis. A bonus is paid where production is completed faster than the time allowed; the bonus is paid at half of the time rate for production time saved. How much will each of the following employees earn for the week?

Employee	Time rate	Hours worked	Time allowed (output per hour)	Actual production
N Ball	£11.00 per hour	35	30 units	1,010 units
T Smith	£9.00 per hour	37	40 units	1,560 units
L Lewis	£10.00 per hour	38	20 units	820 units
M Wilson	£12.00 per hour	36	25 units	950 units

3.2 Harrison & Company is a manufacturing business. Currently it pays its production-line workers on a time rate basis. Recently the employee representatives have approached the management of the company with a view to seeking alternative labour payment methods. Suggestions have been made that either a piecework system, or a time rate with a production bonus system would be more appropriate.

The office manager has asked you, as an accounts assistant, to draft a report for the management giving advantages and disadvantages of:

- time rate

- piecework

- time rate, plus production bonus

as payment methods for production-line employees. In particular, you are asked to describe two circumstances under which the piecework basis would not be in the interests of employees.

3.3 (a)   A company pays its production-line employees on a piecework basis, but with a guaranteed time rate. How much will each of the following employees earn during the week?

Employee	Time rate	Hours worked	Production	Piecework rate
L Fry	£10.00 per hour	40	1,200 units	30p per unit
R Williams	£12.00 per hour	37	500 units	90p per unit
P Grant	£9.50 per hour	36	725 units	50p per unit

(b)   What are the problems a company might face in operating a piecework system of labour payment?

3.4   Print 'n Go is a print shop that specialises in printing headed notepaper for businesses. It employs two printers, Steve Kurtin and Pete Singh. Both are paid a basic rate per hour for a 35-hour week with two overtime rates: time-and-a-third for weekdays (rate 1), and time-and-a-half for week-ends (rate 2). In addition, a production bonus is paid of 50p per 1,000 copies printed.

Details for last week are as follows:

	Steve Kurtin	Pete Singh
Basic rate per hour	£10.50	£12.00
Total hours worked	39	42
Overtime hours: rate 1	4	3
rate 2	–	4
Number of copies printed	45,000	57,000

You are to

- calculate the gross wages earned by each employee for last week

- calculate the piecework rate per 1,000 copies printed that would be equal to the gross wages earned by Steve Kurtin for the week, assuming the same output level of 45,000 copies.

3.5 Wyvern Fabrication Company has two departments – moulding and finishing. Data relating to labour for a four-week period is given on the labour cost sheet below.

The company uses a bonus scheme whereby employees receive 50 per cent of the time saved in each department, paid at the actual labour rate per hour. This is not included in the actual wages cost, which shows actual hours multiplied by the actual wage rate.

LABOUR COST SHEET for the four weeks ended 26 February 20-7		
	MOULDING	FINISHING
Actual wages cost (£)	£41,160	£45,450
Time allowed	4,000 hours	5,000 hours
Time taken	4,100 hours	4,500 hours
Time saved		
Bonus (£)		
Total labour cost (£)		

You are to calculate the total labour cost for each department.

3.6 The direct workers of Haven Limited are paid a basic wage of £10.20 per hour. For time worked above 40 hours per week, they receive overtime pay at time-and-a-half. For two particular weeks, we have the following information for a team of 10 direct workers:

Week 1: Total hours worked = 450 hours, including 50 hours of overtime.

Week 2: Total hours worked = 400 hours, including 20 hours of non-production work, clearing up and re-organising a section of the factory during a machine breakdown.

For each of the two given weeks you are to:

·   calculate the gross earnings in total for the team of 10 employees.

·   state how much of the gross earnings would normally be treated as an indirect labour cost.

3.7 You are an accounts assistant at Durning Limited and have been asked to help with calculating labour costs.

The cost accountant has given you the following time sheet for one of Durning Limited's employees, T Mantle, who is paid as follows:

- For a basic six-hour shift every day from Monday to Friday – basic pay

- For any overtime in excess of the basic six hours on any day from Monday to Friday – the extra hours are paid at time-and-a-half (basic pay plus an overtime premium equal to half of basic pay)

- For three contracted hours each Saturday morning – basic pay

- For any hours worked in excess of three hours on a Saturday or any hours worked on a Sunday – double-time (basic pay plus an overtime premium equal to basic pay)

You are to complete the time sheet columns headed basic pay, overtime premium and total pay (enter a zero figure, '0', in the columns where nothing is to be paid).

Employee's weekly time sheet for week ending 15 April 20-6

	Hours spent on production	Hours worked on indirect work	Notes	Basic pay £	Overtime premium £	Total pay £
Employee: T Mantle			Profit Centre: Finishing			
Employee number: 170			Basic pay per hour: £14.00			
Monday	6	0				
Tuesday	5	2	8am-10am maintenance			
Wednesday	7	0				
Thursday	6	3	9am-12 noon training			
Friday	8	0				
Saturday	5	0				
Sunday	0	0				
Total	37	5				

3.8 Breeden Bakery Limited makes 'homestyle' cakes which are sold to supermarket chains. The payroll for the week ended 26 March 20-4 has been completed with the following amounts to pay:

	£
net wages to be paid to employees	£7,500
Income Tax and National Insurance Contributions (NIC) to HMRC	£1,450
pension contributions to be paid to the pension fund	£750
Total	£9,700

direct labour costs	6,500
indirect labour costs	2,700
administration labour costs	500
Total	9,700

As an accounts assistant at Breedon Bakery you have been given the following tasks:

Task 1

Prepare wages control account for the week ended 26 March 20-4:

Dr	**Wages Control Account**	Cr
£		£

Task 2

All of the direct labour costs are for the manufacture of fruit cakes. The following cost accounting codes are in use to record labour costs:

code number	description
3300	production – fruit cakes
3500	production overheads
3700	non-production overheads – administration
5200	wages control

Complete the table below to record the journal entries which show how the total cost of the payroll is split between the various cost centres of the business.

20-4	Code number	Debit £	Credit £
26 March	3300		
26 March	5200		
26 March	3500		
26 March	5200		
26 March	3700		
26 March	5200		

3.9   Icod Limited manufactures golf clubs. The following data relates to the production of its 'Mulligan' brand of clubs for October 20-4:

Total direct labour hours worked	16,000 hours
Normal time hours	14,400 hours
Overtime hours	1,600 hours
Normal time rate per hour	£10 per hour
Overtime premium per hour	£5 per hour

In the company's cost book-keeping system all direct labour overtime payments are included in direct costs.

The following cost accounting codes are in use to record labour costs:

code number	description
1500	production – 'Mulligan' clubs
5000	wages control

You are to:

·   calculate the total cost of direct labour for October

·   show the cost book-keeping entries, together with account codes, in order to transfer the direct labour costs to production

4 Expenses

this chapter covers...

In Chapter 1 we saw how costs can be classified by element as materials, labour and expenses. In this chapter we focus on expenses and explain

- expenses as an element of cost
- the distinction between capital expenditure and revenue expenditure
- the distinction between direct expenses and indirect expenses
- the book-keeping entries for expenses
- the behaviour of fixed, semi-variable and variable costs
- the use of the high/low method to identify the amounts of fixed and variable costs
- the preparation of a schedule of forecast revenue and costs

EXPENSES – AN ELEMENT OF COST

The third main element of cost is that of expenses, ie any cost that cannot be classified as materials or labour. Expenses include items such as rent, rates, telephone, lighting, heating, royalties paid to the designer of a product, special items bought in for a particular product, etc.

It is important that expenses are classified correctly in order that costs can be calculated accurately and accounting statements can show the true financial position of the business. To achieve this, as shown by the diagram below, we need to distinguish between:

- capital expenditure and revenue expenditure
- direct expenses and indirect expenses
- fixed costs and variable costs

Note that both direct and indirect expenses can be either fixed or variable in behaviour – see page 102.

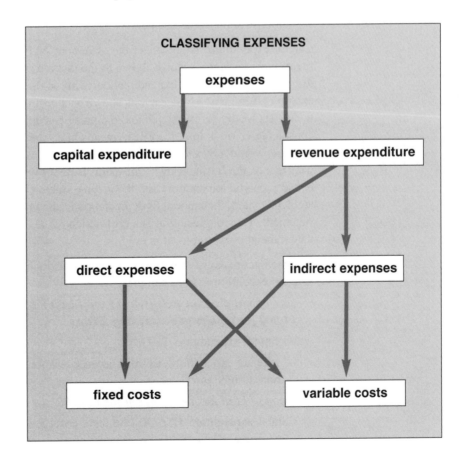

CAPITAL EXPENDITURE AND REVENUE EXPENDITURE

Capital expenditure is expenditure incurred on the purchase, alteration or improvement of non-current assets (fixed assets). For example, the purchase of a car for use in the business is capital expenditure. Included in capital expenditure are costs such as:

- delivery costs of non-current assets
- installation of non-current assets
- improvement (but not repair) of non-current assets
- legal costs of buying property

Revenue expenditure is expenditure incurred on running costs. For example, the cost of petrol or diesel for the car (above) is revenue expenditure. Included in revenue expenditure are the running costs of:

- maintenance and repair of non-current assets
- making, selling and distributing the goods or products in which the business trades
- administration of the business

Capital expenditure is shown in the statement of financial position, while revenue expenditure is a cost shown in the income statement. It is important to classify these types of expenditure correctly in the accounting system. For example, if the cost of the car was shown as a cost in the income statement, then costs would be overstated and the profit for the year would be reduced considerably, or a loss recorded; meanwhile, the statement of financial position would not show the car as a non-current asset – clearly this is incorrect as the business owns the asset. Note, however, that there is a link between capital expenditure and the income statement: as non-current assets are depreciated, the amount of depreciation is shown as a cost in the income statement. Thus depreciation is a cost which relates to the time period over which the non-current asset is used.

In some circumstances we must take care to distinguish between capital and revenue expenditure. For example:

- *cost of building an extension to the factory £30,000, which includes £1,000 for repairs to the existing factory*
  - capital expenditure, £29,000
  - revenue expenditure, £1,000 (because it is for repairs to an existing non-current asset)
- *a plot of land has been bought for £20,000, the legal costs are £750*
  Capital expenditure £20,750 (the legal costs are included in the capital expenditure, because they are the cost of acquiring the non-current asset, ie the legal costs are capitalised).

- *own employees used to install a new air conditioning system: direct labour £1,000, materials £1,500*

  Capital expenditure £2,500 (an addition to the property). Note that, in cases such as this, revenue expenditure, ie direct labour and materials purchases, will need to be reduced to allow for the transfer to capital expenditure.

- *own employees used to repair and redecorate the premises: direct labour £500, materials £750*

  Revenue expenditure £1,250 (repairs and redecoration are running costs).

- *purchase of a new machine £10,000, payment for installation and setting up £250*

  Capital expenditure £10,250 (costs of installation and setting up of a non-current asset are capitalised).

Only by classifying capital expenditure and revenue expenditure correctly can costs be ascertained properly and the income statement and statement of financial position reflect accurately the financial position of the business. It is especially important to identify revenue expenditure in the costing of output; a product that is costed wrongly (for example at too high a price) may not sell well because the selling price is too expensive for buyers. Identification of capital expenditure is important for knowing the assets owned by a business, which are shown on the statement of financial position. If you, as an accounts assistant, are unsure about the allocation of costs between capital and revenue, you should always refer queries to the accounts supervisor.

DIRECT EXPENSES AND INDIRECT EXPENSES

For cost accounting purposes, revenue expenditure needs to be classified by nature as either a direct expense or an indirect expense:

- direct expense – an expense that can be identified directly with each unit of output
- indirect expense – other expenses which cannot be identified directly with specific units of output

The correct identification of these expenses will enable us to obtain a more accurate cost for each unit of output of the business or organisation.

direct expenses

Examples of direct expenses include:

- royalties payable to the designer of a product
- special items bought in for a particular product or job
- hire of specialist machinery/equipment for a particular product or job
- consultant's fees related to a particular product or job
- power costs of running machinery (provided that the machinery is separately metered and is used for a particular product or job)
- depreciation methods linked directly to output, eg units of output method (where depreciation is calculated by reference to the number of units for the year)

indirect expenses

Examples of indirect expenses include:

- factory and office rent and rates
- telephone costs
- power costs of running machinery (where machinery is used for a variety of products or jobs, or where power consumption is low and it is not worthwhile for the costing system to analyse the amount of the direct expense)
- heating and lighting
- insurance
- cost of running vehicles
- depreciation methods not linked directly to output, eg straight-line and reducing balance methods

BOOK-KEEPING FOR EXPENSES

The cost book-keeping entries to record expenses – the transfer of expenses to production and to overheads – form part of the book-keeping system for costing.

The cost of direct expenses – which is attributable to output – is charged to production. The cost of indirect expenses is charged to overheads and split between:

- production overheads
- non-production overheads, such as
  - selling and distribution
  - administration
  - finance

The cost book-keeping entries are:

- **transfer of direct expenses to production**
  - debit production
  - credit expense
- **transfer of indirect expenses to production overheads**
  - debit production overheads
  - credit expense
- **transfer of indirect expenses to non-production overheads**
  - debit non-production overheads, eg selling and distribution, administration, finance
  - credit expense

These cost book-keeping entries are shown diagrammatically as follows:

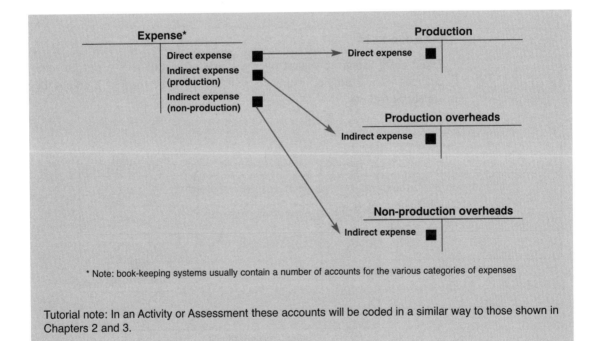

* Note: book-keeping systems usually contain a number of accounts for the various categories of expenses

Tutorial note: In an Activity or Assessment these accounts will be coded in a similar way to those shown in Chapters 2 and 3.

Direct expenses are included with the costs of direct materials and direct labour to give a total of direct costs (prime cost). Indirect expenses are included in the total of indirect costs (overheads) of a business. For a service business, a major proportion of the costs are likely to be in the form of indirect costs; by contrast, a manufacturing business is likely to have a greater proportion of direct costs. We shall be looking at the layout of the manufacturing account in Chapter 7.

FIXED AND VARIABLE COSTS

It is important in costing to appreciate the *behaviour of costs* – in particular to realise that not all costs increase or decrease in line with increases or decreases in output. As seen in Chapter 1 (page 16), 'Classification of costs by behaviour', all costs in the short-term are:

- fixed, or
- semi-variable, or
- variable

We shall be studying the relationship between fixed and variable costs in detail later in the book (Chapter 9). In particular, we will be looking at the technique of break-even analysis – the point at which costs are exactly equal to income.

fixed costs

Fixed costs remain constant over a range of output levels, despite other changes – for example, insurance, rent, rates. In the form of a graph, they appear as follows:

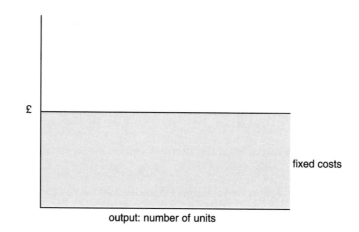

Note that money amounts are shown on the vertical axis and units of output on the horizontal axis.

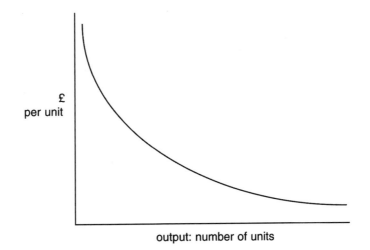

For fixed costs, the *cost per unit* falls as output increases, as follows:

For example, with rent of £40,000 per year:

- at output of 4,000 units, equals £10 per unit
- at output of 10,000 units, equals £4 per unit

Whilst it is sensible to seek to achieve maximum output in order to reduce the cost per unit, fixed costs do not remain fixed at all levels of production. For example, a decision to double production is likely to increase the fixed costs – an increase in factory rent, for example, because an additional factory may need to be rented. Fixed costs are described as **stepped fixed costs**, because they increase by a large amount all at once; graphically, the cost behaviour is shown as a step:

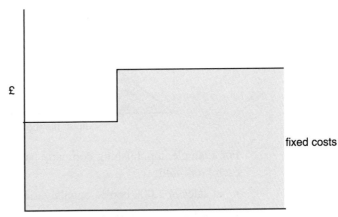

semi-variable costs

These combine both a fixed and a variable cost. For example, a telephone bill comprises the fixed rental for the line, together with the variable amount for each call made. Such a *mixed cost* is expressed graphically as:

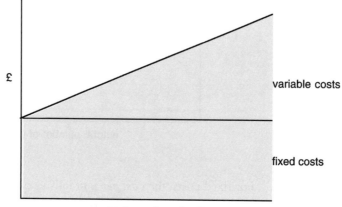

variable costs

Variable costs alter directly with changes in output levels, ie as activity increases, then the cost increases. Examples include direct materials, direct labour, direct expenses such as royalties. Graphically, variable costs appear as follows:

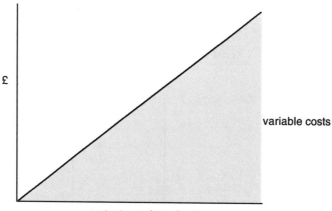

For example, a publishing company paying a royalty of £1 to an author for each book sold:

- at sales of 1,000 books, equals variable cost of £1,000 royalties

- at sales of 10,000 books, equals variable cost of £10,000 royalties

The cost per unit remains constant at all levels of output (unless there are economies of scale, eg bulk discount), as follows:

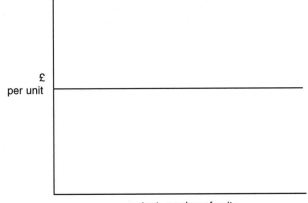

all costs are variable

Whilst we have made the distinction between fixed and variable costs, it is important to appreciate that these cost behaviours hold only in the short term – in the long term, all costs are variable. The example we have seen earlier is of factory rent as a fixed cost but, if production increases, it may result in a larger, or another, factory being rented at an additional cost.

FIXED AND VARIABLE COSTS IN DECISION-MAKING

Identifying costs as being fixed, semi-variable or variable helps with decision-making – the business might be able to alter the balance between fixed and variable costs in order to increase profits. A product could be made:

- either, by using a labour-intensive process, with a large number of employees supported by basic machinery
- or, by using expensive machinery in an automated process with very few employees

In the first case, the cost structure will be high variable costs (direct labour) and low fixed costs (straight-line depreciation of machinery). In the second case, there will be low variable costs, and high fixed costs. Management will need to examine the relationship between the costs – together with the likely sales figures, and the availability of finance with which to buy the machinery – before making a decision.

More specifically, a knowledge of the behaviour of costs can be used to help management to:

- identify the amount of fixed costs within a semi-variable cost
- prepare schedules of forecast revenue and costs
- identify the point at which costs are exactly equal to income – known as the break-even point (covered in Chapter 9)

IDENTIFYING THE AMOUNT OF FIXED AND VARIABLE COSTS

With semi-variable costs we have already seen how these combine both a fixed and a variable cost. It is important in cost accounting to be able to identify the amount of each, as this will help with decision-making. Where the total costs are known at two levels of output, the amounts of fixed and variable costs can be identified using the 'high/low' method.

example

- at output of 1,000 units, total costs are £7,000
- at output of 2,000 units, total costs are £9,000

What are the fixed costs? What are the variable costs?

Using the 'high/low' method to identify the fixed and variable costs:

- The low output and costs are deducted from the high output and costs, as follows:

	high output	2,000 units	£9,000
less	low output	1,000 units	£7,000
equals	differences	1,000 units	£2,000

- The amount of the variable cost per unit is now calculated as:

$$\frac{\text{difference in cost}}{\text{difference in units}} \quad = \quad \frac{£2,000}{1,000} \quad = \quad £2 \text{ variable cost per unit}$$

- Therefore, at 1,000 units of output the cost structure is:

		total cost	£7,000
less	variable costs (1,000 units x £2 per unit)		£2,000
equals	fixed costs		£5,000

- Check this now at 2,000 units of output when the cost structure is:

		£
	variable costs (2,000 units x £2 per unit)	£4,000
add	fixed costs (as above)	£5,000
equals	total costs	£9,000

The 'high/low' method can only be used when variable costs increase by the same money amount for each extra unit of output (ie there is a constant unit variable cost), and where there are no stepped fixed costs.

SCHEDULE OF FORECAST REVENUE AND COSTS

Once fixed and variable costs are known for the three elements of costs – materials, labour and expenses – at a particular level of output, it is relatively simple to calculate what the costs will be at changed levels of output. For example, if variable materials costs at an output of 1,000 units are £2,000 then, at an output of 1,100 units, they will be £2,200 (ie a 10 per cent increase in both output and cost). By contrast, the fixed expense of factory rent of, say, £5,000 will be unchanged if output increases by 10 per cent. (Note that such calculations assume a constant unit variable cost and that there are no stepped fixed costs.)

Such changes in costs can be incorporated, as part of the planning process, into a formal schedule of **forecast revenue and costs**. This calculates total revenues and costs and shows the cost per unit and profit per unit at changed (either increased or decreased) activity levels, as shown in the Case Study which follows.

Case Study

FORECAST REVENUE AND COSTS

situation

Speedpen Limited, which manufactures quality rollerball pens, has forecast its revenue and costs for 20-5 on the basis of sales and output of 100,000 units as follows:

			£
•	sales revenue		200,000
•	variable costs	– materials	75,000
		– labour	50,000
		– expenses	10,000
•	fixed costs	– labour	32,500
		– overheads	20,500

The sales department thinks that demand for the product is more likely to be 110,000 units, or could be as high as 125,000 units.

You have been asked to prepare a forecast schedule of revenue and costs based on sales and outputs of 100,000 units, 110,000 units and 125,000 units. The schedule is to show total cost, total profit, cost per unit, and profit per unit at each level of output.

solution

20-5 **FORECAST REVENUE AND COSTS**			
UNITS PRODUCED AND SOLD	100,000	110,000	125,000
	£	£	£
Sales revenue	200,000	220,000	250,000
Variable costs			
Materials	75,000	82,500	93,750
Labour	50,000	55,000	62,500
Expenses	10,000	11,000	12,500
	135,000	148,500	168,750
Fixed costs			
Labour	32,500	32,500	32,500
Overheads	20,500	20,500	20,500
	53,000	53,000	53,000
Total cost	188,000	201,500	221,750
Total profit	12,000	18,500	28,250
Cost per unit	1.88	1.83	1.77
Profit per unit	0.12	0.17	0.23

Notes:

- Sales revenue per unit is calculated at £2.00 (ie £200,000 ÷ 100,000 units)
- Variable costs per unit are: materials, £0.75 (ie £75,000 ÷ 100,000 units); labour, £0.50; expenses, £0.10
- At the higher activity levels simply multiply the unit costs by 110,000 and 125,000
- Fixed costs remain fixed at the higher levels of output
- Total cost is total variable costs plus total fixed costs
- Cost per unit is total cost divided by output (note that cost per unit has been rounded to the nearest penny)

- The costs at higher activity levels assume that:
  - there is a constant unit for variable cost up to this volume
  - there are no stepped fixed costs
- The fall in cost per unit as output increases occurs because the fixed costs are being spread over a greater number of units, ie the fixed cost per unit falls
- As cost per unit falls, so profit per unit increases (always provided that the selling price per unit can be maintained)

USING THE HIGH/LOW METHOD AND THE FORECAST OF REVENUE AND COSTS

In this chapter we have focused on expenses and, in particular, have seen the behaviour of fixed, semi-variable and variable costs. We have seen how a semi-variable cost combines both a fixed and a variable cost – and have used the high/low method to identify the amounts of fixed and variable costs.

In the Case Study which follows we use the high/low method in conjunction with the schedule of forecast revenue and costs – a combination which is often used in Assessments.

Case Study

PREPARING FOR ASSESSMENT: REVENUE AND COSTS, INCLUDING SEMI-VARIABLE COSTS

situation

Cannit Limited makes cans for customers in the food and drink industry. The company has prepared a forecast for the next quarter for one of its cans, AB24. This can is produced in batches and the forecast is based on producing and selling 800 batches. One of the customers of Cannit Limited has indicated that it may be significantly increasing its order level for can AB24 for the next quarter and it appears that activity levels of 1,000 batches and 1,500 batches are feasible.

The semi-variable costs should be calculated using the high/low method. If 2,000 batches are sold the total semi-variable cost will be £6,500 and there is a constant unit variable cost up to this volume.

Complete the table below and calculate the estimated profit per batch of AB24 at the activity levels of 1,000 and 1,500 batches.

Batches produced and sold	800	1,000	1,500
	£	£	£
Sales revenue	24,000		
Variable costs:			
• Direct materials	4,400		
• Direct labour	6,800		
• Overheads	4,800		
Semi-variable costs:	4,100		
• Variable element			
• Fixed element			
Total cost	20,100		
Total profit	3,900		
Profit per batch (to 2 decimal places)	4.88		

solution

- Sales revenue is £30.000 per batch (£24,000 ÷ 800 batches)
- Direct materials are £5.50 per batch (£4,400 ÷ 800)
- Direct labour is £8.50 per batch (£6,800 ÷ 800)
- Overheads are £6.00 per batch (£4,800 ÷ 800)

Each of these can be multiplied by 1,000 and 1,500 to give the revenue and costs at these activity levels.

The semi-variable cost is split between the amounts for fixed and variable costs by using the high/low method:

	high output	2,000	batches	£6,500
less	low output	800	batches	£4,100
equals	difference	1,200	batches	£2,400

- The amount of the variable cost per batch is £2.00 (£2,400 ÷ 1,200 batches)
- The amount of the fixed cost is £2,500 (at 800 batches £4,100 − [800 x £2.00])

The schedule of revenue and costs completed for activity levels of 1,000 and 1,500 batches is as follows:

Batches produced and sold	800	1,000	1,500
	£	£	£
Sales revenue	24,000	30,000	45,000
Variable costs:			
• Direct materials	4,400	5,500	8,250
• Direct labour	6,800	8,500	12,750
• Overheads	4,800	6,000	9,000
Semi-variable costs:	4,100		
• Variable element		2,000	3,000
• Fixed element		2,500	2,500
Total cost	20,100	24,500	35,500
Total profit	3,900	5,500	9,500
Profit per batch (to 2 decimal places)	4.88	5.50	6.33

Service businesses

Whilst this Case Study has used the schedule of revenue and costs for a manufacturing business, the same format can be used for a service business. For example, a bus company could calculate revenues and costs on the basis of miles travelled, and a hospital could calculate revenues and costs on the basis of the number of bed nights.

Chapter Summary

- Expenses, together with materials and labour, form the three main elements of cost.

- Expenses are classified between:
  - capital expenditure and revenue expenditure
  - direct expenses and indirect expenses
  - fixed costs and variable costs

- Identification of revenue expenditure is important in the costing of output; identification of capital expenditure is important for knowing the assets owned by a business.

- Direct expenses are charged to production.

- Indirect expenses are charged to overheads and split between:
  - production overheads
  - non-production overheads, such as selling and distribution, administration, finance

- The behaviour of costs means that not all costs increase or decrease in line with increases or decreases in output; all costs in the short-term are:
  - fixed, or
  - semi-variable, or
  - variable

- A knowledge of the behaviour of costs enables:
  - identification of the amounts of fixed and variable costs within a semi-variable cost
  - preparation of a schedule of forecast revenue and costs
  - identification of the break-even point

Key Terms

capital expenditure	expenditure incurred on the purchase, alteration or improvement of non-current assets
revenue expenditure	expenditure incurred on running costs
direct expense	an expense that can be identified directly with each unit of output
indirect expense	other expenses which cannot be identified directly with specific units of output
overheads	the indirect costs of materials, labour and expenses
fixed costs	costs which remain fixed over a range of output levels
stepped fixed cost	fixed cost that increases by a large amount all at once
semi-variable costs	costs which combine a fixed and variable element
variable costs	costs which vary directly with output
high/low method	method used to identify the amounts of fixed and variable costs within total costs
forecast revenue and costs	schedule which shows the calculation of total cost, total profit, cost per unit, and profit per unit at particular levels of output

Activities

4.1 Define:

(a) capital expenditure

(b) revenue expenditure

Give two examples of each.

4.2 Define:

(a) direct expenses

(b) indirect expenses

Give two examples of each.

4.3 Fred Jarvis normally works as a production-line employee of Wyevale Plastics. However, for the past four weeks he has been building an extension to the company's warehouse.

How should his wages for this period be dealt with in the accounts? Why is this?

4.4 Explain the behaviour of the costs, as shown by the following graphs:

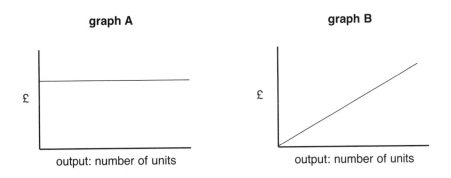

Graph (a) shows the cost of the rent of a factory.

Graph (b) shows the wages of production-line employees who are paid on a piecework basis.

4.5   Classify the following costs (tick the appropriate column):

		capital expenditure	revenue expenditure
(a)	purchase of vehicles		
(b)	depreciation of vehicles		
(c)	payment of office rent		
(d)	salaries of office staff		
(e)	legal fees relating to the purchase of property		
(f)	re-decoration of office		
(g)	installation of air-conditioning in office		
(h)	wages of own employees used to build extension to the stockroom		
(i)	installation and setting up of a new machine		

4.6   Classify the following costs (tick the appropriate column):

		direct expenses	indirect expenses	either*
(a)	hire of machinery for a particular job			
(b)	office rent			
(c)	cleaning materials			
(d)	power costs			
(e)	royalty paid to designer for each unit of output			
(f)	sales staff car expenses			
(g)	depreciation of production machinery			
(h)	consultant's fees relating to a particular job			
(i)	heating and lighting			

*explain your reasons for classifying costs in this column

4.7   Classify the following costs (tick the appropriate column):

		fixed	semi-variable	variable
(a)	rates of business premises			
(b)	royalty paid to designer for each unit of output			
(c)	car hire with fixed rental and charge per mile			
(d)	employees paid on piecework basis			
(e)	straight-line depreciation			
(f)	units of output depreciation			
(g)	direct materials			
(h)	telephone bill with fixed rental and a charge for each call made			
(i)	office salaries			

4.8   Eveshore Pottery Limited manufactures a range of 'souvenir' mugs, cups and saucers, plates, etc, which sell well to visitors from abroad who are seeking a memento of 'Olde England'. A number of different costs have been incurred during the last month, and you are asked to classify them into:

·   direct materials

·   indirect materials

·   direct labour

·   indirect labour

·   direct expenses

·   indirect expenses

The costs are:

(a) cleaning materials for the machines

(b) wages of factory supervisor

(c) clay from which the 'pots' are made

(d) 10p royalties payable to the designer for each 'Eveshore Plate' made

(e) salary of office assistant

(f) electricity used to heat the kilns

(g) rates of factory

(h) depreciation of office equipment

(i) wages of production-line workers

(j) salesperson's salary

(k) interest charged on bank overdraft

If you believe alternative classifications exist, argue the case and state if you need further information from the company.

Of the overhead costs, ie indirect materials, indirect labour and indirect expenses, you are to indicate which would be classified as:

• production overheads

• selling and distribution overheads

• administration overheads

• finance overheads

4.9 Bodytone Limited manufactures two types of exercise equipment – a treadmill and an exercise cycle. The general expenses account for the month ended 30 June 20-2 has a debit balance of £28,250. This balance is analysed as:

	£
• direct expenses – treadmills	5,450
• direct expenses – exercise cycles	3,170
• production overheads	12,950
• non-production overheads – selling and distribution	3,860
• non-production overheads – administration	2,820
	28,250

The following cost accounting codes are in use to record expenses:

code number	description
2100	production: treadmills
2200	production: exercise cycles
3500	production overheads
4200	non-production overheads: selling and distribution
4400	non-production overheads: administration
5150	general expenses

As an accounts assistant at Bodytone Limited you have been given the following tasks:

Task 1

Prepare general expenses account for the month ended 30 June 20-2:

Dr	General Expenses Account (5150)		Cr
20-2	£	20-2	£
30 June Balance b/d	28,250		

Task 2

Complete the table below to record the journal entries which show how the total cost of general expenses is split between production, production overheads and non-production overheads.

20-2	Code number	Debit £	Credit £
30 June	2100		
30 June	5150		
30 June	2200		
30 June	5150		
30 June	3500		
30 June	5150		
30 June	4200		
30 June	5150		
30 June	4400		
30 June	5150		

4.10 The accounts supervisor of Nerca Manufacturing Limited has provided you with the following information:

- at 10,000 units of output, total costs are £50,000

- at 15,000 units of output, total costs are £65,000

You are to use the high/low method to identify the amount of fixed costs. The supervisor tells you that there is a constant unit variable cost up to this volume, and that there are no stepped fixed costs.

4.11 Monica Manufacturing has forecast its revenue and costs for 20-8 on the basis of sales and output of 250,000 units as follows:

		£
sales revenue		1,000,000
variable costs	– materials	400,000
	– labour	325,000
	– expenses	100,000
fixed costs	– labour	96,500
	– overheads	67,500

The sales department thinks that demand for the product is more likely to be 300,000 units, or could be as high as 350,000 units.

You are to complete the table below and calculate the estimated cost per unit and profit per unit at the different activity levels. (Note: you may assume that there is a constant unit variable cost up to this volume, and that there are no stepped fixed costs.)

20-8 FORECAST REVENUE AND COSTS			
UNITS PRODUCED AND SOLD	250,000	300,000	350,000
	£	£	£
Sales revenue			
Variable costs			
Materials			
Labour			
Expenses			
Fixed costs			
Labour			
Overheads			
Total costs			
Total profit			
Cost per unit (to 2 decimal places)			
Profit per unit (to 2 decimal places)			

4.12 Boxster Limited makes boxes for customers in the food and drink industry. The company has prepared a forecast for the next quarter for one of its boxes, BB4. This box is produced in batches and the forecast is based on selling and producing 1,000 batches.

One of the customers of Boxster Limited has indicated that it may be significantly increasing its order level for box BB4 for the next quarter and it appears that activity levels of 1,200 batches and 2,000 batches are feasible.

The semi-variable costs should be calculated using the high/low method. If 3,000 batches are sold the total semi-variable cost will be £7,500 and there is a constant unit variable cost up to this volume.

Complete the table below and calculate the estimated profit per batch of BB4 at the different activity levels.

Batches produced and sold	1,000	1,200	2,000
	£	£	£
Sales revenue	35,000		
Variable costs:			
• Direct materials	7,500		
• Direct labour	10,500		
• Overheads	6,000		
Semi-variable costs:	4,500		
• Variable element			
• Fixed element			
Total cost	28,500		
Total profit	6,500		
Profit per batch (to 2 decimal places)	6.50		

5 Overheads

this chapter covers...

In this chapter we turn our attention to the way in which the overheads of a business are incorporated into the cost of the output. In particular we look at:

- *the need to recover the cost of overheads through units of output*
- *the process of allocating and apportioning the cost of overheads into the units of output*
- *the different bases of apportionment of overheads*
- *apportionment of service department costs, using the direct and step-down methods*
- *the commonly-used overhead absorption rates and their relative merits in given circumstances*
- *the book-keeping entries for overheads*

OVERHEADS

In Chapter 1 'An Introduction to Cost Accounting' we saw that costs could be classified as follows:

DIRECT MATERIALS	INDIRECT MATERIALS
+ DIRECT LABOUR	+ INDIRECT LABOUR
+ DIRECT EXPENSES	+ INDIRECT EXPENSES
= TOTAL DIRECT COSTS (PRIME COST)	= TOTAL OVERHEADS

Direct costs can be identified directly with each unit of output, but indirect costs (overheads) cannot be identified directly with each unit of output.

Overheads do not relate to particular units of output but must, instead, be shared amongst all the cost units (units of output to which costs can be charged) to which they relate. For example, the cost of the factory rent must be included in the cost of the firm's output.

The important point to remember is that all the overheads of a business, together with the direct costs (materials, labour and expenses) must be covered by revenue from the firm's output – the sales of products or services. This point is demonstrated in the Case Study which follows.

Case Study

COOLHEADS: A HAIRDRESSING BUSINESS

situation

CoolHeads is a new hairdressing business, being set up by Nathan and Morgan in a rented shop.

Nathan and Morgan are preparing their price list. They must set the prices at a level which covers their costs and gives them a profit.

They have details of the costs of all the materials they need (shampoos, colourings and so on) from a specialist supplier. Nathan and Morgan have decided the rate to charge to the business for their own work and they do not intend to employ anyone else for the time being.

But there are other costs which they will also incur – their overheads – and they are not so sure how they will work these into their pricing structure. Nathan asks:

'What about the shop rent and rates we have to pay? What about the electricity, the insurance, the telephone bill and all the advertising we have to do? How are we going to cover these costs?'

'How much will it cost us in total to deal with each customer?'

'How do we make sure that we are going to make a profit?'

solution

For pricing purposes, Nathan and Morgan need to include overheads in the cost of each item on their price list.

In a small business like this, the whole business can be a single cost centre. All the overheads can be allowed for in a single rate to charge for a hair cut.

Suppose Nathan and Morgan estimate that their total overheads for the first year of trading will be £27,000. They expect to be working on hairstyling for 1,500 hours each during the year, ie a total of 3,000 hours between them.

Therefore, they could decide in advance that each hour of their work should be charged £27,000 ÷ 3,000 = £9 for overheads. A job that takes two hours to complete would then be charged 2 x £9 = £18 for overheads.

Notice that in a service business such as hairdressing, direct materials costs are likely to be relatively small in comparison with the cost of direct labour and overheads. It is essential for Nathan and Morgan to consider the cost of overheads when they are setting their prices and the hourly rate is one possible way of doing this. This is called an 'overhead absorption rate' and we will look in more detail at this idea later in this chapter (page 128).

In larger businesses and organisations, overheads are usually classified by function under headings such as:

- factory or production, eg factory rent and rates, indirect factory labour, indirect factory materials, heating and lighting of factory
- selling and distribution, eg salaries of sales staff, vehicle costs, delivery costs
- administration, eg office rent and rates, office salaries, heating and lighting of office, indirect office materials
- finance, eg bank interest

Each of these functions or sections of the business is likely to be what is known as a cost centre, a term which was defined in Chapter 1 as follows:

Cost centres are sections of a business or organisation to which costs can be charged.

As well as cost centres, businesses may also have profit centres and investment centres – all three types of centres are collectively called responsibility centres.

In order to deal with the overheads we need to know the responsibility centres of the organisation. This will depend on the size of the business and the way in which the work is organised.

COLLECTING OVERHEADS IN RESPONSIBILITY CENTRES

Depending on the type of cost, overheads are either *allocated* to responsibility centres – cost centres, profit centres or investment centres – or they are *apportioned* to centres.

allocation of overheads

Some overheads belong entirely to one particular centre, for example:

* the wages of a supervisor who works in only one centre

* the rent of a separate building in which there is only one centre

* the cost of indirect materials that have been issued to one particular centre

Overheads like these can therefore be allocated to the centre to which they belong.

Allocation of overheads is the charging to a particular responsibility centre of overheads that are incurred entirely by that centre.

apportionment of overheads

Overheads that cannot be allocated to a particular centre have to be shared or **apportioned** between those responsibility centres that have shared the benefits of the relevant cost.

Apportionment of overheads is the sharing of overheads over a number of responsibility centres to which they relate. Each centre is charged with a proportion of the overhead cost.

For example, a department which is a cost centre within a factory will be charged a proportion of the factory rent and rates. Another example is where a supervisor works within two departments, both of which are separate cost centres: the indirect labour cost of employing the supervisor is shared between the two cost centres.

With apportionment, a suitable **basis** – or method – must be found to apportion overheads between centres; the basis selected should be related to the type of cost. Different methods might be used for each overhead.

Look at the example on the next page.

OVERHEAD	BASIS OF APPORTIONMENT
rent, rates	floor area (or volume of space) of centres
heating, lighting	floor area (or volume of space) of centres
buildings insurance	floor area (or volume of space) of centres
buildings depreciation	floor area (or volume of space) of centres
machinery insurance	cost or value of machinery and equipment
machinery depreciation	value of machinery; or machine usage (hours)
canteen	number of employees in each centre
supervisory costs	number of employees in each centre, or labour hours worked by supervisors in each centre

It must be stressed that apportionment is used for those overheads that cannot be allocated to a particular centre. For example, if a college's Business Studies Department occupies a building in another part of town from the main college building, the rates for the building can clearly be allocated to the Business Studies cost centre. By contrast, the rates for the main college building must be apportioned amongst the cost centres on the main campus.

review of allocation and apportionment

It is important that the allocation and apportionment of overheads are reviewed at regular intervals to ensure that the methods being used are still valid. For example:

- *allocation*

  The role of a supervisor may have changed – whereas previously the supervisor worked in one department only, he or she might now be working in two departments

- *apportionment*

  Building work may have expanded the floor area of a department, so that the apportionment basis needs to be reworked

Any proposed changes to allocation and apportionment must be discussed with senior staff and their agreement obtained before any changes to methods are implemented. Accounting personnel will often have to consult with personnel (such as managers and supervisors) working in operational departments, to discuss how overheads are charged to their departments, and to resolve any queries.

apportionment and ratios

It is important to understand the method of apportionment of overheads using ratios. For example, overheads relating to buildings are often shared in the ratio of the floor area used by the cost centres.

Now read through the Worked Example and the Case Study which follow.

WORKED EXAMPLE: APPORTIONMENT USING RATIOS

A business has four cost centres: two production departments, A and B, and two non-production cost centres, stores and maintenance. The total rent per year for the business premises is £12,000. This is to be apportioned on the basis of floor area, given as:

	production dept A	production dept B	stores	maintenance
Floor area (square metres)	400	550	350	200

Step 1
Calculate the total floor area: 400 + 550 + 350 + 200 = 1,500 square metres

Step 2
Divide the total rent by the total floor area: £12,000 ÷ 1,500 = £8
This gives a rate of £8 per square metre.

Step 3
Multiply the floor area in each cost centre by the rate per square metre. This gives the share of rent for each cost centre. For example, in Production Department A, the share of rent is 400 x £8 = £3,200. The results are shown in the table:

	production dept A	production dept B	stores	maintenance
Floor area (square metres)	400	550	350	200
Rent apportioned	£3,200	£4,400	£2,800	£1,600

Step 4
Check that the apportioned amounts agree with the total rent:
£3,200 + £4,400 + £ 2,800 + £1,600 = £12,000.

Case
Study

1.850

1.600

PILOT ENGINEERING LIMITED:
OVERHEAD ALLOCATION AND APPORTIONMENT

situation

Pilot Engineering Limited, which makes car engine components, uses some of the latest laser equipment in one department, while another section of the business continues to use traditional machinery. Details of the factory are as follows:

Department X is a 'hi-tech' machine shop equipped with laser-controlled machinery which cost £80,000. This department has 400 square metres of floor area. There are three machine operators: the supervisor spends one-third of the time in this department.

Department Y is a 'low-tech' part of the factory equipped with machinery which cost £20,000. The floor area is 600 square metres. There are two workers who spend all their time in this department: the supervisor spends two-thirds of the time in this department.

The overheads to be allocated or apportioned are as follows:

1	Factory rates	£12,000
2	Wages of the supervisor	£21,000
3	Factory heating and lighting	£2,500
4	Depreciation of machinery	£20,000
5	Buildings insurance	£2,000
6	Insurance of machinery	£1,500
7	Specialist materials for the laser equipment	£2,500

How should each of these be allocated or apportioned to each department?

solution

The recommendations are:

1 Factory rates – apportioned on the basis of floor area.

2 Supervisor's wages – apportioned on the basis of time spent, ie one-third to Department X, and two-thirds to Department Y. If the time spent was not known, an alternative basis could be established, based on the number of employees.

3 Factory heating and lighting – apportioned on the basis of floor area.

4 Depreciation of machinery – apportioned on the basis of the cost of machinery.

5 Buildings insurance – apportioned on the basis of floor area.

6 Insurance of machinery – apportioned on the basis of the cost of machinery.

7 Specialist materials for the laser equipment – allocated to Department X because this cost belongs entirely to Department X.

It is important to note that there are no fixed rules for the apportionment of overheads – the only proviso is that a fair proportion of the overhead is charged to each department which has shared the benefits of the relevant cost. Methods of apportionment will need to be reviewed at regular intervals to ensure that they are still valid; changes can only be implemented with the agreement of senior staff.

The apportionment of overheads for Pilot Engineering Limited is as follows (sample workings are shown below the table):

overhead	basis of apportionment	total	dept X	dept Y
		£	£	£
Factory rates	Floor area	12,000	4,800	7,200
Wages of supervisor	Time spent	21,000	7,000	14,000
Heating and lighting	Floor area	2,500	1,000	1,500
Dep'n of machinery	Cost of machinery	20,000	16,000	4,000
Buildings insurance	Floor area	2,000	800	1,200
Machinery insurance	Cost of machinery	1,500	1,200	300
Specialist materials	Allocation	2,500	2,500	–
		61,500	33,300	28,200

workings

For example, the floor areas of the two departments are:

Dept X	400	square metres
Dept Y	600	square metres
Total	1,000	square metres

Factory rates are apportioned as follows:

$$\frac{£12,000}{1,000} = £12 \text{ per square metre}$$

Dept X rates:	£12 x 400 =	£4,800
Dept Y rates	£12 x 600 =	£7,200
Total (check)		£12,000

SERVICE DEPARTMENTS

Many businesses have departments which provide services within the business; for example, maintenance, transport, stores or stationery. Each service department is likely to be a cost centre, to which a proportion of overheads is charged. As service departments do not themselves have any cost units to which their overheads may be charged, the costs of each service department must be re-apportioned to the production departments (which do have cost units to which overheads can be charged). A suitable basis of re-allocation must be used, for example:

- the overheads of a maintenance department might be re-apportioned to production departments on the basis of value of machinery or equipment, or on the basis of time spent in each production department

- the overheads of a stores or stationery department could be re-apportioned on the basis of value of goods issued to production departments

- the overheads of a subsidised canteen could be re-apportioned on the basis of the number of employees

Re-apportionment of service department overheads is considered in the next section.

RE-APPORTIONMENT OF SERVICE DEPARTMENT OVERHEADS

The overheads of service departments are charged to production cost centres using one of the following techniques:

- **direct apportionment** is used where service departments provide services to production departments only

- the **step-down method** is used where service departments provide services to production departments *and* to other service departments

To illustrate re-apportionment, we will apply these techniques to a business with two production departments, A and B, and two service departments, stores and maintenance. After allocation and apportionment of production overheads, the totals are:

	total	production dept A	production dept B	stores	maintenance
	£	£	£	£	£
Overheads	20,400	10,000	5,000	2,400	3,000

direct apportionment

Here the service departments do not provide services to one another. Their costs are directly apportioned to production departments using a suitable basis. In the example on the previous page:

- stores overheads are re-apportioned on the basis of the number of stores requisitions – department A has made 150 requisitions; department B has made 50

- maintenance overheads are re-apportioned on the value of machinery – department A has machinery with a net book value of £20,000, department B's machinery has a value of £10,000

Using direct apportionment, the overheads of the service departments are re-apportioned as shown in the table below. The method of calculation using ratios is the same as we used for apportionment.

Notice that the total is taken out of the service cost centre column when it is shared between the production cost centres.

	total	production dept A	production dept B	stores	maintenance
	£	£	£	£	£
Overheads	20,400	10,000	5,000	2,400	3,000
Stores	–	1,800	600	(2,400)	–
Maintenance	–	2,000	1,000	–	(3,000)
	20,400	13,800	6,600	–	–

Thus all the overheads have now been charged to the production departments where they can be 'absorbed' into the cost units which form the output of each department. We will see how the absorption is carried out later in this chapter.

step-down method

This is used where, as well as to production departments, one service department provides services to another. Using the example, the stores department deals with requisitions from the maintenance department, but no maintenance work is carried out in the stores department. Under the step-down method we re-apportion firstly the overheads of the stores department (because it does not receive any services from the maintenance department), and secondly the overheads of the maintenance department:

- stores requisitions
  - department A 150
  - department B   50
  - maintenance   50
- value of machinery
  - department A £20,000
  - department B £10,000

The re-apportionment of the production overheads of the service departments, using the step-down method, is as follows:

	total	production dept A	production dept B	stores	maintenance
	£	£	£	£	£
Overheads	20,400	10,000	5,000	2,400	3,000
Stores	–	1,440	480	(2,400)	480
				–	*3,480
Maintenance	–	2,320	1,160	–	(3,480)
	20,400	13,760	6,640	–	–

* Note that a new total is calculated for the maintenance department before it is re-apportioned. £480 from stores is added to the original £3,000 overheads in the maintenance department.

All the overheads have now been charged to the production departments.

ALLOCATION AND APPORTIONMENT – A SUMMARY

The diagram on the next page summarises the allocation and apportionment of overheads that we have seen in this chapter. It shows:

- allocation of overheads directly to cost centres
- apportionment of overheads on an equitable basis to cost centres
- re-apportionment of service department costs to production cost centres

The Case Study which follows on page 132 is a comprehensive example of allocation and apportionment – it is based on an AAT sample Assessment task.

Case Study

1.850

1.600

PREPARING FOR ASSESSMENT: ALLOCATION AND APPORTIONMENT OF OVERHEADS

Tutorial note:
* This Case Study is based on an AAT sample Assessment task.
* Note that the task gives the floor area for support cost centres and not for production cost centres – this means that any costs apportioned by floor area must be charged to the support cost centres. When reapportionment takes place the costs will be charged to production cost centres in the proportion that they have used the support centres.

situation

You work as an accounts assistant for Korecki Limited, a manufacturing business. The company has two production cost centres: cutting and assembly – and three support cost centres: maintenance, stores and administration.

Korecki Limited's budgeted overheads for the next financial year are:

	£	£
Depreciation of equipment		3,900
Power for production machinery		4,680
Rent and rates		8,450
Light and heat		3,250
Indirect labour costs:		
Maintenance	45,400	
Stores	27,250	
Administration	62,100	
Totals	134,750	20,280

The following information is also available:

Department	Net book value/ carrying amount of equipment	Production machinery power usage (KwH)	Floor space (square metres)	Number of employees
Production cost centres:				
Cutting	175,000	25,500		6
Assembly	85,000	13,500		8
Support cost centres:				
Maintenance			300	3
Stores			200	2
Administration			150	4
Total	260,000	39,000	650	23

Overheads are allocated or apportioned on the most appropriate basis. The total overheads of the support cost centres are then reapportioned to the two production centres, using the direct method.

- 75% of the maintenance cost centre's time is spent maintaining production machinery in the cutting production centre and the remainder in the assembly production centre.
- The stores cost centre makes 60% of its issues to the cutting production centre, and 40% to the assembly production centre.
- Administration supports the two production centres equally.
- There is no reciprocal servicing between the three support cost centres.

You are to use the information to allocate and apportion the budgeted overheads for the next financial year.

solution

Before completing an apportionment table you identify that:

- indirect labour is to be allocated to the support cost centres
- all other overheads are to be apportioned to the production centres and support cost centres, using a suitable basis

You note that you have not been given the floor space (area) for the two production cost centres; however, your supervisor tells you to apportion those costs which are based on floor space to the support cost centres. By doing this the costs will be charged to the production cost centres in the proportion that they have used the support cost centres.

The basis of apportionment you decide to use is:

- depreciation of equipment – net book value of equipment
- power for production machinery – power usage
- rent and rates – floor space
- light and heat – floor space

As noted earlier, the indirect labour of the support centres will be allocated.

The apportionment table, including the re-apportionment of the service cost centres, is completed as follows:

	Basis of apportionment	Cutting £	Assembly £	Maintenance £	Stores £	Admin £	Totals £
Depreciation of equipment	NBV* of equipment	2,625	1,275				3,900
Power for production machinery	Power usage	3,060	1,620				4,680
Rent and rates	Floor space			3,900	2,600	1,950	8,450
Light and heat	Floor space			1,500	1,000	750	3,250
Indirect labour	Allocated			45,400	27,250	62,100	134,750
Totals		5,685	2,895	50,800	30,850	64,800	155,030
Reapportion Maintenance		38,100	12,700	(50,800)			
Reapportion Stores		18,510	12,340		(30,850)		
Reapportion Administration		32,400	32,400			(64,800)	
Total overheads to production centres		94,695	60,335				155,030

* or carrying amount

OVERHEAD ABSORPTION

Once overheads have been allocated or apportioned to production cost centres, the final step is to ensure that the overheads are charged to cost units. In the language of cost accounting this is known as 'absorption' or 'recovery', ie the cost of overheads is charged to the cost units which pass through that particular production department.

We saw in the Case Study of CoolHeads (page 121), how overheads could be allowed for when deciding on selling prices.

Similarly, if you take a car to be repaired at a garage, the bill may be presented as follows:

	£
Parts	70.00
Labour: 3 hours at £40 per hour	120.00
Total	190.00

Within this bill are the three main elements of cost: materials (parts), labour and overheads. The last two are combined as labour – the garage mechanic is not paid £40 per hour; instead the labour rate might be £15 per hour, with the rest, ie £25 per hour, being a contribution towards the overheads and profit of the garage. Other examples are accountants and solicitors, who charge a 'rate per hour', part of which is used to contribute to the cost of overheads and profit.

To be profitable, a business must ensure that its selling prices more than cover all its costs:

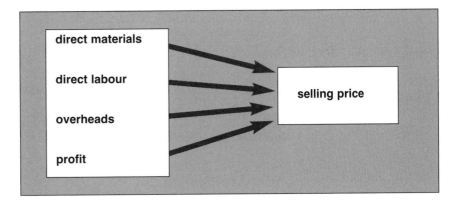

calculating overhead absorption rates

In order to absorb the overheads of a department, there are two steps to be followed:

1   calculation of the overhead absorption rate (OAR)

2   application of this rate to actual work done

The overhead absorption rate is calculated using estimated or budgeted figures as follows, for a given time period:

$$OAR = \frac{total\ budgeted\ cost\ centre\ overheads}{total\ planned\ work\ in\ the\ cost\ centre}$$

The amount of work must be measured in a suitable way – for a manufacturing business this is usually:

•   direct labour hours, or

•   machine hours

Other organisations – especially those which provide a service – will use other ways, eg a bus company may well use miles travelled as an overhead absorption rate.

These methods are illustrated below.

direct labour hour method of calculation

With this method, production overhead is absorbed on the basis of the number of direct labour hours worked. It is most commonly used where labour is intensive.

1   Calculation of the overhead absorption rate, using budgeted (expected) figures:

$$\frac{total\ cost\ centre\ overheads}{total\ direct\ labour\ hours\ (in\ cost\ centre)} = cost\ per\ direct\ labour\ hour$$

2   Application of the rate:

direct labour hours worked x overhead absorption rate

= overhead absorbed

Example

Department A   total budgeted cost centre overheads for year   £40,000
expected direct labour hours for year   5,000
actual direct labour hours in March   450

1   Overhead absorption rate:

$$\frac{£40,000}{5,000 \text{ hours}} = £8 \text{ per direct labour hour}$$

2   Application of the rate:

450 hours x £8 = £3,600 of overhead absorbed in March

machine hour method of calculation

Here the production overhead is absorbed on the basis of machine hours. It is most commonly used where machine use is intensive.

1   Calculation of the overhead absorption rate, using budgeted (expected) figures:

$$\frac{\textit{total cost centre overheads}}{\textit{total machine hours (in cost centre)}} = \textit{cost per machine hour}$$

2   Application of the rate:

machine hours worked x overhead absorption rate

= overhead absorbed

Example

Department B   total budgeted cost centre overheads for year   £216,000
expected machine hours for year   36,000
actual machine hours in March   3,500

1   Overhead absorption rate:

$$\frac{£216,000}{36,000 \text{ hours}} = £6 \text{ per machine hour}$$

2   Application of the rate:

3,500 hours x £6 = £21,000 of overhead absorbed in March

other methods, eg miles travelled, of calculation

Here the overhead is absorbed on the basis of miles travelled.

1 Calculation of the overhead absorption rate, using budgeted (expected) figures:

$$\frac{\textit{total cost centre* overheads}}{\textit{total miles travelled (in cost centre)}} = \textit{cost per mile travelled}$$

* for a bus company, a cost centre could be a route number, a bus or a garage

2 Application of the rate:

miles travelled x overhead absorption rate

= overhead absorbed

Example

Buses on route 73   total budgeted cost centre overheads for year   £100,000
                     expected miles travelled for year   200,000
                     actual miles travelled in March   18,000

1   Overhead absorption rate:
        $$\frac{£100,000}{200,000 \text{ miles}} = £0.50 \text{ per mile travelled}$$

2   Application of the rate:
        18,000 miles travelled x £0.50 = £9,000 of overhead absorbed in March

which method to use?

Only one overhead absorption rate will be used in a particular department, and the method selected must relate to the reason why the costs are incurred. For example, a cost centre which is machine based, where most of the overheads incurred relate to machinery, will use a machine hour basis.

The direct labour hour method is a very popular method (eg the garage mentioned earlier) because overheads are absorbed on a time basis. Thus the cost unit that requires twice the direct labour of another cost unit will be charged twice the overhead. However this method will be inappropriate where some units are worked on by hand while others quickly pass through a machinery process and require little direct labour time.

A machine hour rate is particularly appropriate where expensive machinery is used in the department. However, it would be unsuitable where not all products pass through the machine but some are worked on by hand: in the latter case, no overheads would be charged to the cost units.

It is important to select the best method of overhead absorption for the particular business, otherwise wrong decisions will be made on the basis of the costing information. The particular absorption method selected for a department will need to be reviewed at regular intervals to ensure that it is still valid. For example, the direct labour hour method is unlikely to continue to be appropriate where a machine has been brought in to automate processes that were previously carried out by hand. Any proposed changes must be discussed with senior personnel and their agreement obtained before any changes to methods are implemented. The changes will need to be discussed with personnel (such as managers and supervisors) working in operational departments to explain how overheads will be charged to their departments in the future, and any queries will need to be resolved.

In this chapter, we have calculated overhead absorption rates based on:

- direct labour hours – for a manufacturing business
- machine hours – for a manufacturing business
- miles travelled – for a bus company

There are other possible bases which could be used. For example, overheads could be charged as a percentage of:

- direct material cost
- direct labour cost
- prime cost

The principles are the same for any method of absorption:

- the rate to use is calculated in advance using estimates
- the rate is applied to the actual work done

For example, if the estimates showed that it would be necessary to add 50% on to the direct labour cost for overheads, then a job having a direct labour cost of £6,000 would absorb £6,000 x 50% = £3,000 of overheads, making a total of £9,000.

using a pre-determined rate

Most businesses and organisations calculate a pre-determined overhead absorption rate for each department. This is then applied to all production passing through that department.

The OAR is calculated in advance using estimates – this avoids having to calculate the rate regularly, which may result in changes over quite short time periods. Instead the rate is smoothed out over fluctuations in cost and activity over a longer accounting period.

Appropriate consultation will need to be made with personnel from the operating departments before a pre-determined rate is established for a particular department.

OVER- OR UNDER-ABSORPTION OF OVERHEADS

In the Case Study of CoolHeads (page 121) we saw that Nathan and Morgan estimated that their total overheads for the first year of trading would be £27,000. They expected to be working on hairstyling for 1,500 hours each during the year, ie a total of 3,000 hours between them.

Therefore, they could have decided in advance that each hour of their work should be charged £27,000/3,000 = £9 for overheads. A job taking two hours to complete would then be charged 2 x £9 = £18 for overheads. This is a simple example of the absorption of overheads using a pre-determined rate. (The word 'recovery' is sometimes used instead of 'absorption' – it means the same.)

At the end of CoolHeads' first year, it is most unlikely that Nathan and Morgan will find that everything went exactly according to plan. They may have spent more or less on the overheads than £27,000. They may have worked on styling for more or less than 3,000 hours in total.

They will find, therefore, that the amount of overheads they have absorbed into the cost of their actual work during the year is not the same as the amount they have spent. If the amount absorbed is the greater, the difference is called 'over-absorption' or 'over-recovery' of overheads. If the amount absorbed is less than the amount spent, the difference is called 'under-absorption' or 'under-recovery'.

Over-absorption or under-absorption (recovery) is the difference between the total amount of overheads absorbed (recovered) in a given period and the total amount spent on overheads.

The following worked example shows a calculation for over-absorption – with the overhead absorption rate based on direct labour hours.

Example
Department C

overhead absorption rate (based on direct labour hours)	£6.00 per labour hour
actual labour hours in year	6,300 hours
actual overheads for year	£36,000

- actual overheads for the department are £36,000
- actual overhead absorbed: 6,300 hours x £6.00 per hour = £37,800
- over-absorption of overhead: £37,800 – £36,000 = £1,800

At the end of the financial year, an adjustment is made to the income statement for the total over-absorbed or under-absorbed overhead.

On first impressions, over-absorption of overheads seems to be a 'bonus' for a business – profits will be higher; however, it should be remembered that the overhead rate may have been set too high. As a consequence, sales might have been lost because the selling price has been too high. The overhead absorption rate (OAR) will need to be reviewed with the manager and supervisors of the operational department if over-absorption continues on a regular basis – they may be able to explain the reason for the difference.

With under-absorption, the actual overhead absorbed is less than the actual overheads for the department. For example, if in Department C (above) actual labour hours in the year were 5,500, the calculations would be:

- actual overheads for the department are £36,000

- actual overhead absorbed: 5,500 hours x £6.00 per hour = £33,000

- under-absorption of overhead: £36,000 – £33,000 = £3,000

BOOK-KEEPING ENTRIES FOR OVERHEADS

In this section we look at the cost book-keeping entries to record the transfer of the cost of overheads to production, together with the entries for over- or under-absorption of overheads (which are transferred to the income statement). These entries form part of the book-keeping system for costing.

A production overheads account is used to:
- transfer production overheads to production
- credit the amount of over-absorbed overheads to the income statement
- charge the amount of under-absorbed overheads to the income statement

The cost book-keeping entries are:

- **transfer production overheads (amount absorbed) to production**
  - debit production
  - credit production overheads

- **credit over-absorbed overheads to the income statement**
  - debit production overheads
  - credit income statement

  Here, the amount of over-absorbed overheads reduces the total cost of production, and so increases profits.

- **charge under-absorbed overheads to the income statement**
  - debit income statement
  - credit production overheads

  Here the amount of under-absorbed overheads adds to the total cost of production, and so reduces profits.

These cost book-keeping entries are shown diagrammatically as shown below.

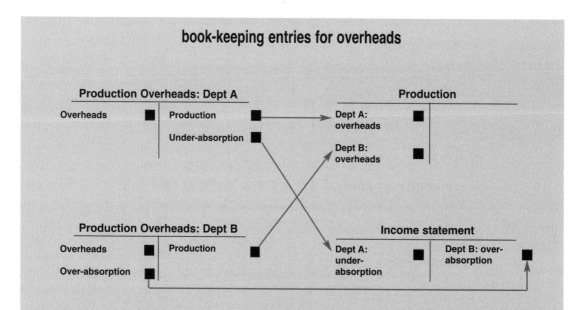

book-keeping entries for overheads

Note: Instead of transferring the over- or under-absorption of overheads direct to the income statement, an alternative is to use a holding account for the amounts. At the end of the financial year, the balance of this account is then transferred to the income statement – as either a debit or a credit entry, depending on the balance.

BOXIT LIMITED: BOOK-KEEPING FOR OVERHEADS

Case Study

situation

Boxit Limited manufactures and sells cardboard boxes which are used for packaging and storage. The boxes pass through two departments – cutting and assembly. Details of overheads for the departments for the four weeks ended 24 March 20-8 are as follows:

Cutting Department

- overhead absorption rate is £10.00 per machine hour
- machine hours worked were 1,000
- actual cost of production overhead was £11,000

Assembly Department

- overhead absorption rate is £4.00 per direct labour hour
- direct labour hours worked were 2,000
- actual cost of production overhead was £7,500

The following cost accounting codes are in use to record overheads:

code number	description
2200	production
2500	production overheads: cutting department
2600	production overheads: assembly department
5500	income statement

As an accounts assistant at Boxit Limited, you are asked to prepare the two production overheads accounts and to fill in the table below to record the journal entries for the overheads and for the over- and under-absorption of overheads.

20-8	Code number	Debit £	Credit £
24 March	2200		
24 March	2500		
24 March	2200		
24 March	2600		
24 March	5500		
24 March	2500		
24 March	2600		
24 March	5500		

solution

The production overheads accounts are prepared as follows:

Dr		**Production Overheads Account: Cutting Department**		Cr
	£			£
Bank (overheads incurred)	11,000	Production		10,000
		Income statement		
		(under-absorption)		1,000
	11,000			11,000

Dr		**Production Overheads Account: Assembly Department**		Cr
	£			£
Bank (overheads incurred)	7,500	Production		8,000
Income statement				
(over-absorption)	500			
	8,000			8,000

The cost book-keeping entries are:

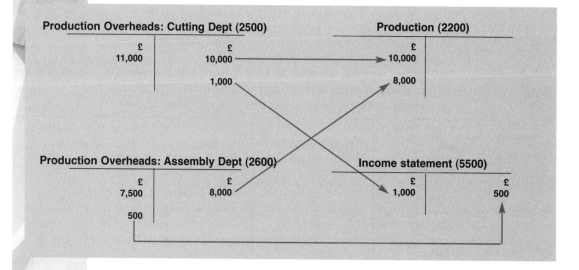

The cost book-keeping entries are recorded on the table as follows:

20-8	Code number	Debit £	Credit £
24 March	2200	£10,000	
24 March	2500		£10,000
24 March	2200	£8,000	
24 March	2600		£8,000
24 March	5500	£1,000	
24 March	2500		£1,000
24 March	2600	£500	
24 March	5500		£500

In this way, the cost of the pre-determined overhead rates is charged to production, while the amount of over- or under-absorption of overheads is transferred to the income statement.

Chapter Summary

- Direct costs can be charged directly to cost units.

- Indirect costs (overheads) cannot be charged to cost units immediately.

- Overheads are:
  - allocated to a specific responsibility centre, if they belong entirely to that centre
  - apportioned between centres, if they are shared

- Apportionment is done on a suitable basis, using ratios of floor area, numbers of employees and so on.

- Methods of allocation and apportionment should be reviewed regularly.

- The total overheads allocated and apportioned to the service cost centres are then re-apportioned to production cost centres using either direct apportionment or the step-down method.

- After re-apportionment of the service cost centre overheads, the total overheads in each production cost centre can be calculated.

- All the above steps can be carried out using expected or budgeted overhead amounts.

- Overhead absorption rates are calculated using the total expected or budgeted overheads in each cost centre.

- An overhead absorption rate is calculated as follows:

$$overhead\ absorption\ rate\ =\ \frac{total\ budgeted\ cost\ centre\ overheads}{total\ planned\ work\ in\ cost\ centre}$$

where the planned amount of work may be measured, often in terms of direct labour hours or machine hours for a manufacturing company, although service sector organisations will use other methods, eg miles travelled for a bus company.

- Overhead absorption rates are applied to the actual work carried out. A direct labour hour absorption rate is applied as follows, for example:

Direct labour hours worked x overhead absorption rate

= overhead absorbed

- At the end of a given period, the amount of overhead absorbed may differ from the amount actually spent on the overheads. The difference is either an over-absorption (when the amount absorbed is greater than the amount spent) or an under-absorption (when the amount absorbed is less than the amount spent).

- Cost book-keeping entries are made to record:

  – the transfer of overheads to production

  – the transfer of over- or under-absorption of overheads to the income statement

Key Terms

overheads	indirect costs, made up of
	indirect materials + indirect labour + indirect expenses
cost centres	sections of a business to which costs can be charged
allocation of overheads	the charging to a particular responsibility centre of overheads that are incurred entirely by that centre

apportionment of overheads	the sharing of overheads over a number of responsibility centres to which they relate – each centre is charged with a proportion of the overhead cost
service department	a non-production cost centre that provides services to other cost centres in the business
re-apportionment of service department overheads	the sharing of the total overheads from a service department, a proportion being charged to each cost centre it serves; after all re-apportionment has been carried out, the overheads will be charged to production cost centres only
direct apportionment	method of re-apportionment used where service departments provide services to production departments only
step-down	method of re-apportionment used where service departments provide services to production departments *and* to other service departments
absorption (recovery) of overheads	the charging of overheads to cost units (units of output)
overhead absorption rate (OAR)	the rate used to charge overheads to cost units – calculated in advance, as: budgeted total overhead ÷ planned amount of work
basis of absorption	the measurement of work used to calculate the overhead absorption rate, for example: • direct labour hours • machine hours
over- or under-absorption (recovery)	the difference between the total amount of overheads absorbed (recovered) in a given period and the total amount spent on overheads

Activities

5.1   Distinguish between:
  • allocation of overheads
  • apportionment of overheads

5.2   Wyvern Fabrication Company has two production departments – moulding and finishing.

The company charges overheads on the basis of machine hours and the following overhead analysis information is available to you (note that service department overheads have already been apportioned to production departments):

OVERHEAD ANALYSIS SHEET		
	MOULDING	FINISHING
Budgeted total overheads (£)	9,338	3,298
Budgeted machine hours	1,450	680
Budgeted overhead absorption rate (£)		

Details of a particular job of work are as follows:

JOB OVERHEAD ANALYSIS SHEET		
	MOULDING	FINISHING
Job machine hours	412	154
Budgeted overhead absorption rate (£)		
Overhead absorbed by job (£)		

You are to:

(a)   Calculate the overhead absorption rate for each of the two departments and complete the overhead analysis sheet.

(b)   Calculate the production overhead absorbed by the job and complete the job overhead analysis sheet.

(c)   Suggest another overhead absorption rates that the company might use and comment on the circumstances that would make it appropriate.

5.3 ABC Limited is a manufacturing business with three cost centres: Departments A, B and C. The following are the expected factory overheads for the forthcoming year:

Rent and rates	£7,210
Depreciation of machinery	£10,800
Supervisor's salary	£12,750
Insurance of machinery	£750

Departmental information is:

	Dept A	Dept B	Dept C
Floor area (sq m)	300	150	250
Value of machinery	£25,000	£15,000	£10,000
Number of production-line employees	8	4	3

You are to:

(a) Apportion the overheads to the cost centres, stating the basis of apportionment.

(b) Calculate the overhead absorption rate (to two decimal places) of each department, based on direct labour hours. Note that the factory works a 37 hour week for 48 weeks in a year.

5.4 Wye Engineering Limited offers specialist engineering services to the car industry. It has two production departments – machining and finishing – and a service department which maintains the machinery of both departments. Expected production overheads for the forthcoming year are:

	£
Rent and rates	5,520
Buildings insurance	1,320
Insurance of machinery	1,650
Lighting and heating	3,720
Depreciation of machinery	11,000
Supervisory salaries	30,000
Maintenance department salary	16,000
Factory cleaning	4,800

The following information is available:

	Machining	Finishing	Maintenance
Floor area (square metres)	300	200	100
Number of employees	6	3	1
Value of machinery	£40,000	£15,000	–

The factory works a 35 hour week for 47 weeks each year.

You are to:

(a) Prepare an analysis of production overheads showing the basis of allocation and apportionment to the three departments of the business.

(b) Re-apportion the service department overheads to production departments on the basis of value of machinery.

(c) Calculate an overhead absorption rate based on direct labour hours for each of the two production departments.

(d) Discuss alternative overhead absorption rates that the company could use.

5.5 Mercia Tutorial College has two teaching departments – business studies and general studies – and two service departments – administration and technical support. The overheads of each department are as follows:

	£
• business studies	40,000
• general studies	20,000
• administration	9,600
• technical support	12,000

The basis for re-apportioning the overheads of the service departments is:

• technical support, on the value of equipment in each department – business studies, £50,000; general studies, £25,000; administration, £25,000

• administration, on the number of students in the teaching departments – business studies, 500; general studies, 250

You are to use the step-down method to re-apportion the two service department overheads to the two teaching departments.

5.6 Rossiter and Rossiter is a firm of chartered accountants, with two partners. Overhead costs for next year are estimated to be:

	£
Office rent	10,000
Office salaries	30,000
Rates	4,800
Heating and lighting	2,400
Stationery	2,000
Postage and telephone	5,100
Car expenses	5,600

The two partners plan to work for 47 weeks next year. They will each be in the office for 40 hours per week, but will be working on behalf of their clients for 35 hours per week.

(a)   What is the overhead absorption rate per partner hour?

(b)   If each partner wishes to earn a salary of £30,000 per year, what is the combined hourly rate per partner, which includes overheads and their salaries?

(c)   If both partners actually work on their clients' behalf for 37 hours per week, what will be the total over-absorption of overheads for the year?

5.7 A friend of yours is about to start in business making garden seats. She plans to make two different qualities – 'Standard' and 'De Luxe'. Costs per unit for direct materials and labour are expected to be:

	Standard	De Luxe
	£	£
Direct materials	12.50	20.00
Direct labour:		
3 hours at £8.00 per hour	24.00	–
3.5 hours at £10.00 per hour	–	35.00
	36.50	55.00
Machine hours	1	2.5

Production overheads are expected to be £1,000 per month.

Production is expected to be 80 'Standard' seats and 40 'De Luxe' seats per month.

(a)   Suggest two different methods by which overheads can be absorbed.

(b)   Calculate the production cost of each of the two qualities of garden seats using the two different methods of overhead absorption.

(c)   Compare the results of your calculations and suggest to your friend the most appropriate method of overhead absorption for this business.

5.8 Durning Limited manufactures and sells household furniture. The company's operations are organised by departments, as follows:

·   Warehouse

·   Manufacturing

·   Sales

·   Administration

The budgeted and actual fixed overheads of the company for November 20-1 were as follows:

	£
Depreciation of fixed assets	9,150
Rent	11,000
Other property overheads	6,200
Administration overheads	13,450
Staff costs:	
− warehouse	3,600
− indirect manufacturing	9,180
− sales	8,650
− administration	5,940
Total budgeted and actual fixed overheads	67,170

The following information is also relevant:

Department	% of floor space occupied	Net book value/ carrying amount of non-current assets £000
Warehouse	15%	120
Manufacturing	60%	400
Sales	10%	20
Administration	15%	60
	100%	600

Overheads are allocated and apportioned between departments using the most appropriate basis.

Task 1

Please see next page.

Task 2

Manufacturing fixed overheads are absorbed on the basis of budgeted machine hours. The budgeted number of machine hours for November 20-1 was 10,000 hours.

You are to calculate the budgeted fixed overhead absorption rate for the manufacturing department for November 20-1.

Task 1

Complete the following table showing the allocation and apportionment of fixed overheads between the four departments.

Fixed overheads for November 20-1	Basis	Total £	Warehouse £	Manufacturing £	Sales £	Administration £
Depreciation		9,150				
Rent		11,000				
Other property overheads		6,200				
Administration overheads		13,450				
Staff costs		27,370				
		67,170				

5.9 You work as an accounts assistant at the Trevaunance Hotel which is part of a group of hotels. Each month it is one of your tasks to record and report cost information to head office.

The Trevaunance Hotel has fifty bedrooms and its operations are organised into five departments, as follows:

- Accommodation
- Restaurant
- Bar
- Kitchen
- Administration

The budgeted and actual fixed overheads for the Trevaunance Hotel for August 20-3 were as follows:

	£
Bedroom repairs	3,200
Electricity	1,700
Rent	9,000
Kitchen repairs	1,025
Staff costs:	
– accommodation	4,550
– restaurant	6,740
– bar	3,045
– kitchen	2,310
– administration	6,950
Other property overheads	4,000
Total budgeted and actual fixed overheads	42,520

The following information is also relevant:

Department	% of floor space occupied	Metered electricity costs £
Accommodation	65%	550
Restaurant	15%	250
Bar	10%	150
Kitchen	5%	700
Administration	5%	50
	100%	1,700

Overheads are allocated and apportioned to the five departments using the most appropriate basis. The total administration overheads are then re-apportioned to the other four departments using the following percentages:

- Accommodation   60%
- Restaurant   20%
- Bar   10%
- Kitchen   10%

Task 1

Complete the following table showing the allocation and apportionment of fixed overheads between the five departments.

Fixed overheads for August 20-3	Basis	Total £	Accommodation £	Restaurant £	Bar £	Kitchen £	Administration £
Bedroom repairs		3,200					
Electricity		1,700					
Rent		9,000					
Kitchen repairs		1,025					
Staff costs		23,595					
Other property overheads		4,000					
		42,520					( )
Administration		42,520					( )

Task 2

Kitchen fixed overheads are absorbed on the basis of budgeted labour hours. The budgeted number of labour hours for the kitchen during August 20-3 was 1,000 hours.

You are to calculate the budgeted fixed overhead absorption rate per labour hour for the kitchen for August 20-3.

5.10 You work as an accounts assistant for Sekula Limited, a manufacturing business. The company has two production cost centres: moulding and finishing – and three support cost centres: maintenance, stores and administration.

Sekula Limited's budgeted overheads for the next financial year are:

	£	£
Depreciation of production machinery		1,950
Power for production machinery		2,604
Rent and rates		4,275
Light and heat		2,925
Indirect labour costs:		
Maintenance	32,200	
Stores	17,150	
Administration	28,450	
Totals	77,800	11,754

The following information is also available:

Department	Net book value/ carrying amount of equipment	Production machinery power usage (KwH)	Floor space (square metres)	Number of employees
Production cost centres:				
Moulding	80,000	16,000		4
Finishing	50,000	8,000		5
Support cost centres:				
Maintenance			120	2
Stores			150	1
Administration			180	2
Total	130,000	24,000	450	14

Overheads are allocated or apportioned on the most appropriate basis. The total overheads of the support cost centres are then reapportioned to the two production centres, using the direct method.

- 75% of the maintenance cost centre's time is spent maintaining production machinery in the moulding production centre and the remainder in the finishing production centre.

- The stores cost centre makes 60% of its issues to the moulding production centre, and 40% to the finishing production centre.

- Administration supports the two production centres equally.

- There is no reciprocal servicing between the three support cost centres.

You are to complete the apportionment table below using the data above.

	Basis of apportionment	Moulding £	Finishing £	Maintenance £	Stores £	Admin £	Totals £
Depreciation of production machinery							
Power for production machinery							
Rent and rates							
Light and heat							
Indirect labour							
Totals							
Reapportion Maintenance							
Reapportion Stores							
Reapportion Administration							
Total overheads to production centres							

5.11 Wentworth Limited's budgeted overheads and activity levels for the next quarter are:

	Cutting	Assembly
Budgeted overheads (£)	165,600	318,750
Budgeted direct labour hours	18,400	12,750
Budgeted machine hours	8,280	4,250

1. **What would be the budgeted overhead absorption rate for each department if this were set based on their both being heavily automated?**

   (a) cutting £9 per hour; assembly £25 per hour

   (b) cutting £9 per hour; assembly £75 per hour

   (c) cutting £20 per hour; assembly £25 per hour

   (d) cutting £20 per hour; assembly £75 per hour

   Answer (a) or (b) or (c) or (d)

2. **What would be the budgeted overhead absorption rate for each department if this were set based on their both being labour intensive?**

   (a) cutting £9 per hour; assembly £25 per hour

   (b) cutting £9 per hour; assembly £75 per hour

   (c) cutting £20 per hour; assembly £25 per hour

   (d) cutting £20 per hour; assembly £75 per hour

   Answer (a) or (b) or (c) or (d)

Additional data

At the end of the quarter actual overheads incurred were found to be:

	Cutting	Assembly
Actual overheads (£)	158,200	322,250

3. **Assuming that exactly the same amount of overheads was absorbed as budgeted, what were the budgeted under or over absorptions in the quarter?**

   (a) cutting over absorbed £7,400; assembly over absorbed £3,500

   (b) cutting over absorbed £7,400; assembly under absorbed £3,500

   (c) cutting under absorbed £7,400; assembly under absorbed £3,500

   (d) cutting under absorbed £7,400; assembly over absorbed £3,500

   Answer (a) or (b) or (c) or (d)

5.12 AggieSurf Limited manufactures and sells surfboards. The boards pass through two departments – moulding and finishing. Details of overheads for the departments for the four weeks ended 26 May 20-6 are as follows:

Moulding Department

- overhead absorption rate is £8.00 per machine hour
- machine hours worked were 600
- actual cost of production overhead was £5,000

Finishing Department

- overhead absorption rate is £5.00 per direct labour hour
- direct labour hours worked were 1,500
- actual cost of production overhead was £7,000

The following cost accounting codes are in use to record overheads:

code number	description
3000	production
3400	production overheads: moulding department
3500	production overheads: finishing department
6000	income statement

As an accounts assistant at AggieSurf Limited, you are asked to prepare the two production overheads accounts and to fill in the following table to record the journal entries for the overheads and the over- and under-absorption of overheads.

20-6	Code number	Debit £	Credit £
26 May	3000		
26 May	3400		
26 May	3000		
26 May	3500		
26 May	6000		
26 May	3400		
26 May	3500		
26 May	6000		

6 Methods of costing

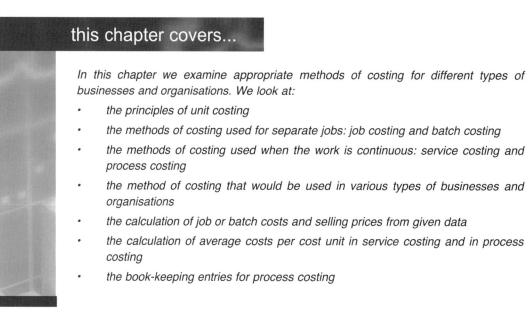

UNIT COSTING

One of the main aims of costing is to establish the cost of one **cost unit** of work, whatever kind of work it is.

The cost unit must be a suitable way of measuring the work of an organisation – examples include:

- for a manufacturing business, per item manufactured

- for a chemical business, per kilogram (kg) or litre of output

- for a transport company, per passenger mile/kilometre (km)

- for a nursing home, per day for each resident

- for a hospital, per day per patient, or per operation

The principles of unit costing are the same whatever method of costing is used by the business or organisation. The unit cost of production or output is always calculated as:

$$\frac{total\ cost\ of\ production/output}{number\ of\ cost\ units} \quad = \quad unit\ cost$$

The total cost of production comprises:

direct costs

- – direct materials

- – direct labour

- – direct expenses

indirect costs

- – production overheads

Non-production overheads – such as administration, selling and distribution – can also be added to give a figure for total cost.

Study the worked example set out on the next page.

WORKED EXAMPLE – unit costing

A toy manufacturer makes a popular type of doll. During the four-week period which has just ended 10,000 dolls were produced, with the following costs:

Product: doll	
Direct costs	
Direct materials	£16,500
Direct labour	£17,500
Direct expenses	£5,000
Indirect costs	
Production overheads	£15,000
Total cost of production	£54,000
Number of dolls produced	10,000
Unit cost of production	£5.40

The unit cost was calculated as

$$\frac{\text{total cost of production}}{\text{number of dolls produced}} \quad = \frac{£54,000}{10,000} \quad = £5.40 \text{ per doll}$$

The addition of non-production overheads – such as administration, selling and distribution – gives a figure for total cost, which can be marked-up with the company's profit percentage, here 30 per cent. To continue with the figures for the production of dolls:

Total cost of production (see above)	£54,000
Non-production overheads	£15,000
Total cost	£69,000
Profit mark-up of 30% on £69,000	£20,700
Selling price	£89,700
Number of dolls produced	10,000
Unit cost (including profit)	£8.97

In this chapter we will be looking at a number of different costing methods and will see that most calculate a unit cost of production.

We look firstly at costing methods for specific orders, and secondly at costing methods for continuous work (page 169).

COSTING METHODS FOR SPECIFIC ORDERS

Specific order costing is where customers order what they want, before it is made. Thus, the customer places the specific order, and agrees to buy the product before the work is done.

Many service businesses also carry out work to customers' requirements, for example, accountants and solicitors. Each piece of work is different and is kept separate from the others.

Costing methods which are used by business to collect costs and to calculate the total cost of their output include:

- job costing
- batch costing

These are used in conjunction with absorption costing to recover the cost of overheads. Remember that businesses must recover their overheads in the total price charged to their customers – this applies both to manufacturing businesses and to service industries, such as banks, shops and transport companies.

Case Study

RACERS LIMITED: MANUFACTURING RACING BIKES

situation

Otto Kranz, a former cycling champion, is setting up a company to manufacture racing bikes. The business is to be called Racers Limited.

Otto is aware that he has two very distinct markets into which to sell his bikes:

- Some of his bikes will be produced to the specific requirements of individual customers for international level competition racing – this is the area which really interests Otto. He can charge a premium price for these custom-built designs.

- He also has to sell to the mass-market for quality racing bikes which will be made in batches of 20 to standard designs. These will be sold in specialist shops and are cheaper, both to manufacture and in terms of selling price.

But Otto is confused about how he is going to cost out these two different methods of production – the 'one-off' and the standard design. He says:

'I can record the costs of the direct materials and labour hours used to make the 'one-off' bike and the batches of 20. But what about the overheads? Will I need more than one costing system here?'

solution

Racers Limited is likely to use two different methods of costing, depending on the kind of work being done:

- job costing – for the one-off designs
- batch costing – for the mass-market bikes

JOB COSTING

Job costing is used where each job can be separately identified from other jobs and costs are charged to the job.

The job becomes the cost unit to which costs are charged.

Examples of job costing include engineering firms that produce 'one-offs' to the customer's specifications, printing businesses, vehicle repairs, jobbing builders, painters and decorators.

The diagram below shows the main steps involved in job costing.

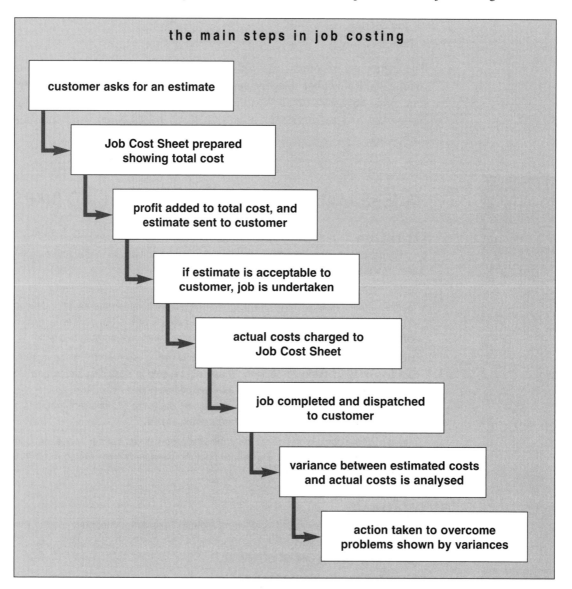

the main steps in job costing

customer asks for an estimate

Job Cost Sheet prepared
showing total cost

profit added to total cost, and
estimate sent to customer

if estimate is acceptable to
customer, job is undertaken

actual costs charged to
Job Cost Sheet

job completed and dispatched
to customer

variance between estimated costs
and actual costs is analysed

action taken to overcome
problems shown by variances

The important points to note from the diagram are:

- each job is given a number, in order to identify it

- a separate job cost sheet is prepared for each job, listing the estimates of direct materials, direct labour, direct expenses and overheads (most businesses nowadays use a computer system to help with their costing and, in practice, the job cost sheet is held as a computer record on a database)

- the actual costs incurred are compared with the estimated costs, and the differences (called 'variances') between the two are analysed; action can then be taken to correct the variances, which will help when preparing future estimates

Case Study

FASHION AID:
JOB COSTING A CHARITY PROGRAMME

situation

The youth group at a local church has decided to organise an evening fashion show, to be called 'FashionAid'. The objective of the show is to raise money to send to a children's charity working in Central Africa. One of the organisers has asked for your help in arranging the printing of a programme for the evening's events. You approach Pearshore Printers for an estimate of the cost of printing 500 copies of a sixteen page programme.

solution

Pearshore Printers allocate a reference number to the job. They prepare a Job Cost Sheet on their computer database as follows:

JOB NO. 6789 'FashionAid' Programme: 500 copies	£
Direct Materials	
Paper for text: white glossart paper code 135	82.00
Paper for cover: coated board code 235	55.00
Printing plates	25.00
Direct Labour	
Printing: 5 hours at £12.00 per hour	60.00
Finishing: 2 hours at £9.00 per hour	18.00
Overheads (based on direct labour hours)	
7 hours at £20.00 per hour	140.00
TOTAL COST	380.00
Profit (40% of total cost)	152.00
SELLING PRICE	532.00

These estimated costs will be obtained as follows:

- *direct materials,* from the inventory records for materials already held, and from the firm's Purchasing Department for items that need to be bought in especially for this job
- *direct labour,* from the payroll records of the different grades of labour to be employed on this job
- *overheads,* from the pre-determined overhead absorption rate based, for this job, on direct labour hours

Assuming that the price is acceptable to the customer, the job will go ahead and Pearshore Printers will record the actual costs of the job. These can then be compared with the estimated costs, and any differences or 'variances' between the two can be investigated. For example, it might be that actual labour costs are much higher than was estimated – this could mean that the employees took longer to do the job than was expected, or that pay rates had increased, or that more skilled staff – earning higher rates of pay – were used to do the job. This type of analysis, called 'variance analysis', will be covered in Chapter 8.

BATCH COSTING

Batch costing is used where the output consists of a number of identical items which are produced together as a batch.

Examples of batch costing include a bakery producing a batch of standard white loaves, and then a batch of croissants; or a clothing factory producing a batch of jackets, and then a batch of trousers. Each batch is the cost unit to which the costs are charged. Once the batch has been produced, the cost per unit is calculated as follows:

$$\frac{total\ batch\ cost}{number\ of\ units\ of\ output} = cost\ per\ unit$$

In essence, batch costing is very similar to job costing, but in a batch a number of identical units are produced. The batch is costed as a job during manufacture and the costs are collected together. Upon completion of the batch, the cost per unit can be calculated.

Batch numbers are frequently used to identify the output of a particular time – examples include paint colours, wallpaper production. The reason for identifying batches in this way is that there might be slight production variations – for example, in the quantities of raw materials used.

AMBER LIMITED:
BATCH COSTING FOR CHILDREN'S CLOTHES

situation

Amber Limited is a company that designs and manufactures children's clothes. The company's products are noted for their design flair, and the use of fabrics that appeal to children and also wear well. The clothes sell through specialist shops and department stores.

This week, Amber Limited is making a batch of 1,000 sequin dresses for a department store. The costs of the batch are expected to be:

- direct materials, £3,500

- direct labour: cutting, 100 hours at £11 per hour

    sewing, 200 hours at £10 per hour

    finishing, 100 hours at £12 per hour

- the overhead absorption rate is £6 per direct labour hour

- a profit mark-up of 40% is added to the total cost

The accounts supervisor asks you, an accounts assistant, to calculate the cost of producing the batch of sequin dresses, and to add the profit mark-up. She also asks you to calculate the company's cost per dress and the selling price per dress.

solution

Batch cost: 1,000 sequin dresses		
	£	£
Direct materials		3,500
Direct labour:		
cutting, 100 hours at £11 per hour	1,100	
sewing, 200 hours at £10 per hour	2,000	
finishing, 100 hours at £12 per hour	1,200	
		4,300
Overheads: 400 direct labour hours at £6 per hour		2,400
TOTAL COST		10,200
Profit (40% x £10,200)		4,080
SELLING PRICE		14,280

- cost per unit = $\dfrac{\text{total batch cost}}{\text{number of units of output}}$ = $\dfrac{£10,200}{1,000}$ = £10.20

- selling price $= \dfrac{\text{total batch cost} + \text{profit}}{\text{number of units of output}} = \dfrac{£14,280}{1,000} = £14.28$

As with most types of costing, the estimated costs above will need to be compared with the actual costs of making the batch. Any significant differences or 'variances' will need to be investigated.

SUMMARY – SPECIFIC ORDER COSTING

The diagram which follows summarises the costing methods for specific orders.

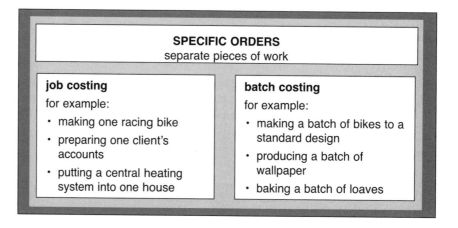

SPECIFIC ORDERS
separate pieces of work

job costing
for example:
- making one racing bike
- preparing one client's accounts
- putting a central heating system into one house

batch costing
for example:
- making a batch of bikes to a standard design
- producing a batch of wallpaper
- baking a batch of loaves

COSTING METHODS FOR CONTINUOUS WORK

In both manufacturing and service industries, work may be done continuously rather than in separate jobs. This requires specific costing methods appropriate to those types of business. For example:

- a bus company runs a continuous service of buses, available for customers to use and customers pay for their use of the service – the business will be costed using the **service costing** method

- in the manufacture of chocolate bars, production is a continuous process and the chocolate bars are available for customers to buy at all times – the business will be costed using the **process costing** method

These two methods are summarised as follows:

CONTINUOUS WORK

service costing	**process costing**
for example:	for example:
• running a nursing home	• making chocolate bars
• providing a bus service	• brewing beer or cider
• providing banking services	• manufacturing paint or chemicals

---

We will now look at these two methods in turn.

SERVICE COSTING

This method of costing applies to service industries. By using service costing, the cost per passenger mile of a bus or train service, the cost of cleaning an office, and the cost per student hour at a school or college, can be calculated. (However, a bus company quoting for a trip to the seaside for a pensioners' group, or a college tendering for an in-house course, would use job costing.)

WORKED EXAMPLE

service costs

A nursing home has capacity for twenty residents at any one time. The home achieves an occupancy rate of 90%, ie an average of eighteen beds are occupied at any one time. Costs for last year were:

	£
direct costs	
food and other supplies	54,580
nursing and medical staff	232,680
other support services	45,300
indirect costs	
overheads	58,820
	391,380

The cost per day of each resident is calculated as follows:

- The occupancy in days is (20 residents x 365 days) x 90% = 6,570 days

- Cost per day per resident is:

$$\frac{\text{total cost}}{\text{number of days}} = \frac{£391,380}{6,570} = £59.57 \text{ per resident}$$

- This is the unit cost for this organisation

PROCESS COSTING

This method of costing is used for continuous manufacturing processes, such as the manufacture of chocolate bars, cider, chemicals and so on. The process continually produces identical units of output.

The total costs of the process for a given time period are collected together. To obtain an average cost per unit of output, the total cost is divided by the number of units of output in the period.

$$\textit{cost per cost unit} = \frac{\textit{total costs of continuous work for the period}}{\textit{total cost units for the period}}$$

WORKED EXAMPLE

process costing

Chox Limited manufactures chocolate bars in a continuous process. In a given time period 400,000 bars are made and the costs of the process are as follows:

	£
Direct materials (ingredients)	40,000
Direct labour (machine operators)	24,000
Production overheads	32,000
Total costs of production for period	96,000

$$\text{Unit cost of production} = \frac{£96,000}{400,000} = £0.24 \text{ per bar}$$

Many products pass through more than one separate process before they are completed. For example, the unleaded petrol with which you fill the tank of your car started the production process as crude oil – this is passed through a number of refining processes before it is suitable to use in cars. Similarly, the production of chemicals starts with raw materials which pass through various processes – often with further chemicals being added – before the finished product is completed.

In process costing we need to know the costs of each process in order to find out the total cost of the finished goods, and also the cost per unit.

WORKED EXAMPLE

costing two processes

Greengrass Limited manufactures 'Weed 'n Feed' – a combined lawn weedkiller and fertiliser. The product is made in two separate processes, with direct materials being added at each process.

In a given time period 20,000 kg are made and the costs of the processes are as follows:

	£	£
Direct materials	5,000	
Direct labour	4,000	
Production overheads	4,000	
Total costs of process 1		13,000
(passed to process 2)		

PROCESS 1

	£	£
Direct materials	2,000	
Direct labour	3,000	
Production overheads	5,000	
Total costs of process 2		10,000

PROCESS 2

Total cost of production		23,000

FINISHED GOODS

Cost per unit:

$$\frac{\text{total cost of production}}{\text{units produced}} = \frac{£23,000}{20,000 \text{ kg}} = £1.15 \text{ per kg}$$

The book-keeping entries for process costing are explained on pages 174-185.

PROCESS COSTING AND WORK-IN-PROGRESS

Process costing is straightforward if all the items on the production line are completed at the end of the accounting period. In a more complex environment there will be items that have been started but not completed. This is known as **part-finished goods** or **work-in-progress** – see also Chapter 2 (page 57).

For example, the production line at a car factory will always have cars which vary from being only just started, to those nearing the end of the line which are almost complete.

In calculating the cost per unit, it is necessary to take into account the degree of completeness of the work-in-progress. This is done by making equivalent unit calculations:

number of units in progress x percentage of completeness   =   equivalent units

Thus, 100 units which are exactly 40% complete are equal to 40 completed units.

The formula for calculating the cost per unit now becomes:

$$\frac{\text{total cost of production}}{\text{number of units of output + equivalent units-in-progress}} = \text{cost per unit}$$

WORKED EXAMPLE

work-in-progress

Cradley Cider Company brews a popular local cider at its cider house in rural Herefordshire. The figures for the first month of the new season's production of its award-winning 'Triple X' variety are:

total cost of production	£8,500
units completed	800 barrels
units in progress	100 barrels

The units in progress are exactly half-finished. The equivalent units in progress, and the cost per barrel, for the month are as follows:

completed units		=	800 barrels
equivalent units	100 x 50%	=	50 barrels
cost per unit	$\dfrac{£8,500}{800 + 50}$	=	£10 per barrel

Although, in the example above, it was assumed that the work-in-progress was exactly half-finished, this may well not be the case for all the elements of cost. For example, while direct materials might be 100% complete, direct labour, and overheads might be 50% complete. Allowance has to be made for these differences in the calculation of the valuation of work-in-progress, and the layout used in the example below is one way in which the calculations can be made.

WORKED EXAMPLE

work-in-progress

The Toy Manufacturing Company makes a plastic toy called a 'Humber-Wumber'. The figures for the first month's production are:

direct materials	£6,600
direct labour	£3,500
production overheads	£4,000
units completed	900
units in progress	200

The units in progress are complete as regards materials, but are 50% complete for direct labour and overheads.

Cost element	Costs	Completed Units	Work-in-progress			Total Equivalent Units	Cost per Unit	WIP value
			Units	% complete	Equivalent Units			
	A	B	C	D	E	F	G	H
					C x D	B + E	A ÷ F	E x G
	£			%			£	£
Direct materials	6,600	900	200	100	200	1,100	6.00	1,200
Direct labour	3,500	900	200	50	100	1,000	3.50	350
Production overheads	4,000	900	200	50	100	1,000	4.00	400
Total	14,100						13.50	1,950

Note: columns are lettered to show how calculations are made.

Using an average cost basis, the cost per unit of the first month's production, and the month-end valuation figure for work-in-progress (WIP) is as follows:

900 completed units at £13.50 each	=	£12,150
work-in-progress valuation	=	£1,950
total costs for month	=	£14,100

BOOK-KEEPING ENTRIES FOR PROCESS COSTING

In this section we look at the cost book-keeping entries to record process costing transactions. The account to be used is a *process account*, which carries out a similar function to the production account that we have used previously for the book-keeping entries.

The basic layout of a process account, which has inputs on the debit side and outputs on the credit side, is shown below.

Dr				Process Account			Cr
	Quantity	Unit cost	Total cost		Quantity	Unit cost	Total cost
		£	£			£	£
Inputs to the process: • transfer from previous process • direct materials • direct labour • direct expenses • production overheads				Outputs from the process: • transfer to next process, or • transfer to finished goods			

Note:

- there are columns for the quantity of goods (eg kg, litres) input to, and output from, the process

- there are money columns for the unit cost (eg cost per kg, cost per litre), and for the total

- inputs to the process can include a transfer from a previous process (if any), and any direct costs and production overheads that are added to this stage of the process

- outputs from the process are either a transfer to the next process or, if this is the last or only process, to finished goods

- where there is more than one process involved in production, each will have a separate account, eg 'Process 1 Account', 'Process 2 Account' (the Case Study on page 186 illustrates the use of two processes)

aspects of process costing

An important feature of process costing is that you don't always get out what you put in to the process. This is illustrated by the example of ordering a steak in a restaurant; the menu will say '250g fillet steak' (explaining that this is the uncooked weight); what comes on the plate will weigh rather less because, when the steak is grilled, fat and liquids are cooked away. Thus, in the 'process' of cooking a steak, the output is less than the input. This is unlike other costing, where the input always equals the output, for example, input the materials for 100 cars, and the output will be 100 cars.

The aspect of process costing where you don't get out what you put in is mainly described as a *normal loss*. This is an unavoidable loss arising from the production process. For example, the normal loss on a 250g steak might be 50g. Normal losses, which occur as a result of factors such as evaporation, breakage, sampling and testing, are included as part of the cost of the output.

Once a standard of normal loss has been established for a process, this then forms the expectation for future processing. Any variation from this normal loss is treated separately in the book-keeping and will be either:

- *abnormal loss*, where the loss is greater than normal, or
- *abnormal gain*, where the loss is less than normal

If any of the normal losses can be sold as *scrap sales*, the amount of money so received is treated as a reduction in the total costs of the process. Examples include: wood chippings and shavings sold off from wood processing, scrap metal from an engineering company.

With normal loss, abnormal loss, abnormal gain, and scrap sales to consider, there are seven possible outcomes from process costing. These are shown in the following diagram:

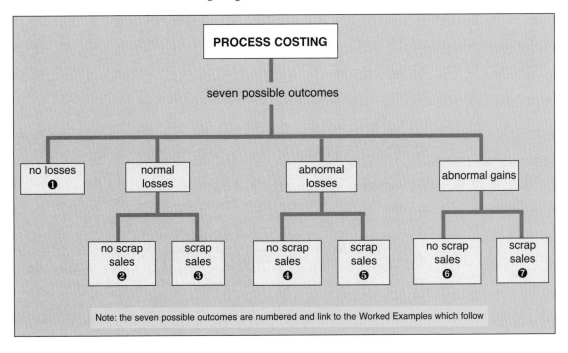

no losses within the process

Here the process account is debited with inputs and credited with the output, which is transferred either to the next process or to finished goods.

The cost book-keeping entries are:

- **transfer inputs to the process account**
  - debit process account
  - credit materials, labour, production overhead accounts
- **transfer outputs to the next process or to finished goods stock**
  - debit next process account, or finished goods account
  - credit process account

The cost book-keeping entries are shown diagrammatically as follows:

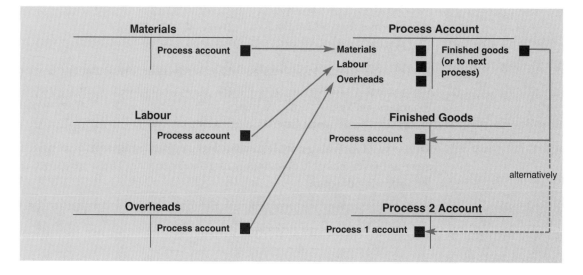

WORKED EXAMPLE 1

no losses within the process

Garden Eezee Limited manufactures granular fertiliser for use on flowers and vegetables. The fertiliser is made in one production process.

For the four weeks ended 30 January 20-4 the company input 11,000 kg of direct materials and had an output of 11,000 kg. The input costs were; materials £6,600, labour £3,300, overheads £1,100. There was no opening or closing inventory at the beginning and end of the process; all output was complete.

The process cost account for the period is prepared as follows:

Dr				Process Account			Cr
	Quantity	Unit cost	Total cost		Quantity	Unit cost	Total cost
	(kg)	£	£		(kg)	£	£
Materials	11,000	0.60	6,600	Finished goods	11,000	1.00	11,000
Labour		0.30	3,300	(or to next process)			
Overheads		0.10	1,100				
	11,000		11,000		11,000		11,000

Note: • here the inputs of materials, labour and overheads total £1.00 (60p + 30p + 10p)

– this figure will be used in subsequent Worked Examples

• inputs could also include the costs of a previous process

normal losses, with no scrap sales

Here the process account is credited with the expected amount of the normal loss. The amount is recorded in the quantity column only, with no amounts in the money columns. In this way, the cost of the normal loss is included as part of the costs of the output.

WORKED EXAMPLE 2

normal losses, with no scrap sales

Garden Eezee Limited has had to change the chemical composition of its granular fertiliser in order to comply with new European Union regulations. As a result of this, not all of the output can be sold to gardeners. The company's scientists have established that, with an input of 11,000 kg of raw materials there will be an output of 10,000 kg and a normal loss of 1,000 kg.

For the four weeks ended 27 February 20-4, the process account is prepared as follows (with the same input costs from Worked Example 1):

Dr				Process Account			Cr
	Quantity	Unit cost	Total cost		Quantity	Unit cost	Total cost
	(kg)	£	£		(kg)	£	£
Inputs (see	11,000	1.00	11,000	Normal loss	1,000	–	–
Worked Example 1)				Finished goods	10,000	1.10	11,000
				(or to next process)			
	11,000		11,000		11,000		11,000

The cost of the normal losses is included as part of the costs of the output, so the cost per unit is:

$$\frac{\text{input cost}}{\text{expected output (input} - \text{normal loss)}} \qquad = \quad \frac{\pounds11,000}{10,000 \text{ kg}} \quad = \pounds1.10 \text{ per kg}$$

The cost of the output is transferred to finished goods (or to the next process).

normal losses, with scrap sales

If any of the normal losses from a process can be sold – called 'scrap sales' – the process account is credited with the revenue. The amount of such revenue is recorded in the money column against the normal loss. In this way, the revenues from scrap sales reduce the cost of the output.

WORKED EXAMPLE 3

normal losses, with scrap sales

Garden Eezee Limited is now able to sell its normal losses to a specialist reprocessing company. The price it receives for the scrap sales is 50p per kg.

For the four weeks ended 26 March 20-4 the process account is prepared as follows (with the same input costs and normal loss as Worked Example 2):

Dr				**Process Account**			Cr
	Quantity	Unit cost	Total cost		Quantity	Unit cost	Total cost
	(kg)	£	£		(kg)	£	£
Inputs (see Worked Example 1)	11,000	1.00	11,000	Normal loss (scrap sales)	1,000	0.50	500
				Finished goods (or to next process)	10,000	1.05	10,500
	11,000		11,000		11,000		11,000

The value of the scrap sales reduces the cost per unit of the expected output to:

$$\frac{\text{input cost} - \text{scrap value of normal loss}}{\text{expected output (input} - \text{normal loss)}} \qquad = \qquad \frac{\pounds11,000 - \pounds500}{10,000 \text{ kg}}$$

$$= \pounds1.05 \text{ per kg}$$

Normal loss account is debited with £500 by transfer from the process account. The revenues from scrap sales are then credited to this account and debited to either bank account (cash received), or receivable's account (sold on credit terms). Normal loss account then appears as:

Dr	Normal Loss Account			Cr
	£			£
Process account	500	Bank/receivables		500

abnormal losses, with no scrap sales

An abnormal loss is, as we have seen, where output is lower than after a normal loss. For example:

	kg
input	11,000
less normal loss	1,000
expected output	10,000
actual output	9,400
abnormal loss	600

Clearly, if there are recurring abnormal losses, the managers will wish to investigate the causes and to take corrective action. Causes of abnormal losses can include poor quality raw materials, wastage and spillages caused by poor handling, faults in the process.

For cost book-keeping, the value of the abnormal loss is credited to the process account at the same cost per unit as the expected output; the value is debited to a separate *abnormal loss account*. These cost book-keeping entries are shown diagrammatically as follows:

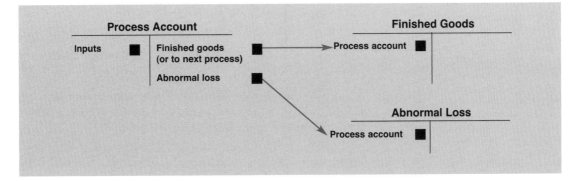

WORKED EXAMPLE 4

abnormal losses, with no scrap sales

For the four weeks ended 23 April 20-4, Garden Eezee Limited inputs 11,000 kg of direct materials. Output transferred to finished goods is 9,400 kg – the difference of 1,600 kg being made up of a normal loss of 1,000 kg and an abnormal loss of 600 kg. For technical reasons, none of the losses was able to be sold as scrap.

The process account is prepared as follows (with the same input costs as Worked Example 1):

Dr				**Process Account**			Cr
	Quantity	Unit cost	Total cost		Quantity	Unit cost	Total cost
	(kg)	£	£		(kg)	£	£
Inputs (see Worked Example 1)	11,000	1.00	11,000	Normal loss	1,000	–	–
				Finished goods (or to next process)	9,400	1.10	10,340
				Abnormal loss	600	1.10	660
	11,000		11,000		11,000		11,000

Both the transfer to finished goods (or to the next process) and the abnormal loss are valued at the cost per unit of the expected output, ie

$$\frac{\text{input cost}}{\text{expected output}} \quad = \quad \frac{£11,000}{10,000 \text{ kg}} \quad = £1.10 \text{ per kg}$$

The amount of abnormal loss is debited to abnormal loss account:

Dr	**Abnormal Loss Account**		Cr
	£		£
Process account	660		

At the end of the financial year, the balance of abnormal loss account is debited to the income statement. In this way, abnormal losses are treated as a period cost instead of being included with the closing inventory valuation.

abnormal losses, with scrap sales

Where there are revenues from scrap sales for both normal losses and abnormal losses, we must be careful to distinguish between the two amounts:

- revenues for scrap sales from normal losses are credited to the process account (where they reduce the cost of the output – including the abnormal loss)

- revenues for scrap sales from abnormal losses are credited to abnormal loss account (where they reduce the amount of the abnormal loss and, at the end of the financial year, the amount debited to the income statement)

WORKED EXAMPLE 5

abnormal losses, with scrap sales

Here the details are the same as Worked Example 4, except that all losses – both normal and abnormal – are sold to a specialist reprocessing company at a price of 50p per kg.

For the four weeks ended 21 May 20-4, the process account and abnormal loss account are prepared as follows (with the same input costs and normal and abnormal loss as Worked Example 4):

Dr				**Process Account**			Cr
	Quantity	Unit cost	Total cost		Quantity	Unit cost	Total cost
	(kg)	£	£		(kg)	£	£
Inputs (see Worked Example 1)	11,000	1.00	11,000	Normal loss	1,000	0.50	500
				Finished goods (or to next process)	9,400	1.05	9,870
				Abnormal loss	600	1.05	630
	11,000		11,000		11,000		11,000

Both the transfer to finished goods (or to the next process) and the abnormal loss are valued at the cost per unit of the expected output, ie

$$\frac{\text{input cost} - \text{scrap value of normal loss}}{\text{expected output}} = \frac{£11,000 - £500}{10,000 \text{ kg}} = £1.05 \text{ per kg}$$

The amount of abnormal loss (600 kg x £1.05 per kg = £630) is debited to abnormal loss account; the revenues from scrap sales from either bank or receivables are then credited to abnormal loss account.

Dr		**Abnormal Loss Account**		Cr
	£		£	
Process account	630	Bank/receivables (600 kg x 50p)	300	

If there are no more abnormal losses, the balance of this account (£630 – £300 = £330) will be debited as an expense to the income statement at the end of the company's financial year.

Normal loss account is debited with £500 by transfer from the process account; revenues from scrap sales are credited to the account (as in Worked Example 3):

Dr		**Normal Loss Account**		Cr
	£		£	
Process account	500	Bank/receivables	500	

abnormal gains, with no scrap sales

An abnormal gain is, as we have seen, where output is higher than after a normal loss. For example:

	kg
input	11,000
less normal loss	1,000
expected output	10,000
actual output	10,200
abnormal gain	200

If there are recurring abnormal gains, the managers will wish to investigate the causes with a view to reducing the amount of the normal loss. Causes of abnormal gains can include good quality raw materials, less wastage and spillage caused by improved handling techniques, improved processing caused by the introduction of better machinery.

For cost book-keeping, the value of the abnormal gain is debited to the process account at the same cost per unit as the expected output; the value is credited to a separate *abnormal gain account*. The cost book-keeping entries are shown diagrammatically as follows:

WORKED EXAMPLE 6

abnormal gains, with no scrap sales

For the four weeks ended 18 June 20-4, Garden Eezee Limited inputs 11,000 kg of direct materials. Output transferred to finished goods is 10,200 kg – the difference of 800 kg being made up of a normal loss of 1,000 kg and an abnormal gain of 200 kg. For technical reasons, none of the losses was able to be sold as scrap.

The process account is prepared as follows (with the same input costs as Worked Example 1)

Dr				Process Account			Cr
	Quantity	Unit cost	Total cost		Quantity	Unit cost	Total cost
	(kg)	£	£		(kg)	£	£
Inputs (see Worked Example 1)	11,000	1.00	11,000	Normal loss	1,000	–	–
Abnormal gain	200	1.10	220	Finished goods (or to next process)	10,200	1.10	11,220
	11,200		11,220		11,200		11,220

Both the transfer to finished goods (or to next process) and the abnormal gain are valued at the cost per unit of the expected output, ie

$$\frac{\text{input cost}}{\text{expected output}} \quad = \frac{£11,000}{10,000 \text{ kg}} \quad = £1.10 \text{ per kg}$$

The amount of the abnormal gain is credited to abnormal gain account:

Dr		Abnormal Gain Account		Cr
	£			£
		Process account		220

At the end of the financial year, the balance of abnormal gain account is credited to the income statement. In this way, abnormal gains are treated as a period gain instead of being included with the closing inventory valuation.

abnormal gains, with scrap sales

Where there are normal losses (with a scrap sales value) and abnormal gains, we must be careful to distinguish between the two amounts:

- the value of the full amount of normal losses is credited to the process account (notwithstanding the fact that normal losses are reduced because of the abnormal gains)

- the value of abnormal gains is debited to the process account and credited to abnormal gains account (at the cost per unit of the expected output)

WORKED EXAMPLE 7

abnormal gains, with scrap sales

Here the details are the same as Worked Example 6, except that normal losses have a scrap value of 50p per kg.

For the four weeks ended 16 July 20-4, the process account and abnormal gain account are prepared as follows (with the same input costs and abnormal gain as Worked Example 6):

Dr				Process Account				Cr
	Quantity	Unit cost	Total cost		Quantity	Unit cost	Total cost
	(kg)	£	£		(kg)	£	£
Inputs (see Worked Example 1)	11,000	1.00	11,000	Normal loss	1,000	0.50	500
Abnormal gain	200	1.05	210	Finished goods (or to next process)	10,200	1.05	10,710
	11,200		11,210		11,200		11,210

Both the transfer to finished goods (or to next process) and the abnormal gain are valued at the cost per unit of the expected output, ie

$$\frac{\text{input cost} - \text{scrap value of normal loss}}{\text{expected output}} = \frac{£11,000 - £500}{10,000 \text{ kg}} = £1.05 \text{ per kg}$$

Dr		**Abnormal Gain Account**		Cr
	£			£
Normal loss account	100	Process account		210

If there are no more abnormal gains, the balance of this account (£210 – £100 = £110) will be credited to the income statement at the end of the company's financial year

The transactions on abnormal gain account are:

	Quantity	Unit cost	Total cost
	(kg)	£	£
• credit (transfer from process account)	200	1.05	210
• debit (transfer to normal loss account)	200	0.50	100
• balance		0.55	110

The reason for the transfer of £100 to normal loss account is to leave only the amount of the abnormal gain, £110. This is 55p per kg, which is left after deducting the value of normal losses of 50p from the cost per unit of expected output of £1.05. By doing this, we highlight the value of abnormal gains above the normal efficiency of the process.

At the end of the financial year, the balance of abnormal gain account is credited to the income statement.

Dr		**Normal Loss Account**		Cr
	£			£
Process account	500	Bank/receivables		400
		Abnormal gain account		100
	500			500

Here, normal loss account is debited with £500 by transfer from the process account. Credits to the account come from two sources:

- revenue of £400 (ie 800 kg sold at 50p per kg) from bank or receivables
- transfer of £100 (ie 200 kg at 50p per kg) from abnormal gain account

PERRAN CHEMICALS LIMITED: TWO PROCESSES

Tutorial note: This Case Study illustrates normal losses, abnormal losses and abnormal gains using the example of a two-process company.

situation

Perran Chemicals Limited manufactures a product, Xenova, within two separate processes. For the week ended 14 May 20-4 the details were:

- Process 1

    – materials input, 2,000 kg at £4 per kg

    – labour, £720

    – overheads, £1,440

- Process 2

    – materials input, 3,100 kg at £6 per kg

    – labour, £960

    – overheads, £480

Normal outputs are:

- Process 1, 80% of input
- Process 2, 90% of input

All losses are sold at a scrap value of £1 per kg to a specialist reprocessing company.

There was no work-in-progress at either the beginning or end of the week.
Output during the week was 1,400 kg from Process 1 and 4,200 kg from Process 2.
As an accounts assistant at Perran Chemicals Limited you are asked to prepare the process 1 account, process 2 account, normal loss account, abnormal loss account, and abnormal gain account for the week ended 14 May 20-4. Note: show the cost per unit of expected output to the nearest penny.

solution

Dr				Process 1 Account			Cr
	Quantity	Unit cost	Total cost		Quantity	Unit cost	Total cost
	(kg)	£	£		(kg)	£	£
Materials	2,000	4.00	8,000	Normal loss (20%)	400	1.00	400
Labour			720	Transfer to process 2	1,400	6.10	8,540
Overheads			1,440	Abnormal loss	200	6.10	1,220
	2,000		10,160		2,000		10,160

Dr				Process 2 Account				Cr
	Quantity	Unit cost	Total cost		Quantity	Unit cost	Total cost	
	(kg)	£	£		(kg)	£	£	
Transfer from				Normal loss (10%)	450	1.00	450	
process 1	1,400	6.10	8,540	Finished goods	4,200	6.95	29,172	
Materials	3,100	6.00	18,600					
Labour			960					
Overheads			480					
	4,500		28,580					
Abnormal gain	150	6.95	1,042					
	4,650		29,622		4,650		29,622	

Dr	Normal Loss Account		Cr
	£		£
Process 1 account	400	Bank/receivables	400
Process 2 account	450	Abnormal gain account	*150
		Bank/receivables	300
	850		850

* see abnormal gain account

Dr	Abnormal Loss Account		Cr
	£		£
Process 1 account	1,220	Bank/receivables (200 kg x £1.00)	200

Dr	Abnormal Gain Account		Cr
	£		£
Normal loss account	*150	Process 2 account	1,042
* 150 kg x £1.00 per kg			

Tutorial notes (amounts calculated to the nearest penny):

- In process 1, the cost per unit of expected output is:

$$\frac{£10,160 - £400}{1,600 \text{ kg*}} = £6.10 \text{ per kg}$$

  * ie 2,000 kg x 80%

- In process 2, the cost per unit of expected output is:

$$\frac{£28,580 - £450}{4,050 \text{ kg**}} = £6.95 \text{ per kg}$$

  ** ie 4,500 kg x 90%

- At the end of the financial year:

  – the balance of abnormal loss account, here £1,020 (ie £1,220 - £200), is debited to the income statement

  – the balance of abnormal gain account, here £892 (ie £1,042 - £150), is credited to the income statement

Chapter Summary

- The method chosen for cost accounting within a business depends on the kind of work being done.

- In manufacturing and in service industries, work may consist of separately identifiable jobs or it may be continuous.

- Separately identifiable jobs are usually done to a customer's specific order.

- Costs are calculated for each separately identifiable job.

- The costing method to be used for specific orders (separate jobs) is:

  – job costing for a single unit of work

  – batch costing for a batch of identical units

- The costing method to be used for continuous work is:

  – process costing for continuous manufacturing processes

  – service costing for continuous services

- To obtain a cost per cost unit for continuous work, the total costs for a time period are first collected together, then divided by the number of cost units produced or provided in the time period, ie

  $$cost \ per \ cost \ unit = \frac{total \ costs \ of \ continuous \ work \ for \ the \ period}{total \ cost \ units \ for \ the \ period}$$

- If there is work-in-progress at the end of the period, the number of equivalent complete units is calculated, for example 500 units that are 50% complete are equivalent to 500 x 50% = 250 completed units.

- Book-keeping for process costing uses a process account to calculate the cost per unit of expected output. Possible outcomes of process costing to be recorded in the accounts are:
  - no losses within the process
  - normal losses, with or without scrap sales
  - abnormal losses, with or without scrap sales
  - abnormal gains, with or without scrap sales

  At the end of a financial year, the balance of abnormal loss account is debited to the income statement, while the balance of abnormal gain account is credited.

Key Terms

costing method	a technique used to collect costs and to calculate the total cost of output
job/batch costing	a form of specific order costing which applies costs to jobs/batches
service costing	a form of costing for service industries; costs are averaged to find the cost per unit
job cost sheet	sheet (or record on a computer database) which shows the estimated and actual direct and indirect costs for a particular job
variance	the difference between an estimated cost and an actual cost
process costing	method of costing applied to continuous manufacturing processes
work-in-progress (WIP)	part-finished goods at a particular time
equivalent units	number of units in progress x percentage of completeness
cost per unit	$\dfrac{total\ costs}{number\ of\ units\ (including\ equivalent\ units)}$
process account	book-keeping account used in process costing to calculate the cost per unit of expected output
normal loss	an unavoidable loss arising from the production process
abnormal loss	where the loss in a process is greater than the normal loss
abnormal gain	where the loss in a process is less than the normal loss

Activities

6.1 State, with reasons, the method of costing you think would be appropriate for:
- an accountant
- a bus company
- a baker
- a sports centre
- a hotel

6.2 A clothing manufacturer has been asked to give a quotation for the supply of a batch of uniforms for a band. Materials for the uniforms will be:

- 100 metres of cloth at £7.50 per metre

- 75 metres of braiding at £4.00 per metre

It is estimated that the job will take the machinists a total of 35 hours.

They are paid at the rate of £10.00 per hour.

The overhead absorption rate is £8.50 per direct labour hour.

You are to:

(a) calculate the cost of the job

(b) calculate the selling price if the company is to make a profit of 20% on the cost price

6.3 Rowcester Engineering Limited is asked to quote for the supply of a replacement cylinder head for a large stationary engine installed in a local factory.

The item will need to be cast in the foundry and then passed to the finishing shop for machining to specification.

Materials needed will be a 100 kg ingot of high-strength steel, which costs £10 per kg.

Direct labour will be 10 hours in the foundry, and 15 hours in the finishing shop, of which 12 hours will be machine hours.

Foundry workers are paid £10 per hour, while machine operators in the finishing shop are paid £12 per hour.

Overheads are charged on the basis of 80% of direct labour cost in the foundry, and on the basis of £20 per machine hour in the finishing shop.

Profit is to be 25% of cost price.

You are to complete the following Job Cost Sheet to show the estimated total cost of the job, and the selling price.

```
                        JOB COST SHEET
                      Replacement Cylinder Head
                                                                £
    Direct Materials

    Direct Labour
    Foundry:
    Finishing:

    Overheads
    Foundry:
    Finishing:                                              _____
    TOTAL COST
    Profit                                                  _____
    SELLING PRICE                                           _____
```

6.4 City Transit plc is a small train operating company which runs passenger rail services on a commuter line in a large city. The line links the docks area, which has been redeveloped with flats and houses, with the city centre, and then runs on through the suburbs. An intensive service is operated from early morning to late at night carrying people to and from work, schoolchildren, shoppers and leisure travellers.

The tracks that City Transit uses are leased from the track owner, Railnet plc.

The modern fleet of six diesel trains is owned and maintained by City Transit.

The following information is available in respect of last year's operations:

	cost	estimated life
Diesel trains	£1,300,000 each	20 years

Depreciation is on a straight-line basis, assuming a residual value of £100,000 for each train.

Leasing charges for track	£1,000,000 pa
Maintenance charges for trains	£910,000 pa
Fuel for trains	£210,000 pa
Wages of drivers and conductors	£480,000 pa
Administration	£520,000 pa

There were 2.5 million passenger journeys last year with an average distance travelled of five miles.

You are to calculate the cost per passenger mile of operating the railway for last year.

6.5 A manufacturer of plastic toys has the following information concerning the first month of production:

Direct materials £11,500

Direct labour £9,000

Production overheads £18,000

Toys completed 20,000

Toys in progress 5,000

The work-in-progress is complete as regards materials, but is 50% complete as regards direct labour and production overheads.

You are to complete the following layout to show the cost per toy of the first month's production and the month-end valuation for work-in-progress.

Cost element	Costs	Completed Units	Work-in-progress			Total	Cost	WIP
			Units	% complete	Equivalent Units	Equivalent Units	per Unit	valuation
	A	B	C	D	E	F	G	H
					C x D	B + E	A ÷ F	E x G
	£						£	£
Direct materials								
Direct labour								
Production overheads								
Total								

6.6 Agro Chemicals Limited produces a chemical, which is made in one production process.

For the four weeks ended 27 February 20-8, the company input 22,000 litres of direct materials, had an output of 20,000 litres and a normal loss of 2,000 litres. The input costs were: materials £5,500, labour £3,300, overheads £2,200. Normal losses were sold to a specialist reprocessing company for 20p per litre.

There was no opening or closing inventory at the beginning and end of the process; all output was complete.

As an accounts assistant, you are to complete the following process account and the normal loss account for the four weeks ended 27 February 20-8.

Dr				Process Account				Cr
	Quantity	Unit cost	Total cost			Quantity	Unit cost	Total cost
	(litres)	£	£			(litres)	£	£
Materials					Normal loss			
Labour					Finished goods			
Overheads								

Dr	Normal Loss Account		Cr
	£		£

6.7 GrowFast Limited produces a granular lawn fertiliser, which is made in one production process.

For the four weeks ended 21 May 20-7, the company input 42,000 kg of direct materials, had an output of 39,500 kg – the difference of 2,500 kg was made up of a normal loss of 2,000 kg and an abnormal loss of 500 kg.

The input costs were: materials £10,500, labour £4,200, overheads £2,100. All losses were sold to a specialist reprocessing company for 20p per kg.

There was no opening or closing inventory at the beginning and end of the process; all output was complete.

As an accounts assistant, you are to complete the following process account, the abnormal loss account, and the normal loss account for the four weeks ended 21 May 20-7.

Dr				Process Account				Cr
	Quantity	Unit cost	Total cost			Quantity	Unit cost	Total cost
	(kg)	£	£			(kg)	£	£
Materials					Normal loss			
Labour					Finished goods			
Overheads					Abnormal loss			

Dr		Normal Loss Account		Cr
	£			£

Dr		Abnormal Loss Account		Cr
	£			£

6.8 RP Industries Limited produces a liquid furniture polish called 'EasyShine'. The product is made in two production processes before completion and transfer to finished goods.

For the four weeks ended 26 November 20-6, details of production of 'EasyShine' were as follows:

	Process 1	Process 2
Direct materials (10,000 litres)	£5,000	–
Labour	£4,000	£1,800
Overhead	£2,000	£1,350
Normal loss in process	10% of input	5% of input
Output	9,000 litres	8,300 litres
Scrap value of all losses	£0.40 per litre	£0.50 per litre

There was no opening or closing inventory at the beginning and end of either process; all output was complete. All losses were sold to a specialist reprocessing company.

As an accounts assistant, you are to complete the following process 1 account, process 2 account, normal loss account, and abnormal loss account for the four weeks ended 26 November 20-6. Note: show the cost per unit of expected output to the nearest penny.

Dr			Process 1 Account				Cr
	Quantity (litres)	Unit cost £	Total cost £		Quantity (litres)	Unit cost £	Total cost £
Materials				Normal loss			
Labour				Transfer to			
Overheads				process 2			

Dr				Process 2 Account				Cr
	Quantity	Unit cost	Total cost			Quantity	Unit cost	Total cost
	(litres)	£	£			(litres)	£	£
Transfer from				Normal loss				
process 1				Finished goods				
Labour				Abnormal loss				
Overheads								

Dr	Normal Loss Account		Cr
	£		£

Dr	Abnormal Loss Account		Cr
	£		£

6.9 Zelah Chemicals Limited produces an insect repellant called 'BuzzOff', which is made in one production process.

For the four weeks ended 16 July 20-5, the company input 11,000 litres of direct materials, and had an output of 10,200 litres – the difference of 800 litres was made up of a normal loss of 1,000 litres and an abnormal gain of 200 litres.

The input costs were: materials £5,500, labour £3,850, overheads £2,750. All losses were sold to a specialist reprocessing company for 30p per litre.

There was no opening or closing inventory at the beginning and end of the process; all output was complete.

As an accounts assistant, you are to complete the following process account, abnormal gain account, and normal loss account for the four weeks ended 16 July 20-5.

Dr				**Process Account**				Cr
	Quantity	Unit cost	Total cost		Quantity	Unit cost	Total cost
	(litres)	£	£		(litres)	£	£
Materials				Normal loss			
Labour				Finished goods			
Overheads							
Abnormal gain							

Dr	**Abnormal Gain Account**	Cr
	£	£

Dr	**Normal Loss Account**	Cr
	£	£

6.10 Astra Chemicals Limited uses process costing for its products.

The process account for April for one particular process has been partly completed but the following information is also relevant:

- Three employees worked on this process during April. Each employee worked 35 hours per week for 4 weeks and was paid £10 per hour.

- Overheads are absorbed on the basis of £20 per labour hour.

- Astra Chemicals Limited expects a normal loss of 10% during this process, which it then sells for scrap at 80p per kg.

(a)   Complete the process account below for April.

Description	kg	Unit cost £	Total cost £	Description	kg	Unit cost £	Total cost £
Material AB4	500	1.50		Normal loss		0.80	
Material AC5	200	2.20		Output	900		
Material AD6	300	4.10					
Labour							
Overheads							

(b)   Identify the correct entry for each of the following in a process account.

	Debit ✓	Credit ✓
Abnormal loss		
Abnormal gain		

7 Marginal and absorption costing

this chapter covers...

This chapter focuses on the costing methods of marginal and absorption costing and compares the profit made by a business under each method. The chapter concludes with the layout of a manufacturing account and income statement and where the different types of inventory – raw materials, work-in-progress, finished goods – are shown in the financial statements.

This chapter explains:

* how overheads are treated differently in marginal costing and absorption costing

* how marginal costing works, including the calculation of contribution, and its role in short-term decision-making

* how absorption costing works, including the valuation of closing inventory

* a comparison of profits when marginal costing and absorption costing are used

* the layout of

   – a manufacturing account to show production cost

   – an income statement to show profit for the year

MARGINAL AND ABSORPTION COSTING SYSTEMS

These two costing systems are often used in cost accounting, but for different purposes:

- marginal costing – helps with short-term decision-making
- absorption costing – is used to calculate inventory valuations and profit calculations in financial statements

The use of each system is dependent on the information needs of the business or organisation:

- – 'can we afford to sell 1,000 units of our product each month to Megastores Limited at a discount of 20 per cent?' (use marginal costing)
- – 'what profit have we made this year?' (use absorption costing)

These costing systems use the same costs, but they are treated differently according to their behaviour. We will now look at each of these costing systems in turn and then make a comparison between them.

MARGINAL COSTING

Marginal cost is the cost of producing one extra unit of output

To help with short-term decision-making, costs are classified by their behaviour as either variable costs or fixed costs (with semi-variable costs being split between their fixed and variable parts). Such a classification of costs is used in marginal costing to work out how much it costs to produce each extra unit of output.

Marginal cost is often – but not always – the total of the variable costs of producing a unit of output. For most purposes, marginal costing is not concerned with fixed period costs (such as the rent of a factory); instead it is concerned with variable product costs – direct materials, direct labour, direct expenses, and variable production overheads – which increase as output increases. For most decision-making, the marginal cost of a unit of output is, therefore, the variable cost of producing one more unit.

Knowing the marginal cost of a unit of output enables the managers of a business to focus on the contribution provided by each unit. The contribution is the sales revenue after marginal/variable costs have been paid. The contribution formula is:

selling price less variable cost = contribution

Contribution can be calculated on a per unit basis (as here), or for a batch of output (eg 1,000 units), or for a whole business.

It follows that the difference between the sales revenue and the variable costs of the units sold in a period is the total contribution that the sales of all the units in the period make towards the fixed costs of the business. Once these are covered, the remainder of the contribution is profit.

Thus a business can work out its profit, using a marginal costing statement, for any given period from the total contribution and fixed costs figures:

total contribution less total fixed costs = profit

A marginal costing statement can be prepared in the following format:

		£
	Sales revenue	x
less	Variable costs	x
equals	Contribution	x
less	Fixed costs	x
equals	PROFIT	x

Note from the marginal costing statement how the contribution goes firstly towards the fixed costs and, when they have been covered, secondly contributes to profit.

The relationship between marginal costing, contribution and profit is shown in the Worked Example which follows.

Case Study

WYVERN BIKE COMPANY: MARGINAL COSTING

situation

The Wyvern Bike Company makes 100 bikes each week and its costs are as follows:

Direct materials	£4,000
Direct labour	£5,000
Production overheads	£5,000

Investigations into the behaviour of costs has revealed the following information:

• direct materials are variable costs

• direct labour is a variable cost

• of the production overheads, £2,000 is a fixed cost, and the remainder is a variable cost

The selling price of each bike is £200.

As an accounts assistant at the Wyvern Bike Company, you are asked to:

- calculate the marginal cost of producing each bike
- show the expected contribution per bike
- prepare a marginal costing statement to show clearly the total contribution and the total profit each week

solution

Marginal cost per bike

Variable costs per unit:	£
Direct materials (£4,000 ÷ 100)	40
Direct labour (£5,000 ÷ 100)	50
Production overheads (£3,000* ÷ 100)	30
Marginal cost per bike	120

*   £5,000 – £2,000 fixed costs

Contribution per bike

	Selling price per bike	200
less	Variable cost per bike	120
equals	Contribution per bike	80

Marginal costing statement

		£	£
	Sales £200 x 100 bikes		20,000
less	Variable costs:		
	Direct materials	4,000	
	Direct labour	5,000	
	Production overheads	3,000	
			12,000
equals	Total contribution		8,000
less	Fixed costs (production overheads)		2,000
equals	Profit for the week		6,000

advantages of a marginal costing statement

A marginal costing statement is of benefit to the managers of a business because:

- contribution, ie selling price less variable cost, is clearly identified
- with the marginal cost of output identified, the managers can focus on the contribution provided by the output
- the effect on costs of changes in sales revenue can be calculated
- it helps with short-term decision-making in the forms of
  - break-even analysis
  - margin of safety
  - target profit
  - contribution sales ratio
  - limiting factors
  - 'special order' pricing

We will look at the role of marginal costing in short-term decision-making in Chapter 9.

ABSORPTION COSTING

Absorption costing absorbs the costs of the business amongst the cost units.

Absorption costing answers the question, 'What does it cost to make one unit of output?'

The absorption cost of a unit of output is made up of the following costs:

		£
	Direct materials	x
add	Direct labour	x
add	Direct expenses	x
add	Production overheads (fixed and variable)	x
equals	ABSORPTION COST	x

Note that the production overheads comprise the factory costs of indirect materials, indirect labour, and indirect expenses.

Case Study	WYVERN BIKE COMPANY: ABSORPTION COSTING

WYVERN BIKE COMPANY: ABSORPTION COSTING

situation

The Wyvern Bike Company makes 100 bikes each week and its costs are as follows:

Direct materials	£4,000
Direct labour	£5,000
Production overheads	£5,000

The selling price of each bike is £200.

As an accounts assistant at the Wyvern Bike Company, you are asked to:
* calculate the absorption cost of producing each bike
* calculate the total profit each week

solution

Absorption cost per bike

Total costs per week: £

Direct materials	4,000
Direct labour	5,000
Production overheads	5,000
Total cost	14,000

The absorption cost of producing one bike is:

$$\frac{\text{Total cost}}{\text{Units of output}} = \frac{£14,000}{100\text{ bikes}} = £140\text{ per bike}$$

Profit each week

	Selling price (100 bikes x £200)	20,000
less	Total cost	14,000
equals	Profit for the week	6,000

Conclusion

Profit for the week of £6,000 is the same as with the marginal costing method, so we could say 'Does it matter whether we use marginal or absorption costing?' The answer to this is that it does:

– marginal costing, with its focus on variable costs and contribution, is useful for short-term decision-making

– absorption costing is a simple method of calculating the cost of output and is used in financial statements for inventory valuation

As the Case Study shows, each cost unit bears an equal proportion of the costs of the production overheads of the business. Because of its simplicity, absorption costing is a widely used system which tells us how much it costs to make one unit of output. It works well where the cost units are identical, eg 100 identical bikes, but is less appropriate where some of the cost units differ in quality, eg 100 bikes, of which 75 are standard models and 25 are handbuilt to the customers' specifications. It also ignores the effect of changes in the level of output on the cost structure. For example, if the bike manufacturer reduces output to 50 bikes a week:

- will direct materials remain at £40 per bike? (buying materials in smaller quantities might mean higher prices)

- will direct labour still be £50 per bike? (with lower production, the workforce may not be able to specialise in certain jobs, and may be less efficient)

- will the production overheads remain at £5,000? (perhaps smaller premises can be used and the factory rent reduced)

MARGINAL AND ABSORPTION COSTING COMPARED

Marginal costing tells the managers of a business or organisation the cost of producing one extra unit of output. Nevertheless, we must always remember that one of the objectives of the costing system is to ensure that all the costs of a business or organisation are recovered by being charged to production. This is achieved by means of overhead absorption (see Chapter 5). We will now make a comparison between marginal and absorption costing:

- *marginal costing*

  Marginal costing recognises that fixed period costs vary with time rather than activity, and identifies the variable production cost of one extra unit. For example, the rent of a factory relates to a certain time period, eg one month, and remains unchanged whether 100 units of output are made or whether 500 units are made (always assuming that the capacity of the factory is at least 500 units); by contrast, the production of one extra unit will incur an increase in variable costs, ie direct materials, direct labour, direct expenses (if any), and variable overheads – this increase is the *marginal cost*.

- *absorption costing*

  This technique absorbs all production costs into each unit of output through the use of an overhead absorption rate (see Chapter 5). Therefore the more units that are produced, the cheaper will be the cost per unit – because the overheads are spread over a greater number of units.

The diagram below demonstrates how the terms in marginal costing relate to the same production costs as those categorised under absorption costing terms. As noted above, when using marginal costing it is the behaviour of the cost – fixed or variable – that is important, not the origin of the cost.

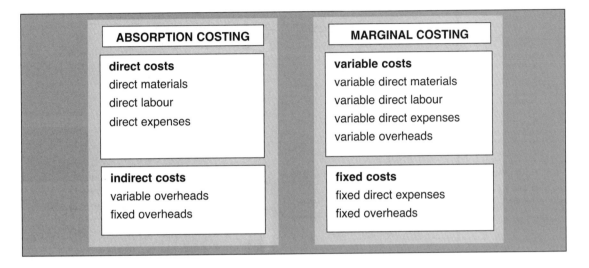

The table on the next page gives a comparison between marginal costing and absorption costing, including a note on the usefulness and the limitations of each.

marginal and absorption costing: profit comparisons

Because of the different ways in which marginal costing and absorption costing treat fixed period costs, the two techniques produce different levels of profit when there is a closing inventory figure. This is because, under marginal costing, the closing inventory is valued at variable production cost; by contrast, absorption cost includes a share of fixed production costs in the closing inventory valuation. This is illustrated in the Case Study which follows, looking at the effect of using marginal costing and absorption costing on the income statement of a manufacturing business.

Note that the marginal cost approach is used to help with short-term decision-making (see Chapter 9). However, for financial statements, absorption costing must be used for inventory valuation purposes in order to comply with IAS 2 (see page 44). Under IAS 2, *Inventories*, the closing inventory valuation is based on the costs of direct materials, direct labour, direct expenses (if any), and production overheads. Note that non-production overheads are not included, as they are charged in full to the income statement in the year to which they relate.

COMPARISON OF MARGINAL AND ABSORPTION COSTING		
	marginal costing	**absorption costing**

main use	• to help with short-term decision-making (see Chapter 9) in the forms of
	  – break-even analysis
	  – margin of safety
	  – target profit
	  – contribution sales ratio
	  – limiting factors
	  – 'special order' pricing
		• to calculate profit
		• to calculate inventory valuation for financial statements

how does it work?	• costs are classified as either fixed or variable • contribution to fixed costs is calculated as selling price less variable costs	• overheads are charged to output through an overhead absorption rate, often on the basis of direct labour hours or machine hours
main focus	• marginal cost • contribution	• all overheads charged to output • calculating profit • calculating inventory values
usefulness	• concept of contribution is easy to understand • useful for short-term decision-making, but no consideration of overheads	• acceptable under IAS 2, *Inventories* • appropriate for traditional industries where overheads are charged to output on the basis of direct labour hours or machine hours
limitations	• costs have to be identified as either fixed or variable • all overheads have to be recovered, otherwise a loss will be made • not acceptable under IAS 2, *Inventories* • calculation of selling prices may be less accurate than other costing methods	• not as useful in short-term decision-making as marginal costing • may provide less accurate basis for calculation of selling prices where overheads are high and complex in nature

CHAIRS LIMITED:
MARGINAL AND ABSORPTION COSTING

situation

Chairs Limited commenced business on 1 January 20-7. It manufactures a special type of chair designed to alleviate back pain. Information on the first year's trading is as follows:

number of chairs manufactured	5,000
number of chairs sold	4,500
selling price	£110 per chair
direct materials	£30 per chair
direct labour	£40 per chair
fixed production overheads	£100,000

The directors ask for your help in producing profit statements using the marginal costing and absorption costing methods. They say that they will use 'the one that shows the higher profit' to the company's bank manager.

solution

CHAIRS LIMITED

Income statement for the year ended 31 December 20-7

	MARGINAL COSTING £	MARGINAL COSTING £	ABSORPTION COSTING £	ABSORPTION COSTING £
Sales revenue at £110 each		495,000		495,000
Variable costs				
Direct materials at £30 each	150,000		150,000	
Direct labour at £40 each	200,000		200,000	
	350,000			
Less Closing inventory (marginal cost)				
500 chairs at £70 each	35,000			
	315,000			
Fixed production overheads	100,000		100,000	
			450,000	
Less Closing inventory (absorption cost)				
500 chairs at £90 each			45,000	
Less Cost of sales		415,000		405,000
PROFIT		80,000		90,000

Tutorial notes:

- Closing inventory is always calculated on the basis of this year's costs:

  marginal costing, variable costs only, ie £30 + £40 = £70 per chair

  absorption costing, variable and fixed costs, ie £450,000 ÷ 5,000 chairs = £90 per chair

- The difference in the profit figures is caused only by the closing inventory figures: £35,000 under marginal costing and £45,000 under absorption costing – the same costs have been used, but fixed production overheads have been treated differently.

- Only fixed production overheads are dealt with differently using the techniques of marginal and absorption costing – both methods charge non-production overheads in full to the income statement in the year to which they relate.

With marginal costing, the full amount of the fixed production overheads has been charged in this year's income statement; by contrast, with absorption costing, part of the fixed production overheads (here, £10,000) has been carried forward in the inventory valuation.

With regard to the directors' statement that they will use 'the one that shows the higher profit', the following points should be borne in mind:

- A higher profit does not mean more money in the bank.

- The two methods simply treat fixed production overheads differently and, in a year when there is no closing inventory, total profits to date are exactly the same – but they occur differently over the years. Over time, profits are identical under both methods.

- For financial statements, Chairs Limited must use the absorption cost inventory valuation of £45,000 in order to comply with IAS 2, *Inventories*.

THE USE OF A MANUFACTURING ACCOUNT

Now that we have seen how a manufacturing business uses absorption costing to value its closing inventory, we can turn our attention to the year-end financial statements and, in particular, the use of a *manufacturing account*.

For preparing financial statements a business needs to have an accounting system that records the costs and revenues for its output, and then shows the profit or loss that has been made for the accounting period. For a business such as a retailer that buys and sells goods, without carrying out any production processes, the accounting system is relatively simple – the figure for revenue is deducted from the amount of purchases (after allowing for changes in the value of opening and closing inventories) and the amount of overheads; a profit is made when revenue exceeds the total costs. For a manufacturer, though, the costs are more complex as they comprise the direct and indirect costs of materials, labour and expenses; also, a manufacturer will invariably have opening and closing inventory in three different forms – direct materials, work-in-progress and finished goods.

In its year-end financial statements a manufacturer prepares:

- a manufacturing account, which shows production (factory) cost

- an income statement, which shows profit for the period

The financial statements, which are part of the double-entry system, use the following outline:

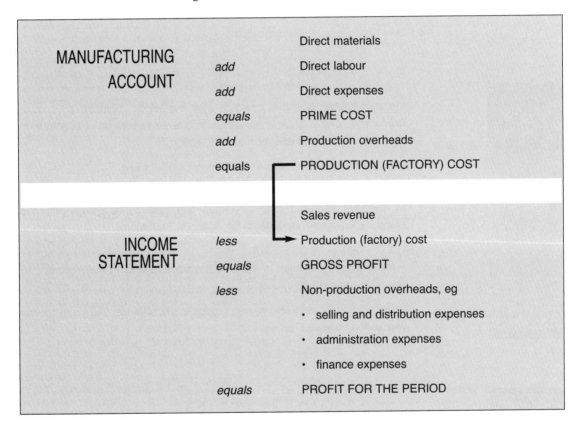

MANUFACTURING ACCOUNT

	Direct materials
add	Direct labour
add	Direct expenses
equals	PRIME COST
add	Production overheads
equals	PRODUCTION (FACTORY) COST

INCOME STATEMENT

	Sales revenue
less	Production (factory) cost
equals	GROSS PROFIT
less	Non-production overheads, eg
	• selling and distribution expenses
	• administration expenses
	• finance expenses
equals	PROFIT FOR THE PERIOD

notes

- Adjustments have to be made to allow for changes in the value of inventory at the start of the accounting period (opening inventory) and at the end of the accounting period (closing inventory) for:

  – direct materials, in the manufacturing account

  – work-in-progress (or partly manufactured goods), in the manufacturing account

  – finished goods, in the income statement

- The income statement shows two levels of profit:
  - gross profit, the difference between selling price and production cost (after allowing for changes in the value of opening and closing inventory)
  - profit for the year, the profit after all costs have been deducted and which belongs to the owner(s) of the business
- Certain expenses might be apportioned on an appropriate basis between the manufacturing account and the income statement – for example, rent and rates might be apportioned 75 per cent to the factory (production overheads) and 25 per cent to the office (non-production overheads)

An example of a manufacturing account and income statement is shown on the next page.

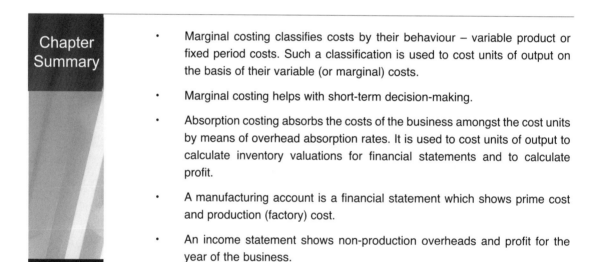

Chapter Summary

- Marginal costing classifies costs by their behaviour – variable product or fixed period costs. Such a classification is used to cost units of output on the basis of their variable (or marginal) costs.

- Marginal costing helps with short-term decision-making.

- Absorption costing absorbs the costs of the business amongst the cost units by means of overhead absorption rates. It is used to cost units of output to calculate inventory valuations for financial statements and to calculate profit.

- A manufacturing account is a financial statement which shows prime cost and production (factory) cost.

- An income statement shows non-production overheads and profit for the year of the business.

Key Terms

marginal cost	the cost of producing one extra unit of output
contribution	selling price – variable cost
absorption cost	the costs of the business are absorbed amongst the cost units through the use of an overhead absorption rate
manufacturing account	an account – part of the double-entry system – which brings together the elements of cost that make up production (factory) cost

ALPHA MANUFACTURING COMPANY
MANUFACTURING ACCOUNT AND INCOME STATEMENT
for the year ended 31 December 20-4

	£	£
Opening inventory of direct materials		5,000
Add Purchases of direct materials		50,000
		55,000
Less Closing inventory of direct materials		6,000
DIRECT MATERIALS USED		49,000
Direct labour		26,000
Direct expenses		2,500
PRIME COST		77,500
Add Production (factory) overheads:		
Indirect materials	2,000	
Indirect labour	16,000	
Indirect expenses:		
Rent of factory	5,000	
Depreciation of factory machinery	10,000	
Factory light and heat	4,000	
		37,000
		114,500
Add Opening inventory of work-in-progress		4,000
		118,500
Less Closing inventory of work-in-progress		3,000
PRODUCTION (FACTORY) COST OF GOODS MANUFACTURED		115,500
Sales revenue		195,500
Opening inventory of finished goods	6,500	
Production (factory) cost of goods manufactured	115,500	
	122,000	
Less Closing inventory of finished goods	7,500	
COST OF SALES		114,500
Gross profit		81,000
Less Non-production overheads:		
Selling and distribution expenses	38,500	
Administration expenses	32,000	
Finance expenses	3,500	
		74,000
Profit for the year		7,000

Note: a layout for a manufacturing account and income statement is given in the Appendix.

Activities

7.1 Coffeeworks Limited manufactures coffee machines for domestic use. The management of the company is considering next year's production and has asked you to help with certain financial decisions.

The following information is available:

Selling price (per machine)	£80
Direct materials (per machine)	£25
Direct labour (per machine)	£20
Fixed production overheads	£270,000 per year

The company is planning to manufacture 15,000 coffee machines next year.

(a)   calculate the marginal cost per coffee machine

(b)   calculate the absorption cost per coffee machine

(c)   prepare an income statement to show the profit or loss if 15,000 coffee machines are sold

7.2 Cook-It Limited makes garden barbecues. The management of the company is considering the production for next year and has asked for help with certain financial decisons.

The following information is available:

Selling price (per barbecue)	£90
Direct materials (per barbecue)	£30
Direct labour (per barbecue)	£25
Fixed production overheads	£150,000 per year

The company is planning to manufacture 10,000 barbecues next year.

REQUIRED

You are to calculate:

•   the marginal cost per barbecue

•   the absorption cost per barbecue

•   the profit or loss if 10,000 barbecues are sold

7.3 Maxxa Limited manufactures one product, the Maxx. For the month of January 20-7 the following information is available:

Number of units manufactured	4,000
Number of units sold	3,000
Selling price	£8 per unit
Direct materials for month	£5,000
Direct labour for month	£9,000
Fixed production overheads for month	£6,000

There was no finished goods inventory at the start of the month. Both direct materials and direct labour are variable costs.

REQUIRED

You are to produce income statements using marginal costing and absorption costing methods.

7.4 Activtoys Limited commenced business on 1 January 20-1. It manufactures the 'Activ', an outdoor climbing frame. Information on the first year's trading is as follows:

Number of climbing frames manufactured	1,500
Number of climbing frames sold	1,300
Selling price	£125 per frame
Direct materials	£25 per frame
Direct labour	£30 per frame
Fixed production overheads	£82,500

REQUIRED

(a) The directors ask for your help in producing income statements using the marginal costing and absorption costing methods. They say that they will use "the one that gives the higher profit" to show to the company's bank manager.

(b) Write a note to the directors explaining the reason for the different profit figures and commenting on their statement.

7.5 Durning Limited manufactures one product, the Durn. For the month of April 20-4 the following information is available:

Number of units manufactured	10,000
Number of units sold	8,000
Selling price	£4 per unit
Direct materials for month	£8,000
Direct labour for month	£16,000
Fixed production overheads for month	£10,000

There was no finished goods inventory at the start of the month. Both direct materials and direct labour are variable costs.

REQUIRED

(a) produce income statements for April 20-4, using:

- marginal costing

- absorption costing

(b) explain briefly the reason for the difference between recorded profits under the alternative costing methods

7.6 Which one of the following does not appear in a manufacturing account?

(a) depreciation of factory machinery

(b) indirect labour

(c) depreciation of office equipment

(d) factory light and heat

Answer (a) or (b) or (c) or (d)

7.7 For a manufacturing business, which type of inventory is recorded in the income statement?

(a) raw materials

(b) work-in-progress

(c) partly manufactured goods

(d) finished goods

Answer (a) or (b) or (c) or (d)

7.8 Allocate the following costs to either the manufacturing account or the income statement by ticking the appropriate column in the table below:

		Manufacturing account	Income statement
(a)	factory rent		
(b)	production supervisors' wages		
(c)	insurance of factory buildings		
(d)	depreciation of office equipment		
(e)	sales commission		
(f)	direct materials purchased		
(g)	advertising		

7.9 The following figures relate to the accounts of Crown Heath Manufacturing Company for the year ended 31 December 20-6:

	£
Inventories at 1 January 20-6:	
Direct materials	10,500
Finished goods	4,300
Inventories at 31 December 20-6:	
Direct materials	10,200
Finished goods	3,200
Expenditure during year:	
Purchases of direct materials	27,200
Factory wages – direct	12,600
Factory wages – indirect	3,900
Factory rent and rates	1,200
Factory power	2,000
Depreciation of factory machinery	900
Repairs to factory buildings	300
Sundry factory expenses	900
Non-production overheads	6,500
Revenue for the year	60,400

You are to prepare the year end:
- manufacturing account
- income statement

Note: a layout for a manufacturing account and income statement is given in the Appendix.

7.10 The following figures relate to the accounts of Barbara Francis, who runs a furniture manufacturing business, for the year ended 31 December 20-7:

	£
Inventory of direct materials at 1 January 20-7	31,860
Inventory of direct materials at 31 December 20-7	44,790
Inventory of finished goods at 1 January 20-7	42,640
Inventory of finished goods at 31 December 20-7	96,510
Purchases of direct materials	237,660
Revenue for the year	796,950
Rent and rates	32,920
Manufacturing wages	234,630
Manufacturing power	7,650
Manufacturing heat and light	2,370
Manufacturing expenses and maintenance	8,190
Salaries	138,700
Advertising	22,170
Office expenses	7,860
Depreciation of plant and machinery	7,450

Rent and rates are to be apportioned 75 per cent to manufacturing and 25 per cent to administration.

You are to prepare the year end:

- manufacturing account
- income statement

Note: a layout for a manufacturing account and income statement is given in the Appendix.

7.11 The following figures relate to the accounts of Ryedale Limited, a manufacturing business, for the year ended 31 October 20-4:

	£
Inventory of direct materials at 1 November 20-3	41,210
Inventory of direct materials at 31 October 20-4	46,380
Inventory of work-in-progress at 1 November 20-3	7,200
Inventory of work-in-progress at 31 October 20-4	8,450
Inventory of finished goods at 1 November 20-3	29,470
Inventory of finished goods at 31 October 20-4	38,290
Purchases of direct materials	311,050
Revenue for the year	874,360
Rent and rates	35,640
Factory wages – direct	180,860
Factory wages – indirect	45,170
Factory power	12,040
Factory heat and light	5,030
Factory sundry expenses and maintenance	10,390
Administration salaries	154,610
Advertising	30,780
Office expenses	10,390
Depreciation of factory plant and machinery	12,500
Depreciation of office equipment	2,500

Additional information:
- factory power is to be treated as a production overhead
- rent and rates are to be allocated 75% to manufacturing and 25% to administration

You are to prepare the year end:
- manufacturing account
- income statement

Note: a layout for a manufacturing account and income statement is given in the Appendix.

8 Aspects of budgeting

this chapter covers...

In this chapter we turn our attention to budgets and how they are used to help with the financial planning of a business or organisation. In particular we see

- the need for budgets as part of the decision-making, planning and control processes
- how budgeted costs and revenues are set
- how budgets are a method of cost control through the use of variances
- how budgets are used in responsibility accounting to make managers and supervisors responsible for the costs and revenues of their section of the business or organisation, and as a way of motivating employees
- the monitoring process for budget reports
- the difference between fixed and flexible budgets, together with a practical example of a flexible budget
- the causes of variances for costs and revenues

WHAT IS A BUDGET?

A budget is a financial plan for a business or organisation that is prepared in advance.

Budgets are based on pre-determined costs and revenues set in advance of production. These will be set for materials, labour, overheads, selling prices and operating profit. Such pre-determined costs and revenues are often referred to as standard costs and standard selling prices.

All businesses need methods of controlling the costs of materials, labour, and overheads that go to make up the finished product. Imagine a car factory where the cost and amount of materials to make the car is not known; where the hours of work and rates of pay are not known, where the cost of overheads is not known. Under such circumstances, the costs could not be controlled, and it would be impossible to quote a selling price for the product. To overcome this problem many businesses establish budgeted costs and revenues for their output in advance of production. Thus a budgeted cost can be calculated for things as diverse as a product manufactured in a factory, a hospital operation, servicing a car, a meal in a restaurant, a passenger-mile on a bus.

Budgeted costs and revenues are set for:

*   **direct materials**

    The quantity and quality of each type of material to be used in producing the output, and the price of such materials is pre-determined. Budgeted materials cost is the expected quantity and quality of materials multiplied by the expected material price.

*   **direct labour**

    The labour hours required to manufacture a quantity of goods or provide a service, together with the cost of the labour is pre-determined. Budgeted labour cost is the expected labour hours multiplied by the expected wage rates.

*   **overheads**

    The expected volume of output within a time period, multiplied by the overhead absorption rate, determines the budgeted overhead cost.

*   **sales revenue**

    The expected volume of sales within a time period multiplied by the expected selling price determines the budgeted sales revenue.

*   **operating profit**

    The expected profit within a time period (note that operating profit is sales revenue minus direct materials, direct labour and overheads).

Budgets are usually set for each of the responsibility centres – cost, profit or investment centres – of the business or organisation. Once budgets have been set, they can be used as part of the decision-making, planning, and control processes:

- **decision-making**

  The budgeted cost can be used to make pricing decisions, and to consider the effect of using different qualities of materials and grades of labour on the cost of the output.

- **planning**

  Budgets can be prepared to plan the production of goods or services for the next accounting period, and to budget for materials, labour, overheads, sales revenue and operating profit.

- **control**

  Monitoring can be carried out on a regular basis to identify cost and revenue variances from the budget, together with a reconciliation of budgeted and actual costs, revenues and operating profit.

BUDGETS AND VARIANCES

A variance is the budgeted cost or revenue minus the actual cost or revenue.

A particular feature of budgets is their use as a method of cost and revenue control. this is done by comparing the budgeted cost or revenue with the actual cost or revenue of the output in order to establish the variance, ie

| budgeted cost or revenue | minus | actual cost or revenue | equals | variance |

Variances can be either *favourable* (F) or *adverse* (A):

- a favourable cost variance is where actual costs are lower than budgeted costs
- an adverse cost variance is where actual costs are higher than budgeted costs
- a favourable revenue variance is where actual revenues are higher than budgeted revenues

- an adverse revenue variance is where actual revenues are lower than budgeted revenues
- a favourable operating profit variance is where actual profit is higher than budgeted profit
- an adverse operating profit variance is where actual profit is lower than budgeted profit

management by exception

The control systems of a business will set down procedures for acting on variances, but only for significant variances. This type of system is known as *management by exception*, ie acting on variances that are exceptional. Managers will normally work to *tolerance limits* – a tolerance limit is an acceptable percentage variance on the budgeted amount. If a cost or revenue exceeds the tolerance limit, the variance will be significant and investigative action will need to be taken. For example, the budgeted labour cost for a production department is £50,000 a month, with a tolerance limit of 5 per cent set. If labour costs in any one month exceed £50,000 x 5%, ie a variance of £2,500, action will have to be taken and the cause investigated.

who needs to know about variances?

Variances against budgeted cost need to be reported to the *appropriate* level of management within the business or organisation. This level will depend on the significance of the variance, as shown in the two extreme examples which follow:

- **the cost of the materials used is going up by 1 per cent**

The managing director is unlikely to be interested – it will be up to the purchasing department to see if there is a way around the increase.

- **a major failure in an automated process has cut output by 50 per cent**

This is a matter to bring to the attention of higher management and the directors of the company: production patterns, purchasing and staffing will have to be re-organised so that production can be increased.

motivating employees

As a means of motivating employees, budgets are an example of *responsibility accounting*. Managers and supervisors are made responsible for the costs and revenues of their section but, in order to be effective, managers must participate in the budget-setting process. As a method of motivation, budgets can be seen by employees as either a 'carrot' or a 'stick', ie as a form of encouragement to achieve the amounts set, or as a form of punishment if pre-determined costs are exceeded or sales revenues not achieved.

reporting and investigating variances

The variances for the cost elements and sales revenues are summarised on a *budget report*. Such reports reconcile the budgeted cost and the actual cost for each cost element (materials, labour, expenses and overheads) and the budgeted revenues, and show the variances. An example of a budget report is shown below. (Note that the budget has been flexed so that costs and revenues are based on the actual volume sold – we will look at how budgets are flexed on page 225.)

	Flexed budget	Actual	Variance	Favourable (F) or Adverse (A)
Volume sold		145,000		
	£000	£000	£000	
Sales revenue	870	899	29	F
Less costs:				
Direct materials	200	170	30	F
Direct labour	260	260	0	0
Overheads	280	320	40	A
Operating profit	130	149	19	F

A budget report shows the variances for each cost element and revenue by comparing the budget amount with the actual amount. For example, from the above budget report:

- cost variance: materials £200,000 – £170,000 = £30,000 favourable (F)
- cost variance: overheads £280,000 – £320,000 = £40,000 adverse (A)
- revenue variance: sales revenue £870,000 – £899,000 = £29,000 favourable (F), because actual revenue is better than the budget

Note that, where the budget and actual figures are the same, there is no variance and this is recorded as '0' (zero) in the variance column.

The effect of variances on operating profit is that:

- favourable cost variances increase profit
- adverse cost variances reduce profit
- favourable revenue variances increase profit
- adverse revenue variances reduce profit

In the budget report the cost and revenue variances are reconciled to the operating profit variance, ie the net amount of the variances for costs and revenues is equal to the operating profit variance – £19,000 in the example on the previous page.

The order for investigating variances shown by the budget report is usually as follows:

• large variances – favourable and adverse

• other adverse variances

• any remaining favourable variances

Note that small variances may not be worth investigating – the cost of the investigation might outweigh the benefits.

The variances need to be investigated by the appropriate level of management:

• less significant variances are dealt with by managers and supervisors

• significant variances need to be referred to a higher level of management who will decide what further investigation is required

Note that constant adverse or favourable variances need to be investigated as the budgeted costs and revenues may have been set incorrectly.

reporting cycle

For budget reports to be used effectively it is essential that employees are trained to record information accurately about actual costs and revenues. The quality of the information must be:

– accurate

– timely

– in the appropriate format, highlighting the major features

The reporting cycle of the budget report will depend on the time periods used. For example, if a business establishes budget reports on the basis of monthly – or four-weekly – periods, then variances are likely to be reported within the first two weeks of the next period – often in the form of a computer report from the finance department. Generally a senior manager will call a meeting at a fixed point in each period – with the staff responsible for the costs and revenues – in order to review variances from the previous period.

revision of budgets

At regular intervals – annually, or more often – the budgeted costs and revenues need to be revised to take note of:

- cost increases caused by inflation, which will affect materials, labour and overheads (although not necessarily to the same extent)
- changes to the specifications and quality of materials, eg an improvement in quality may lead to less wastage and easier, faster, production
- changes to work practices, eg an increase in automation may lead to reduced labour costs, or the employment of different grades of employees
- changes to selling prices, which may be limited by what others are charging for similar products

controllable and non-controllable costs and revenues

When investigating variances, it is important to appreciate that not all of the costs and revenues can be controlled directly by managers and supervisors in the short term. For example, the cost of rent paid on the premises is outside the control of the purchasing manager – the rent being negotiated by the administration manager. Nevertheless, a proportion of rent will be included amongst the budgeted cost of overheads. By contrast the purchasing manager has control over the cost of materials (unless there is a world price – eg for coffee or crude oil – over which he or she can have no influence). Thus we can distinguish between:

- *controllable costs* – costs which can be influenced by the manager/supervisor
- *non-controllable costs* – costs which cannot be influenced by the manager/supervisor in the short term

Sales revenues are often non-controllable as they may be influenced by what others are charging, or the price the market will bear.

Note that, in the longer-term, all costs and revenues are controllable. For example, a business may decide to move to premises where the rent is cheaper, or to close its operations at one location, or even – in the extreme – to cease trading altogether.

MONITORING OF BUDGET REPORTS

A business or organisation using budgets will monitor the outcomes by comparing the budgeted amounts set with the results that actually occurred. An outline of the monitoring process is shown in the following diagram.

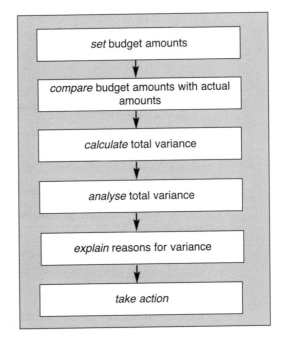

FIXED AND FLEXIBLE BUDGETS

fixed budgets

A fixed budget remains the same whatever the level of activity.

A fixed budget is set at the beginning of the time period for planning purposes and then adhered to and monitored, whatever the circumstances – ie the budgeted figures do not change. Fixed budget are useful in situations where circumstances are stable – for example a departmental budget for a school or a college, where a set amount of money is allowed for buying stationery each year.

flexible budgets

A flexible budget changes with the level of activity and takes into account different cost behaviour patterns.

In reality, situations do change. For example, the sales revenue can vary quite widely from the figure set in the budget: a new product can be more successful than expected – or it can be a complete disaster. In either case the budgeted figures for sales revenue (and production costs too) will be wide of the mark. The answer is to use a *flexible budget*, which is altered for control purposes to vary in line with the level of activity of a business – ie with output of products sold or services provided. By doing this the right costs and revenues are matched and variances can be calculated.

A business may therefore prepare a flexible budget to show different levels of activity. For example, if production is at 80 per cent of the expected amount, then the budget is 'flexed' to 80 per cent and appropriate variances calculated.

flexible budgets – fixed and variable costs

When calculating costs for a flexible budget, certain costs vary with the level of activity, eg

- materials costs for a manufacturing business
- direct labour costs – the production line wages bill

The other costs of making a product or providing a service – the overheads – fall into two categories:

- fixed overheads, eg the rent of a factory
- variable overheads, eg unit costs of telephone calls

The important point to note is that, when preparing a flexible budget, fixed overheads will not change due to changes in the volume of output, but they may change due to price effects (eg the rent is increased). When there is an increase in fixed overheads, it is the actual cost that should be compared with the budget figure.

Case Study

PITMAN PLASTICS LIMITED – FIXED AND FLEXIBLE BUDGETS

situation

Pitman Plastics Limited manufactures plastic kitchenware. The management accountant has extracted the actual cost figures for last month's output and compares them with the budgeted figures:

	budget	actual
	£	£
direct materials	100,000	81,000
direct labour	75,000	60,000
fixed overheads	25,000	26,000
TOTAL	200,000	167,000

The results, on the face of it, look very encouraging – actual costs are £33,000 below budget. The management accountant knows, however, that sales are down during the month and also that production has been running at 80 per cent of normal capacity.

As an accounts assistant at Pitman Plastics Limited, you are asked to produce a flexible budget based on 80 per cent of output.

solution

The fixed budget based on the figures given shows a total <u>favourable</u> variance of costs, being £33,000 below budget. The management accountant knows that this is misleading.

BUDGET REPORT

	Fixed budget	Actual	Variance	Favourable (F) or Adverse (A)
output level	100%			
	£	£	£	
direct materials	100,000	81,000	19,000	F
direct labour	75,000	60,000	15,000	F
fixed overheads	25,000	26,000	1,000	A
TOTAL	200,000	167,000	33,000	F

The flexible budget report, based on costs for 80 per cent output shows a total <u>adverse</u> variance of £2,000. This is a more realistic picture of performance, and is less encouraging.

BUDGET REPORT – 80% output

	Flexed budget	Actual	Variance	Favourable (F) or Adverse (A)
output level	80%			
	£	£	£	
direct materials	80,000	81,000	1,000	A
direct labour	60,000	60,000	0	0
fixed overheads	25,000	26,000	1,000	A
TOTAL	165,000	167,000	2,000	A

summary

In a flexible budget:

- variable costs are flexed to reflect the actual level of activity – in this example they are multiplied by 0.8 to reflect the 80% output level

- fixed overheads are shown at their actual cost, which is compared with the budget figure

CAUSES OF VARIANCES

Budgeted costs and revenues are set in order to give individual departmental managers, who are responsible for aspects of the business' output, suitable targets to aim for. When actual costs are compared with budgeted costs, an investigation can be carried out to find out the causes of the variances and to see what can be done about them for the future. Note, in particular, the way in which variances are calculated down to a responsibility level of an individual employee, or a small section within the business – *responsibility accounting*.

The main causes of variances are listed below.

direct materials	adverse		favourable
inflation	✓		
change in exchange rates	✓	or	✓
alternative materials used	✓	or	✓
more materials wasted	✓		
fewer materials wasted			✓
theft	✓		
change in specifications	✓	or	✓
direct labour			
pay rise	✓		
poor supervision	✓		
different grade of labour used	✓	or	✓
increase in machine speeds			✓
decrease in machine speeds	✓		
fixed overheads			
inflation	✓		
change in exchange rates	✓	or	✓
stepped fixed cost	✓		
change in supplier	✓	or	✓
sales revenue			
increase in price			✓
decrease in price	✓		
increase in volume sold			✓
decrease in volume sold	✓		

Note the following examples of inter-relationship between variances:

- an adverse direct material variance may be resolved by
  - reducing the amount of materials wasted, or
  - buying the materials at a cheaper price, or
  - training staff so that materials are used more efficiently
- an adverse direct labour variance may be resolved by
  - training staff to work more efficiently, or
  - using labour at a lower grade of pay, or
  - reorganising the production process so that staff work more efficiently
- an adverse fixed overhead variance may be resolved by
  - buying from cheaper suppliers (eg telephones, electricity, gas), or
  - more efficient use of overheads (eg sub-letting part of the premises), or
  - making changes to the production process (eg by reviewing the balance between labour work and machine work)

Case Study

1.850

1.600

PREPARING FOR ASSESSMENT: FLEXIBLE BUDGETS

Tutorial note: this Case Study is based on an AAT sample Assessment task.

situation

You work as an accounts assistant for Exbury Limited, a manufacturing business.

Exbury Ltd has the following original budget and actual performance for product 10EX for the year ending 31 December.

	budget	actual
Volume sold	10,000	12,000
	£000	£000
Sales revenue	250	290
Less costs:		
Direct materials	80	90
Direct labour	110	140
Overheads	30	35
Operating profit	30	25

Both direct materials and direct labour are variable costs, but the overheads are fixed.

You are to complete the table below to show a flexed budget and the resulting variances against this budget for the year. Show the actual variance amount, for sales and each cost, in the column headed 'Variance' and indicate whether this is Favourable or Adverse by entering F or A in the final column. If neither F nor A, enter 0.

	Flexed budget	Actual	Variance	Favourable (F) or Adverse (A)
Volume sold		12,000		
	£000	£000	£000	
Sales revenue		290		
Less costs:				
Direct materials		90		
Direct labour		140		
Overheads		35		
Operating profit		25		

solution

You complete the table as follows:

	Flexed budget	Actual	Variance	Favourable (F) or Adverse (A)
Volume sold	12,000	12,000		
	£000	£000	£000	
Sales revenue	300	290	10	A
Less costs:				
Direct materials	96	90	6	F
Direct labour	132	140	8	A
Overheads	30	35	5	A
Operating profit	42	25	17	A

Working notes:

- The budget is flexed from 10,000 to 12,000 units. This is 20 per cent increase (2,000/10,000 x 100).

- The budget figures for sales revenue, direct materials and direct labour are all increased by 20 per cent to give the amount for the flexed budget. For example, sales revenue £250,000 x 1.2 = £300,000.

- For fixed overheads, the actual figure of £35,000 is used. The increase from the budget figure of £30,000 shows an adverse variance of £5,000.

- The variance columns are completed and the total variance, here £17,000, is reconciled with the change in operating profit from that shown by the flexed budget to the actual figure.

Chapter Summary

- Budgets are based on pre-determined costs and revenues set in advance.

- Budgeted costs and revenues are set for:
  - sales revenue
  - direct materials
  - direct labour
  - overheads
  - operating profit (sales revenue minus direct materials, direct labour and overheads)

- Budgets are part of the decision-making, planning and control processes of a business or organisation.

- Variances are used as a method of cost and revenue control. Variances can be either favourable (F) or adverse (A), and are acted upon if they are significant.

- Fixed budgets are set at the beginning of the time period and then adhered to and monitored whatever the circumstances.

- Flexed budgets are altered to vary in line with the level of activity.

- There are a number of reasons why variances occur and, often, there is an inter-relationship between variances – eg an adverse direct material variance may be resolved by reducing wastage or by buying at a cheaper price.

budget	a financial plan for a business or organisation that is prepared in advance
operating profit	sales revenue minus direct materials, direct labour and overheads
variance	budgeted cost or revenue minus actual cost or revenue
favourable variance	where actual costs are lower than budgeted costs, or where actual revenues are higher than budgeted revenues
adverse variance	where actual costs are higher than budgeted costs, or where actual revenues are lower than budgeted revenues
controllable costs	costs which can be influenced by the manager/supervisor
non-controllable costs	costs which cannot be influenced by the manager/supervisor in the short term
fixed budget	budget which remains the same whatever the level of activity
flexible budget	budget which changes with the level of activity and takes into account different cost behaviour patterns

Activities

8.1 The budget for direct labour is £10,800; the actual cost is £12,200. The budget for direct materials is £4,600; the actual cost is £4,350.

Which one of the following statements is correct?

(a) direct labour variance £1,400 adverse; direct materials variance £250 adverse

(b) direct labour variance £1,400 favourable; direct materials variance £250 favourable

(c) direct labour variance £1,400 adverse; direct materials variance £250 favourable

(d) direct labour variance £1,400 favourable; direct materials variance £250 adverse

Answer (a) or (b) or (c) or (d)

8.2   The budget for direct labour is £15,900; the actual cost is £14,800. The budget for direct materials is £8,200; the actual cost is £8,650.

Which one of the following statements is correct?

(a)   direct labour variance £1,100 adverse; direct materials variance £450 adverse

(b)   direct labour variance £1,100 favourable; direct materials variance £450 favourable

(c)   direct labour variance £1,100 adverse; direct materials variance £450 favourable

(d)   direct labour variance £1,100 favourable; direct materials variance £450 adverse

Answer (a) or (b) or (c) or (d)

8.3   A budget for 8,000 units of output shows a direct materials cost of £17,400 and a direct labour cost of £12,600. Actual output is 9,000 units.

Which one of the following gives the correct figures for the flexed budget?

(a)   direct materials £19,575; direct labour £14,175

(b)   direct materials £19,575; direct labour £12,600

(c)   direct materials £17,400; direct labour £14,175

(d)   direct materials £17,400; direct labour £12,600

Answer (a) or (b) or (c) or (d)

8.4   The budget for 10,000 units of output shows a fixed overheads cost of £20,200. Actual output is 12,000 and the actual cost of fixed overheads is £21,000.

For the flexed budget identify whether the following statements are true or false by putting a tick in the relevant column of the table below.

Flexed budget	True	False
Fixed overheads are shown in the flexed budget at a cost of £24,240		
Fixed overheads are shown in the flexed budget at a cost of £21,000		
Fixed overheads are shown in the flexed budget at a cost of £20,200		
There is a fixed overheads variance of £800 adverse		
There is a fixed overheads variance of £2,040 adverse		
There is no fixed overheads variance		

8.5   Identify the correct variance from the causes of variances given by putting a tick in the relevant column of the table below.

Cause of variance	Adverse	Favourable
increase in cost of direct materials		
fewer materials are wasted		
cheaper direct materials are used		
theft of direct materials		
direct labour receives a pay rise		
the supervisor organises the direct labour more efficiently to improve output		
overtime is paid to direct labour		
inflation increases the cost of fixed overheads		
a cheaper electricity supplier is used for the fixed overhead		
selling prices are increased		
there is an increase in the volume of output sold		

8.6   You work as an accounts assistant for Eveshore Limited, a manufacturing business.

You are asked to complete the following fixed budget report, including the actual performance and the variances for last month from the following information:

	budget £	actual £
Direct materials	85,000	83,000
Direct labour	62,000	65,000
Fixed overheads	54,000	59,000

BUDGET REPORT				
	Fixed budget	**Actual**	**Variance**	**Favourable (F) or Adverse (A)**
Output level	100%			
	£	£	£	
Direct materials				
Direct labour				
Fixed overheads				
TOTAL				

8.7 You work as an accounts assistant for Onslow Limited, a manufacturing business.

You have been given the original budget costs and the actual performance for last month for product O14. Actual output was 90 per cent of budgeted output.

You are asked to complete the flexible budget report, below, including the actual performance and the variances for last month from the following information:

	budget £	actual £
Direct materials	4,700	5,200
Direct labour	10,800	8,900
Fixed overheads	4,100	4,500

Both direct materials and direct labour are variable costs.

BUDGET REPORT				
	Flexed budget	**Actual**	**Variance**	**Favourable (F) or Adverse (A)**
Output level	90%			
	£	£	£	
Direct materials				
Direct labour				
Fixed overheads				
TOTAL				

8.8 Wyvern Ltd has the following original budget and actual performance for product WV10 for the year ending 31 December.

	budget	actual
Volume sold	30,000	33,000
	£000	£000
Sales revenue	1,800	1,950
Less costs:		
Direct materials	550	610
Direct labour	340	365
Overheads	650	710
Operating profit	260	265

Both direct materials and direct labour are variable costs, but the overheads are fixed.

You are to complete the following table to show a flexed budget and the resulting variances against this budget for the year. Show the actual variance amount, for sales and each cost, in the column headed 'Variance' and indicate whether this is Favourable or Adverse by entering F or A in the final column. If neither F nor A, enter 0.

	Flexed budget	Actual	Variance	Favourable (F) or Adverse (A)
Volume sold		33,000		
	£000	£000	£000	
Sales revenue		1,950		
Less costs:				
Direct materials		610		
Direct labour		365		
Overheads		710		
Operating profit		265		

8.9 Perran Ltd has the following original budget and actual performance for product P14 for the year ending 31 December.

	budget	**actual**
Volume sold	22,000	27,500
	£000	£000
Sales revenue	1,400	1,675
Less costs:		
Direct materials	300	360
Direct labour	500	645
Overheads	420	480
Operating profit	180	190

Both direct materials and direct labour are variable costs, but the overheads are fixed.

You are to complete the following table to show a flexed budget and the resulting variances against this budget for the year. Show the actual variance amount, for sales and each cost, in the column headed 'Variance' and indicate whether this is Favourable or Adverse by entering F or A in the final column. If neither F nor A, enter 0.

	Flexed budget	**Actual**	**Variance**	**Favourable (F) or Adverse (A)**
Volume sold		27,500		
	£000	£000	£000	
Sales revenue		1,675		
Less costs:				
Direct materials		360		
Direct labour		645		
Overheads		480		
Operating profit		190		

9 Short-term decisions

this chapter covers...

In this chapter we see how cost accounting information is used to help a business or organisation to make short-term decisions. The techniques we will look at include:

- break-even analysis
- margin of safety
- target profit
- contribution sales ratio
- limiting factors
- 'special order' pricing

These techniques make use of the principles of marginal costing, which have been covered in Chapter 7.

SHORT-TERM DECISIONS

what is meant by short-term decisions?

By short-term decisions we mean those actions which will affect the costs and revenues of a business or organisation over the next few weeks and months, up to a maximum of one year ahead. Long-term decisions – see Chapter 10 – affect the costs and revenues of future years. For example, an ice-cream manufacturer might make the following decisions:

- *short-term* – 'we have to increase production over the summer months in order to meet higher sales'
- *long-term* – 'we need to build a production line so that we can make the new Veneto range of ice creams that we are developing.'

types of short-term decisions

The decisions that we will be looking at include:

- Break-even analysis, where the break-even point is the output level (units manufactured or services provided) at which the sales revenue is just enough to cover all the costs. Break-even analysis answers questions such as:
  - what output do we need in order to break-even?
  - at current levels of output we are above break-even, but how safe are we?
  - we have to make a profit of £1,000 per week; what level of output do we need to achieve this?
  - what is the effect on profit if we sell more than we think?
- Limiting factors, where there is a shortage which affects output. Limiting factors include a shortage of materials, skilled labour, machine hours, etc. Once the limiting factor has been identified, the effect of the constraint on output can be minimised in order to achieve the best results for the business or organisation. A knowledge of limiting factors answers questions such as:
  - there is a shortage of materials this week – shall we produce Product Exe or Product Wye?
  - until we complete the training programme we have a shortage of skilled labour; how best can we use the skilled labour that we have available?
  - one of the machines has broken down; both of our products need machine hours – which product takes priority?
- Marginal costing is used in short-term decision-making to identify the fixed and variable costs that are required to make a product or to provide

a service. Once these are known questions about pricing can be answered:

– if we increase prices, sales revenues are expected to fall but how will our profit be affected?

– if we decrease prices, sales revenues are expected to increase but how will our profit be affected?

– a potential customer wants to buy our product but at a lower price than we usually charge; how will our profit be affected?

what information is needed?

Decision-making, both in the short-term and long-term, is concerned with the future and always involves making a choice between alternatives. To help with decision-making it is important to identify *relevant (avoidable) costs* and *irrelevant (unavoidable) costs*.

Relevant costs are those costs that are changed by a decision.

Irrelevant costs are those costs that are not affected by a decision.

In order to make a decision, information is needed about costs and revenues:

- future costs and revenues
  – it is the expected future costs and revenues that are relevant
  – past costs and revenues are only useful in so far as they provide a guide to the future
  – costs already spent (called *sunk costs*) are irrelevant to decision-making
- differential costs and revenues
  – only those costs which alter as a result of decision-making are relevant and are avoidable costs
  – where costs are the same for each alternative, they are irrelevant and are unavoidable costs
  – thus any cost that changes when a decision is made is a relevant cost

In the short-term, a business or organisation always attempts to make the best use of existing resources. This involves focusing on the relevant costs and revenues that will change as a result of a decision being made, such as:

- selling prices
- variable costs and the variable element of semi-variable costs
- contribution per unit of output, which is selling price minus variable cost
- marginal cost, which is the cost of producing one extra unit of output

Fixed period costs and the fixed element of semi-variable costs are irrelevant in decision-making as they do not alter in short-term decision-making, eg the rent of a car factory is most likely to be the same when 11,000 cars are produced each year instead of 10,000 previously. Although, remember that, in the long-term, all costs are variable. Also, note that, in the long term, all costs are relevant and avoidable – for example, if a business decided to stop production and cease to trade.

reporting decisions

With decision-making – both short- and long-term – the costing information has to be reported to managers, or other appropriate people, in a clear and concise way. The information should include recommendations which are supported by well-presented reasoning. The decisions will not be taken by the person who has prepared the information, but the decision-makers will be influenced by the recommendations of the report. Remember that managers, and other appropriate people, do not always have an accounting background, so any form of presentation must be set out clearly and must use as little technical accounting terminology as possible.

Methods of presentation include:

- verbal presentations
- written reports/emails/memorandums

Both of these require a similar amount of preparation; the steps are:

- plan the report
- check that the plan deals with the tasks set
- be aware of the context in which the report is written
- express the report, verbal or written, in clear and concise English

written reports

The written report should include:

- an introduction, which sets out the task or the problem
- the content of the report, which explains the steps towards a solution and may include accounting calculations
- a conclusion, which includes a recommendation of the decision to be taken
- an appendix, which can be used to explain fully the accounting calculations, and to detail any sources of reference consulted

In this chapter we will see two written reports on short-term decisions which make recommendations – see pages 256 and 262. The next chapter includes an example of a report for a long-term decision.

verbal presentations

A verbal presentation requires the same preparation and content as a written report and is probably the more difficult to present. Accordingly, verbal presentations often include support material in the form of handouts or computer presentations. Such material can be used to explain accounting data and to make key points and recommendations.

FIXED AND VARIABLE COSTS

Before we can look at short-term decision-making techniques, it is important to understand that costs behave in different ways as the volume of output or activity changes. We have already seen (Chapter 4, pages 102-105) that there are three ways in which costs can behave within a range of output levels. These are summarised as follows:

variable product costs   These are the costs where the cost varies in proportion to the level of output. For example, if a car manufacturer makes more cars it will use more sheet metal – a variable product cost.

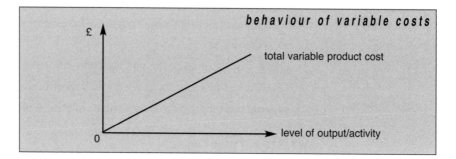

fixed period costs   These are costs that do not normally change when the level of output changes. The cost of insuring a car factory against business risks will not vary in line with the number of cars produced – it is a fixed period cost.

Remember that increases in output may produce a stepped fixed cost, eg an increase in factory rent because an additional factory is needed for the increase in output. The nature of stepped fixed costs is illustrated as follows:

semi-variable costs

These are costs where a part of the cost acts as a variable cost, and a part acts as a fixed cost. Some fuel bills are semi-variable: there is a fixed standing charge and a variable unit charge.

The amount of variable cost within a semi-variable cost can be calculated using the high/low method – see page 106.

costs, contribution and profit

To help with short-term decision-making, costs are classifed by their behaviour as either variable costs or fixed costs (with semi-variable costs being split between their fixed and variable elements). For example, a car manufacturer will need to identify:

- the variable product costs of each car
- the total fixed period costs of running the business over the period

When the manufacturer sells a car it receives the selling price, which covers the variable costs of the car. As the selling price is greater than the variable costs there will also be an amount of money – the contribution – available to pay off the fixed period costs incurred. The contribution formula (which we have seen in Chapter 7) is:

selling price per unit *less* variable cost per unit = contribution per unit

It follows that the difference between the sales income and the variable costs of the units sold in a period is the **total contribution** that the sales of all the units in the period make towards the fixed costs of the business.

A business can work out its profit for any given period from the total contribution and fixed costs figures:

total contribution *less* total fixed costs = profit

An income statement can be prepared in the following format:

		£
	Sales revenue	x
less	Variable costs	x
equals	Contribution	x
less	Fixed costs	x
equals	PROFIT	x

BREAK-EVEN

Break-even is often referred to as CVP (cost, volume, profit) analysis because we look at the costs of output, the volume of output, and the profit made.

Break-even is the point at which neither a profit nor a loss is made.

The break-even point is the output level (units manufactured or services provided) at which the sales revenue is just enough to cover all the costs. Break-even is the point at which the profit (or loss) is zero. The output level can be measured in a way that is appropriate for the particular business or organisation – either units of output or sales revenue. The break-even formula is:

$$\frac{\textit{fixed costs (£)}}{\textit{contribution per unit (£)}} = \textit{number of units to break-even}$$

The formula for break-even in sales revenue is:

break-even point (units of output) x selling price per unit

This can also be calculated using the contribution sales (CS) ratio – see page 251.

In order to use break-even analysis, we need to know:

- selling price (per unit)
- costs of the product
  - variable costs (such as materials, labour) per unit
  - overhead costs, and whether these are fixed or variable
- limitations, such as maximum production capacity, maximum sales

The Case Study of Fluffy Toys Limited which follows shows how the break-even point can be worked out.

Case Study

1.850

1.600

FLUFFY TOYS LIMITED: BREAK-EVEN

situation

Fluffy Toys Limited manufactures soft toys, and is able to sell all that can be produced. The variable product costs (materials and direct labour) of each toy are £10 and the selling price is £20 each. The fixed period costs of running the business are £5,000 per month. How many toys need to be produced and sold each month for the business to cover its costs, ie to break-even?

solution

This problem can be solved by calculation, by constructing a table, or by means of a graph. Which method is used depends on the purpose for which the information is required:

- the *calculation method* is quick to use and is convenient for seeing the effect of different cost structures on break-even point

- the *table method* shows the amounts of fixed and variable costs, sales revenue, and profit at different levels of production

- the *graph method* is used for making presentations – for example, to the directors of a company – because it shows in a visual form the relationship between costs and sales revenue, and the amount of profit or loss at different levels of production

Often the calculation or table methods are used before drawing a graph. By doing this, the break-even point is known and suitable scales can be selected for the axes of the graph in order to give a good visual presentation.

calculation method

The contribution per unit is:

	selling price per unit	£20
less	variable costs per unit	£10
equals	contribution per unit	£10

Each toy sold gives a contribution (selling price less variable costs) of £10. This contributes towards the fixed costs and, in order to break-even, the business must have sufficient £10 'lots' to meet the fixed costs. Thus, with fixed costs of £5,000 per month, the break-even calculation is:

$$\frac{fixed\ costs\ (£)}{contribution\ per\ unit\ (£)} = \frac{£5,000}{£10} = 500\ toys\ each\ month$$

The break-even point is:

– in units of output, 500 toys each month

– in sales revenue, £10,000 each month (500 toys x £20)

table method

units of output	fixed costs	variable costs	total cost	sales revenue	profit/(loss)
	A	B	C	D	
			A + B		D – C
	£	£	£	£	£
100	5,000	1,000	6,000	2,000	(4,000)
200	5,000	2,000	7,000	4,000	(3,000)
300	5,000	3,000	8,000	6,000	(2 000)
400	5,000	4,000	9,000	8,000	(1,000)
500	5,000	5,000	10,000	10,000	nil
600	5,000	6,000	11,000	12,000	1,000
700	5,000	7,000	12,000	14,000	2,000

graph method

A graphical presentation uses money amounts as the common denominator between fixed costs, variable costs, and sales revenue.

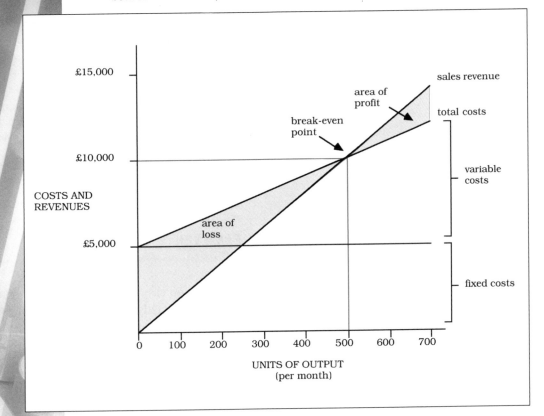

notes to the graph

- With a break-even graph, it is usual for the vertical axis to show money amounts; the horizontal axis shows units of output/sales.
- The sales revenue and total costs lines are straight.
- The fixed costs are unchanged at all levels of output, in this case they are £5,000 (but there might be stepped fixed costs).
- The variable costs commence, on the vertical axis, *from the fixed costs amount*, not from 'zero'. This is because the cost of producing zero units is the fixed costs.
- The fixed costs *and* the variable costs form the *total costs line*.
- The point at which the total costs and sales revenue lines cross is the break-even point.
- From the graph we can read off the break-even point both in terms of units of output, 500 units on the horizontal axis, and in sales revenue, £10,000 on the vertical axis.

- The 'proof' of the break-even chart is:

		£
	Sales revenue (500 units at £20 each)	10,000
less	Variable costs (500 units at £10 each)	5,000
equals	Contribution	5,000
less	Fixed costs	5,000
equals	PROFIT/LOSS	nil

> Tutorial note: Although it is unlikely that you will be asked to draw a break-even graph in assessments, it is good practice and illustrates well the relationship between costs and revenues.

INTERPRETATION OF BREAK-EVEN

When interpreting break-even, it is all too easy to concentrate solely on the break-even point. The graph, for example, tells us much more than this: it also shows the profit or loss at any level of output/sales revenue contained within the graph. To find this, simply measure the gap between sales revenue and total costs at a chosen number of units, and read the money amounts off on the vertical axis (above break-even point it is a profit; below, it is a loss). For example, the graph in the Case Study above shows a profit or loss at:

- 650 units = £1,500 profit
- 600 units = £1,000 profit
- 400 units = £1,000 loss

Break-even analysis, whether by calculation, by table, or by graph, can be used by all types of businesses and organistions. For example, a shop will wish to know the sales it has to make each week to meet costs; a sports centre will wish to know the ticket sales that have to be made to meet costs; a club or society might wish to know how many raffle tickets it needs to sell to meet the costs of prizes and of printing tickets.

Once the break-even point has been reached, the *additional* contribution forms the profit. For example, if the business considered in the Case Study above was selling 650 toys each month, it would have a total contribution of 650 x £10 = £6,500; of this the first £5,000 will be used to meet fixed costs, and the remaining £1,500 represents the profit (which can be read off the break-even graph). This can be shown by means of an income statement as follows:

		£
	Sales revenue (650 units at £20 each)	13,000
less	Variable costs (650 units at £10 each)	6,500
equals	Contribution (to fixed costs and profit)	6,500
less	Monthly fixed costs	5,000
equals	PROFIT FOR MONTH	1,500

LIMITATIONS OF BREAK-EVEN ANALYSIS

The problem of break-even analysis is the assumption that the relationship between sales revenue, variable costs and fixed costs, remains the same at all levels of production. This is a rather simplistic view because, for example, in order to increase sales, a business will often need to offer bulk discounts, so reducing the sales revenue per unit at higher levels. The limitations of break-even analysis can be summarised as follows:

- The assumption is made that all output is sold. There is no point in preparing the cost data, calculating the break-even point, and estimating the profits to be made if the product will not sell in sufficient quantities. However, break-even analysis is useful for a new business in order to establish the level of sales – units or revenue – that must be achieved to reach break-even point. The feasibility of reaching that level of sales must then be considered by the owners.

- All costs and revenues are expressed in terms of straight lines. However, this relationship is not always so. As indicated above selling prices may vary at different quantities sold; in a similar way, as we have seen earlier in the chapter, variable costs alter at different levels as advantage is taken of the lower prices to be gained from bulk buying, and/or more efficient production methods.

- Fixed costs do not remain fixed at all levels of production; instead, as we have seen, there may be stepped fixed costs and, in the long-term, all costs are variable.

- It is not possible to *extrapolate* the graph or calculation; by extrapolation is meant extending the lines on the graph beyond the limits of the activity on which the graph is based. For example, in the Case Study, the graph cannot be extended to, say, 1,000 units of output and the profit read off at this point. The relationship between sales revenues and costs will be different at much higher levels of output – for example, different methods of production might be used.

- The profit or loss shown by the graph or calculations is probably only true for figures close to current output levels – the further away from current figures, the less accurate will be the expected profit or loss.

- A further disadvantage of break-even analysis is that it concentrates too much attention on the break-even point. While this aspect is important, other considerations such as ensuring that the output is produced as efficiently as possible, and that costs are kept under review, are just as important.

BREAK-EVEN: MARGIN OF SAFETY

The margin of safety is the amount by which sales exceed the break-even point. Margin of safety can be expressed as:

- a number of units

- a sales revenue amount

- a percentage, using the following formula

$$\frac{current\ output - break\text{-}even\ output}{current\ output} \times \frac{100}{1} = percentage\ margin\ of\ safety$$

WORKED EXAMPLE

margin of safety

In the Case Study earlier in this chapter, Fluffy Toys Limited, (pages 245-248), if current output is 700 units, while the break-even point is 500 units, the margin of safety is:

- 200 units (ie 700 – 500)

- £4,000 of sales revenue (ie 200 units at £20 each)

- 29 per cent, ie $\frac{700 - 500}{700} \times \frac{100}{1}$

In interpreting this margin of safety we can say that production/sales can fall by these values before the business reaches break-even point and ceases to make a profit.

Margin of safety is especially important in times of recession as it expresses to management the amount of the 'cushion' which current production/revenue gives beyond the break-even point. Where there is a comparison to be made between two or more products, each with different margins of safety, the product with the highest margin of safety is looked on favourably; however, margin of safety is only one factor in decision-making.

BREAK-EVEN: TARGET PROFIT

A further analysis of break-even is to calculate the production and sales revenue in order to give a certain amount of profit – the *target profit*. This is calculated as:

$$\frac{\textit{fixed costs (£) + target profit (£)}}{\textit{contribution per unit (£)}} \quad = \textit{number of units of output}$$

The sales revenue to achieve the target profit is calculated as:

number of units of output x sales revenue per unit (£) = target sales revenue (£)

Thus, if Fluffy Toys Limited (see the Case Study on pages 245-248) required a profit of £2,000 per month, the calculation is:

$$\frac{\textit{£5,000 + £2,000}}{\textit{£10}} \quad = \textit{700 units of output, with a sales revenue of £14,000*}$$

$$\textit{* 700 units x £20 each = £14,000}$$

This target profit can then be shown by means of an income statement as follows:

		£
	Sales revenue (700 units at £20 each)	14,000
less	Variable costs (700 units at £10 each)	7,000
equals	Contribution (to fixed costs and profit)	7,000
less	Monthly fixed costs	5,000
equals	TARGET PROFIT FOR MONTH	2,000

Target profit can also be calculated by making use of the contribution sales ratio (see below).

CONTRIBUTION SALES (CS) RATIO

The contribution sales (CS) ratio – expresses the amount of contribution in relation to the amount of the selling price:

$$\frac{\textit{contribution (£)}}{\textit{selling price (£)}} \quad = \quad \textit{contribution to sales ratio}$$

The ratio, or percentage, can be calculated on the basis of a single unit of production or for the whole business.

In break-even analysis, if fixed costs are known, we can use the CS ratio to find the sales revenue at which the business breaks-even, or the sales revenue to give a target profit.

WORKED EXAMPLE

contribution sales ratio

Referring back to the Case Study (Fluffy Toys Limited), the CS ratio (on a per unit basis) is:

$$\frac{\text{contribution (£)}}{\text{selling price (£)}} \quad = \quad \frac{£10^*}{£20} = 0.5 \text{ or } 50\%$$

* selling price (£20) – variable costs (£10) = contribution £10

Fixed costs are £5,000 per month, so the sales revenue needed to break-even is:

$$\frac{\text{fixed costs (£)}}{\text{CS ratio}} \quad = \quad \frac{£5,000}{0.5 \text{ (see above)}} = \underline{£10,000}$$

As the selling price is £20 per toy, we can get back to the break-even in units of output as follows: £10,000 ÷ £20 = 500 units

If the directors of Fluffy Toys Limited wish to know the sales revenue that must be made to achieve a target profit of £2,000 per month, the CS ratio is used as follows:

$$\frac{\text{fixed costs + target profit}}{\text{CS ratio}} \quad = \quad \text{required level of sales}$$

$$\frac{£5,000 + £2,000}{0.5} \quad = \quad \underline{£14,000}$$

As the selling price is £20 per toy, we can get to the units of output as follows:

£14,000 ÷ £20 = 700 units to achieve a target profit of £2,000.

WHEN TO USE BREAK-EVEN ANALYSIS

Break-even analysis is often used:

before starting a new business

The calculation of break-even point is important in order to see the sales revenue needed by the new business in order to cover costs, or to make a particular level of profit. The feasibility of achieving the level can then be considered by the owner of the business, and other parties such as the bank manager.

when making changes

The costs of a major change will need to be considered by the owners and/or managers. For example, a large increase in production will, most likely, affect the balance between fixed and variable costs. Break-even analysis will be used as part of the planning process to ensure that the business remains profitable.

to measure profits and losses

Within the limitations of break-even analysis, profits and losses can be estimated at different levels of output from current production. Remember that this can be done only where the new output is close to current levels and where there is no major change to the structure of costs – ie it is not possible to extrapolate.

to answer 'what if?' questions

Questions such as 'what if sales revenue falls by 10 per cent?' and 'what if fixed costs increase by £1,000?' can be answered – in part at least – by break-even analysis. The effect on the profitability of the business can be seen, subject to the limitations noted earlier. A question such as 'what if sales revenue increases by 300 per cent?' is such a fundamental change that it can only be answered by examining the effect on the nature of the fixed and variable costs and then re-calculating the break-even point.

to evaluate alternative viewpoints

There are often different ways of production; this is particularly true of a manufacturing business. For example, a product could be made:

- either, by using a labour-intensive process, with a large number of employees supported by basic machinery
- or, by using expensive machinery in an automated process with very few employees.

In the first case, the cost structure will be high variable costs (labour) and low fixed costs (depreciation of machinery). In the second case, there will be low variable costs and high fixed costs. Break-even analysis can be used to examine the relationship between the costs which are likely to show a low break-even point in the first case, and a high break-even point in the second. In this way, the management of the business is guided by break-even analysis; management will also need to know the likely sales revenues, and the availability of money with which to buy the machinery.

LIMITING FACTORS

Limiting factors (or scarce resources) are those aspects of a business which affect output.

Examples of limiting factors include:

- availability of materials

- availability of skilled labour

- availability of machine hours

- finance

- the quantity of the output which can be sold – whether a manufactured product or a service

At any one time there is usually one main limiting factor. It is essential to minimise its effect by optimising resources and maximising profit. After one limiting factor has been dealt with, another one then affects the business – for example, once a shortage of materials has been resolved, the limiting factor might well become a lack of skilled labour.

Where a business sells more than one product, under normal circumstances it will be best to switch output to the product that gives the highest contribution in relation to sales revenue (the contribution sales ratio). For example, a company makes two products, X and Y, with the following costs and revenues:

	Product	X £	Y £
	Selling price per unit	100	200
less	Variable costs per unit	60	140
equals	Contribution per unit	40	60

With no limiting factors, the company should concentrate on making and selling product X. The reason for this is that the contribution sales ratio is 40 per cent (£40 ÷ £100) when compared with product Y, where it is 30 per cent (£60 ÷ £200).

Where there is a limiting factor, for example the availability of skilled labour, a business will switch production to the product which gives the highest contribution from each unit of the limiting factor (eg contribution per direct labour hour). Thus the key to dealing with limiting factors is to:

maximise the contribution per unit of limiting factor

Following this rule will always maximise profits. Where there is a maximum level of output for the selected product, this product should be produced to the full if possible, and any units of limiting factors which remain unused should be 'spilled over' to the next best product. This is illustrated in the Case Study which follows.

Case Study

SOUND SYSTEMS LIMITED: LIMITING FACTORS

situation

Sound Systems Limited is a small company which makes reproduction radios to 1930s' designs (but with year 21st century sound quality!). Two models are made – the 'Windsor' and the 'Buckingham'. Both products require skilled direct labour which cannot be increased in the short term. Demand for the company's products is increasing rapidly and, while the company is taking steps to train new employees, the managing director is unsure of the 'mix' of products that should be produced each week.

Costs and revenues are as follows:

Product		Windsor £	Buckingham £
	Selling price per unit	50	100
less	Variable costs per unit	30	70
equals	Contribution per unit	20	30

- each radio takes two direct labour hours to make
- the number of direct labour hours available each week is 260
- the weekly fixed costs of the business are £2,000
- demand for the Windsor model is currently 100 radios per week, and for the Buckingham it is 80 radios per week

As an accounts assistant, prepare a report for the managing director which gives your recommendations for next week's production. Support your views with a forecast income statement.

solution

Without taking into account the limiting factor of direct labour, the better model for the company to produce is the Windsor, because this gives a higher contribution sales ratio:

- Windsor: £20 contribution on £50 of sales = CS ratio of 40 per cent

- Buckingham: £30 contribution on £100 of sales = CS ratio of 30 per cent

However, as direct labour is the limiting factor, the company should maximise the contribution from each hour of direct labour:

- Windsor: contribution per direct labour hour £20 ÷ 2 hours = £10

- Buckingham: contribution per direct labour hour £30 ÷ 2 hours = £15

To make best use of the limiting factor, the company should produce all of the Buckingham model that can be sold, ie 80 per week. This will utilise 160 direct labour hours (80 units x 2 hours per unit). The remaining 100 direct labour hours (260 hours less 160 hours) will be used to produce 50 of the Windsor model (50 units x 2 hours per unit).

Report for managing director:

REPORT

To:	Managing Director
From:	Accounts Assistant
Date:	Today

Production of Windsor and Buckingham models

Introduction

- You asked for my recommendations for next week's production.

- Until we have completed the training of new employees, the company has insufficient skilled labour to enable us to manufacture both models to meet customer demand. We therefore need to use our skilled labour to the best advantage of the company.

Report

- With insufficient skilled labour we have a limiting factor (or a scarce resource). To make best use of this limiting factor to produce profits for the company, we must maximise the contribution (selling price – variable costs) from each hour of skilled labour.

- The contribution from producing each Windsor radio is £20. As this product requires two hours of skilled labour, the contribution per hour is £20 ÷ 2 hours = £10.

continued on next page

- The contribution from producing each Buckingham radio is £30. As this product also requires two hours of skilled labour, the contribution per hour is £30 ÷ 2 hours = £15.

- To make best use of the limiting factor of skilled labour, the company should produce all of the Buckingham model that can be sold, ie 80 per week. This will take 160 hours of skilled labour (80 radios x 2 hours each) and will leave 100 hours available to produce 50 of the Windsor model (50 radios x 2 hours each).

- Please note that, if this production plan is followed, insufficient Windsor models will be produced to meet demand. This may make it difficult to re-establish the Windsor in the market when full production of this model can be resumed following the completion of training of new employees.

Conclusion

- Based on the concept of maximising the contribution from each hour of skilled labour (the limiting factor), I recommend that the production for next week should be:

  80 Buckingham radios

  50 Windsor radios

- This will give a forecast income statement for next week as follows:

		Windsor £	Buckingham £	Total £
	Sales revenue:			
	50 Windsor at £50 per unit	2,500		2,500
	80 Buckingham at £100 per unit		8,000	8,000
		2,500	8,000	10,500
less	Variable costs:			
	50 Windsor at £30 per unit	1,500		1,500
	80 Buckingham at £70 per unit		5,600	5,600
equals	Contribution	1,000	2,400	3,400
less	Fixed overheads			2,000
equals	PROFIT			1,400

Summary:

The procedures for decision-making with limiting factors are:

- calculate the *contribution per unit of limiting factor* to make the decision as to which product to manufacture – the one with the higher contribution per unit of limiting factor will maximise profits

- calculate the income statement using the *number of units of output* (and not the number of units of limiting factor)

- where there is a maximum level of output for the selected product, use as much of the limiting factor as possible, and then 'spill over' any unused limiting factor to the next best product (as in the Case Study)

Note that, where there are limiting factors, fewer of one or more products will be produced causing a shortfall in the market. It may be difficult to re-establish these products when full production can be resumed after the limiting factor has been resolved. The problem is that often customers want availability of all products and, if one isn't fully available, they won't buy the others (think of a store closing its carpet department and the effect on sales in the furniture department).

'SPECIAL ORDER' PRICING

'Special order' pricing is where a business uses spare capacity to make extra sales of its product at a lower price than its normal selling price.

'Special order' pricing, which makes use of marginal costing techniques, is normally used once the business is profitable at its current level of output, ie it has reached break-even. Additional sales – at 'special order' prices – can be made at a selling price above marginal cost, but below absorption cost. In this way, profits can be increased, provided that the additional sales are spare capacity. The key to increasing profit from additional sales is to ensure that a contribution to profit is made from the special order: the Case Study (below) illustrates this principle.

Case Study

WYVERN BIKE COMPANY: SPECIAL ORDERS

situation

The Wyvern Bike Company produces 100 bikes a week, and sells them for £200 each. Its costs are as follows:

Weekly costs for producing 100 bikes

	£
Direct materials (£40 per bike)	4,000
Direct labour (£50 per bike)	5,000
Production overheads (fixed)	5,000
Total cost	14,000

The owner of the company has been approached by an internet sales company which wishes to buy:

- *either* 50 bikes each week at a price of £120 per bike

- *or* 100 bikes each week at a price of £80 per bike

The bikes can be produced in addition to existing production, with no increase in overheads. The special order is not expected to affect the company's existing sales. How would you advise the owner?

solution

The *absorption cost* of producing one bike is £140 (£14,000 ÷ 100 bikes). The internet sales company is offering either £120 or £80 per bike. On the face of it, with an absorption cost of £140, both orders should be rejected. However, as there will be no increase in production overheads, we can use *marginal costing* to help with decision-making.

The *marginal cost* per bike is £90 (direct materials £40 + direct labour £50), and so any contribution, ie selling price less marginal cost, will be profit:

- **50 bikes at £120 each**

  Although below absorption cost, the offer price of £120 is above the marginal cost of £90 and increases profit by the amount of the £30 extra contribution, ie (£120 – £90) x 50 bikes = £1,500 extra profit.

- **100 bikes at £80 each**

  This offer price is below absorption cost of £140 and marginal cost of £90; therefore there will be a fall in profit if this order is undertaken of (£80 – £90) x 100 bikes = £1,000 reduced profit.

weekly income statements	Existing production of 100 units	Existing production + 50 units @ £120 each	Existing production + 100 units @ £80 each
	£	£	£
Sales revenue (per week):			
100 bikes at £200 each	20,000	20,000	20,000
50 bikes at £120 each	–	6,000	–
100 bikes at £80 each	–	–	8,000
	20,000	26,000	28,000
Less production costs:			
Direct materials (£40 per unit)	4,000	6,000	8,000
Direct labour (£50 per unit)	5,000	7,500	10,000
Production overheads (fixed)	5,000	5,000	5,000
PROFIT	6,000	7,500	5,000

The conclusion is that the first special order from the internet sales company should be accepted, and the second declined. The general rule is that, once the fixed overheads have been recovered (ie break-even has been reached), provided additional units can be sold at a price above marginal cost, then profits will increase.

COST AND REVENUE PLANNING

The principles of marginal costing can also be used to establish the effect of changes in costs and revenues on the profit of the business. Such changes include

– a reduction in selling prices in order to sell a greater number of units of output and to increase profits

– an increase in selling prices (which may cause a reduction in the number of units sold) in order to increase profits

Any change in selling prices and output will have an effect on sales revenues and on variable costs; there may also be an effect on fixed costs. The best way to show such changes is to use a columnar layout which shows costs and revenues as they are at present and then – in further columns – how they will be affected by any proposed changes. This method is used in the Case Study which follows.

Case Study

BROOKES AND COMPANY: COST AND REVENUE PLANNING

situation

Brookes and Company produces tool kits for bikes. The company produces 100,000 tool kits each year and the costs per unit of output are:

	£
Direct materials	2.20
Direct labour	2.00
Variable production overheads	0.80
Fixed production overheads	0.40
Fixed non-production overheads	0.60
	6.00

The selling price per tool kit is £10.00

The managing director of the business has been thinking about how to increase profits for next year. He has asked you, as an accounts assistant, to look at the following two proposals from a cost accounting viewpoint.

Proposal 1

To reduce the selling price of each tool kit to £9.00. This is expected to increase sales by 20,000 kits each year to a total of 120,000 kits. Apart from changes in variable costs, there would be no change in fixed costs.

Proposal 2

To increase the selling price of each tool kit to £12.00. This is expected to reduce sales by 20,000 kits each year to a total of 80,000 kits. Apart from changes in variable costs, there would be a reduction of £5,000 in fixed production overheads.

You are to write a report to the managing director stating your advice, giving reasons and workings. Each of the two proposals is to be considered on its own merits without reference to the other proposal.

solution

The following calculations, presented in columnar format, will form an appendix to the report to the managing director. Note that the three money columns deal with the existing production level, and then the two proposals.

BROOKES AND COMPANY

Cost and revenue planning for next year

	existing output (100,000 units) £	proposal 1 (120,000 units) £	proposal 2 (80,000 units) £
Sales revenue:			
100,000 units at £10.00 per unit	1,000,000		
120,000 units at £9.00 per unit		1,080,000	
80,000 units at £12.00 per unit			960,000
TOTAL REVENUE	1,000,000	1,080,000	960,000
Direct materials at £2.20 per unit	220,000	264,000	176,000
Direct labour at £2.00 per unit	200,000	240,000	160,000
Variable production overhead at £0.80 per unit	80,000	96,000	64,000
Fixed production overhead	40,000	40,000	35,000
Fixed non-production overhead	60,000	60,000	60,000
TOTAL COSTS	600,000	700,000	495,000
PROFIT	400,000	380,000	465,000

Tutorial notes:
- fixed production overheads: 100,000 units at £0.40 per unit (note £5,000 reduction under proposal 2)
- fixed non-production overheads: 100,000 units at £0.60 per unit

REPORT		
To:	Managing Director	
From:	Accounts Assistant	
Date:	Today	

Cost and revenue planning for next year

Introduction

- You asked for my comments on the proposals for next year's production.

- I have looked at the expected profits if
  - we continue to sell 100,000 units each year at a selling price of £10.00 each
  - selling price is reduced to £9.00 per unit, with sales volume expected to increase to 120,000 units each year
  - selling price is increased to £12.00 per unit, with sales volume expected to decrease to 80,000 units each year

Report

- Please refer to the calculations sheet.

- At existing levels of production, the contribution (selling price – variable costs) per unit is:

  £10.00 – (£2.20 + £2.00 + £0.80) = £5.00 per unit x 100,000 units = £500,000

  Fixed costs total £100,000.

  Therefore profit is £400,000.

- For proposal 1, the contribution per unit is:

  £9.00 – (£2.20 + £2.00 + £0.80) = £4.00 per unit x 120,000 units = £480,000

  Fixed costs total £100,000.

  Therefore profit is £380,000.

- For proposal 2, the contribution per unit is:

  £12.00 – (£2.20 + £2.00 + £0.80) = £7.00 per unit x 80,000 units = £560,000

  Fixed costs total £95,000.

  Therefore profit is £465,000.

Conclusion

- Proposal 2 maximises the contribution from each unit of output.

- Although we expect to sell fewer units, the total contribution is greater.

- There is a small reduction in fixed costs under this proposal.

- Before proposal 2 is adopted, we would need to be sure of the accuracy of the expected fall in sales volume.

MARGINAL COSTING IN DECISION-MAKING

We have seen how marginal costing principles can be useful in short-tem decision-making. Nevertheless, there are a number of points that must be borne in mind:

- *fixed period costs must be covered*

  A balance needs to be struck between the output that is sold at above marginal cost and the output that is sold at absorption cost. The overall contribution from output must cover the fixed period costs of the business and provide a profit. Overall output should be sold at a high enough price to provide a contribution to fixed costs.

- *separate markets for marginal cost*

  It is sensible business practice to separate out the markets where marginal cost is used. For example, a business would not quote a price based on absorption cost to retailer A and a price based on marginal cost to retailer B, when A and B are both in the same town! It would be better to seek new markets – perhaps abroad – with prices based on marginal cost.

- *effect on customers*

  One of the problems of using marginal cost pricing to attract new business is that it is difficult to persuade the customer to pay closer to, or above, absorption cost later on. Thus one of the dangers of using marginal cost is that profits can be squeezed quite dramatically if the technique is used too widely.

- *problems of product launch on marginal cost basis*

  There is great temptation to launch a new product at the keenest possible price – below absorption cost (but above marginal cost). If the product is highly successful, it could well alter the cost structure of the business. However, it could also lead to the collapse of sales of older products so that most sales are derived from output priced on the marginal cost basis – it may then be difficult to increase up prices to above absorption cost levels.

- *special edition products*

  Many businesses use marginal costing techniques to sell off older products at a keen price. For example, car manufacturers with a new model due in a few months' time will package the old model with 'special edition' features and sell it at a low price (but above marginal cost).

Chapter Summary

- Short-term decisions are those actions which will affect the costs and revenues over the next few weeks and months.

- Break-even analysis distinguishes between fixed period costs and variable product costs.

- The relationship between sales revenue, fixed costs and variable costs is used to ascertain the break-even point, by means of a calculation, a table, or a graph.

- Break-even analysis can show:

  - break-even point in units of production

  - break-even point in sales revenue

  - profit or loss at a given levels of production and sales revenue

- Break-even analysis has its limitations. Care needs to be taken to make sure that is is applied appropriately.

- Limiting factors (or scarce resources) are those aspects of a business which affect output, eg availability of materials, skilled labour, machine hours. The key to dealing with limiting factors is to *maximise the contribution per unit of limiting factor*.

- 'Special order' pricing is where a business uses spare capacity to make extra sales of its product at a lower price than normal. In order to increase profits the special order selling price must be above marginal cost.

- Marginal costing principles are used in short-term decision-making for break-even, limiting factors, and 'special order' pricing.

Key Terms

relevant costs	those costs that are changed by a decision
irrelevant costs	those costs that are not affected by a decision
sunk costs	past costs which are irrelevant to decision-making
cost behaviour	the way in which costs behave in different ways as the volume of output or activity changes
contribution	selling price less variable cost

cost, volume, profit (CVP) analysis of the costs of output, the volume of output, and the profit made

break even the point at which neither a profit nor a loss is made, calculated in units of output as follows:

$$\frac{fixed\ costs\ (£)}{contribution\ per\ unit\ (£)}$$

margin of safety the amount by which sales exceed the break-even point; calculated as a percentage as follows:

$$\frac{current\ output - break\text{-}even\ output}{current\ output} \times \frac{100}{1}$$

target profit the output that needs to be sold to give a certain amount of profit, calculated in number of units of output as follows:

$$\frac{fixed\ costs\ (£) + target\ profit\ (£)}{contribution\ per\ unit}$$

contribution sales (CS) ratio ratio which expresses the amount of contribution in relation to the amount of the selling price:

$$\frac{contribution\ (£)}{selling\ price\ (£)}$$

CS ratio is used to calculate the sales revenue needed to break-even as follows:

$$\frac{fixed\ costs\ (£)}{CS\ ratio}$$

limiting factor (or scarce resources) those aspects of a business which affect output

marginal cost the cost of producing one extra unit of output

Activities

9.1 Bright Limited estimates that costs and revenue for next month will be:

selling price   £10 per unit

variable cost   £5 per unit

fixed costs for the month   £7,500

Maximum output is 3,000 units per month

As an accounts assistant, you are to complete the following table:

units of output	fixed costs	variable costs	total cost	sales revenue	profit/(loss)
	£	£	£	£	£
0					
500					
1,000					
1,500					
2,000					
2,500					
3,000					

9.2 Mike Etherton, a manufacturer of cricket bats, has the following monthly costs:

Material cost   £8 per bat

Labour cost   £12 per bat

Selling price   £35 per bat

Overheads (fixed)   £12,000

You are to:

(a) Prepare a table showing costs, sales revenue, and profit or loss for production of bats in multiples of 100 up to 1,200.

(b) Draw a graph showing the break-even point.

(c) Prove your answer by calculation.

(d) Read off the graph the profit or loss if 200 bats, and 1,200 bats are sold each month: prove the answer by calculation.

(e) If production is currently 1,000 bats per month, what is the margin of safety, expressed as a percentage and in units?

9.3 Wyvern Limited makes a product which is numbered WV5. The selling price of product WV5 is £28 per unit and the total variable cost is £16 per unit. Wyvern Limited estimates that the fixed costs per quarter associated with this product are £24,000.

(a) **Calculate the budgeted breakeven, in units, for product WV5.**

(b) **Calculate the budgeted breakeven, in £, for product WV5.**

£

(c) **Complete the table below to show the budgeted margin of safety in units, and the margin of safety percentage if Wyvern Limited sells 2,500 units or 4,000 units of product WV5.**

Units of WV5 sold	2,500	4,000
Margin of safety (units)		
Margin of safety percentage		

(d) **If Wyvern Limited wishes to make a profit of £18,000, how many units of WV5 must it sell?**

(e) **If Wyvern Limited reduces the selling price of WV5 by £1, what will be the impact on the breakeven point and the margin of safety, assuming no change in the number of units sold?**

A   The breakeven point will decrease and the margin of safety will increase.

B   The breakeven point will stay the same but the margin of safety will decrease.

C   The breakeven point will decrease and the margin of safety will stay the same.

D   The breakeven point will increase and the margin of safety will decrease.

Answer A or B or C or D.

9.4 Riley Limited has made the following estimates for next month:

Selling price	£25 per unit
Variable cost	£10 per unit
Fixed costs for the month	£300,000
Forecast output	30,000 units
Maximum output	40,000 units

As an accounts assistant, you are to carry out the following tasks:

Task 1

Calculate:

*   the contribution sales ratio

*   the break-even point in units

*   the break-even point in sales revenue

*   the margin of safety in units and sales revenue at the forecast output

*   the number of units to generate a profit of £100,000

Task 2

Calculate the profit at:

*   the forecast output

*   the maximum output

Task 3

One of the managers has suggested that, if the selling price were reduced to £20 per unit, then sales would be increased to the maximum output.

*   For this new strategy, you are to calculate:

    –   the contribution sales ratio

    –   the break-even point in units

    –   the break-even point in sales revenue

    –   the margin of safety in units and sales revenue

    –   the forecast profit

*   Write a report to the general manager advising whether you believe that the new strategy should be implemented. (Use a copy of the report form in the Appendix.)

9.5 Sesame Shoes Limited manufactures shoes at its factory in Wyvern. It has three shoe ranges – the 'Madrid', the 'Paris', and the 'Rome'. The expected monthly costs and sales information for each range is as follows:

Product	'Madrid'	'Paris'	'Rome'
Sales and production units*	5,000	3,000	500
Machine hours per month	2,500	1,200	375
Total sales revenue	£150,000	£120,000	£30,000
Total direct materials	£50,000	£45,000	£10,000
Total direct labour	£25,000	£24,000	£6,000
Total variable overheads	£10,000	£9,000	£1,250

* note: a unit is a pair of shoes

The total expected monthly fixed costs relating to the production of all shoes are £72,800.

As an accounts assistant at Sesame Shoes Limited, you are to carry out the following tasks.

Task 1

Complete the table below to show for each product range the expected contribution per unit.

Product	'Madrid' £	'Paris' £	'Rome' £
Selling price per unit			
Less: Unit variable costs			
Direct materials			
Direct labour			
Variable overheads			
Contribution per unit			

Task 2

If the company only manufactures the 'Madrid' range, calculate the number of units it would need to make and sell each month to cover the fixed costs of £72,800.

Task 3

The breakdown of a machine used in the manufacture of shoes has reduced available machine time from 4,075 to 3,000 hours. The finance director asks you to calculate the contribution of each unit (pair of shoes) per machine hour.

Using the data from Task 1, complete the table below.

Product	'Madrid'	'Paris'	'Rome'
Contribution per unit			
Machine hours per unit			
Contribution per machine hour			

Task 4

Using the data from Task 3, calculate how many units of each of product ranges 'Madrid', 'Paris', and 'Rome' the company should make and sell in order to maximise its profits using 3,000 machine hours.

9.6 Dean Limited makes two products – A and B. Both products are made from the same type of direct materials. These materials are currently in short supply. At present the company can obtain only 500 kilos of the direct materials each week. The production manager seeks your guidance as to the 'mix' of products that should be produced each week. The information available is:

Product		A	B
	Selling price per unit	£150	£200
less	Unit variable costs	£120	£150
equals	Contribution per unit	£30	£50
	Kilos of direct materials per unit	2	4
	Demand per week (in units)	200	150

The weekly fixed overheads of the business are £4,000.

As an accounts assistant, you are to write a report to the production manager giving your recommendations for next week's production. Support your views with a forecast income statement. (Use a copy of the report form in the Appendix.)

9.7 You are an accounts assistant at Durning Foods Limited. The company produces ready meals which are sold in supermarkets and convenience stores. You have just received the following email from the general manager:

EMAIL

From: General Manager

To: Accounts Assistant

Subject: Production line of Indian meals

Date: 8 October 20-8

Please prepare a cost and revenue plan for the Indian meals production line for November.

We plan to sell 36,000 meals in November and will base our projection on the cost and revenue behaviour patterns experienced during July to September.

The cost accounting records show the following for July, August and September:

DURNING FOODS LIMITED: Production line for Indian meals

Actual results for July to September 20-8

	July	August	September
Number of meals sold	33,500	31,000	34,700
	£	£	£
Direct materials	25,125	23,250	26,025
Direct labour	15,075	13,950	15,615
Direct expenses	6,700	6,200	6,940
Overheads for Indian meals production line	12,525	12,150	12,705
Other production overheads	4,000	4,000	4,000
Total cost	63,425	59,550	65,285
Sales revenue	67,000	62,000	69,400
Profit	3,575	2,450	4,115

Task 1

- Use the above information to identify the cost and revenue projections to be used in your projections.

- Use the identified cost and revenue behaviour patterns to complete the projection for November 20-8.

Task 2

After you have completed Task 1, the general manager sends you the following email:

EMAIL
From   General Manager
To   Accounts Assistant
Subject Production line of Indian meals
Date   14 October 20-8

Thank you for your work on the cost and revenue projections for November.

Our Buying Department has found an alternative supplier of materials – meat, rice and sauces. The buyers say that the quality is better than we use at the moment and the price is 20 per cent cheaper. However, we will need to buy in larger quantities to get such good prices. To allow for this, I would like to increase production and sales to 40,000 meals in November.

Could you please recalculate the cost and revenue projections for November 20-8 based on the increased activity and taking advantage of the cheaper prices?

Also, please calculate the break-even point in terms of the number of meals to be sold in November if we make this change. Please include a note of the margin of safety we will have.

- Use your identified cost and revenue behaviour patterns to adjust for the change in material costs and to prepare a revised projection for November 20-8 based on sales of 40,000 meals.

- Calculate the break-even point in terms of meals to be sold in November if the lower priced materials are used.

- Calculate the margin of safety, expressed as a percentage of the increased planned activity for November.

9.8   Westfield Limited makes 2,000 units of product Exe each month. The company's costs are:

monthly costs for making 2,000 units of Exe

	£
direct materials	6,000
direct labour	4,000
production overheads (fixed)	8,000
total cost	18,000

Each unit of Exe is sold for £12.

The management of the company has been approached by a buyer who wishes to purchase:

- *either* 200 units of Exe each month at a price of £6 per unit

- *or* 500 units of Exe each month at a price of £4 per unit

The extra units can be produced in addition to existing production, with no increase in overheads. The special order is not expected to affect the company's existing sales. How would you advise the management?

9.9 Popcan Limited manufactures and sells a soft drink which the company sells at 25p per can. Currently output is 150,000 cans per month, which represents 75 per cent of production capacity. The company has an opportunity to use the spare capacity by producing the product for a supermarket chain which will sell it under their own label. The supermarket chain is willing to pay 18p per can.

Use the following information to advise the management of Popcan Limited if the offer from the supermarket should be accepted:

POPCAN LIMITED

Costs per can

	pence
Direct materials	5
Direct labour	5
Production overheads (variable)	4
Production overheads (*fixed)	6

* fixed production overheads are apportioned on the basis of current output

---

10 Long-term decisions

this chapter covers...

In this chapter we see how cost accounting information is used to help a business or organisation to make long-term decisions. In particular, we focus on capital investment projects. For example, if we need a new photocopier for the office, shall we buy a Toshiba or a Canon model?

The main methods of capital investment appraisal are:

- *payback period*
- *discounted cash flow, also known as net present value*

We look at what capital investment appraisal involves, and then study these two methods by means of a Case Study, and make comparisons between them. Towards the end of the chapter, we look briefly at a further capital investment appraisal method called internal rate of return.

WHAT IS CAPITAL INVESTMENT APPRAISAL?

Capital investment appraisal enables a business or organisation to make decisions as to whether or not to invest in a particular capital investment project and, where there are alternatives, to assist in deciding in which to invest.

You will readily appreciate that, whether at home or at work, resources are limited in supply and, as a result, there is a need to use them in such a way as to obtain the maximum benefits from them. To do this it is necessary to choose between various financial alternatives available; for example, on a personal level, we have to make decisions such as:

Should I save my spare cash in a bank's instant access account, or should I deposit it for a fixed term?

Should I save up for a car, or should I buy on hire purchase?

Which make of car, within my price range, should I buy?

Should I rent a house or should I buy, taking out a mortgage?

While these decisions are personal choices, the management of businesses of all sizes are faced with making choices, as are other organisations such as local authorities and central government.

The management of any business is constantly having to make decisions on *what* goods or services to produce, *where* to produce, *how* to produce, and *how much* to produce. For each major choice to be made, some method of appraisal has to be applied to ensure that, whatever decisions are taken, they are consistent with the objectives of the organisation. This means that it is necessary to look at all the alternatives available and to choose the one that is going to give the most benefit. For example, a business may have to decide whether to replace its existing machinery with new, more up-to-date machinery. If it decides on new machinery, it then has to choose between different makes of machine and different models, each having a different cost and each capable of affecting output in a different way. The decision will affect the performance of the business – its profit or loss and its cash flow.

WHAT IS A CAPITAL INVESTMENT PROJECT?

A capital investment project is the spending of money now in order to receive benefits (or reduce costs) in future years; it is illustrated in the diagram on the next page.

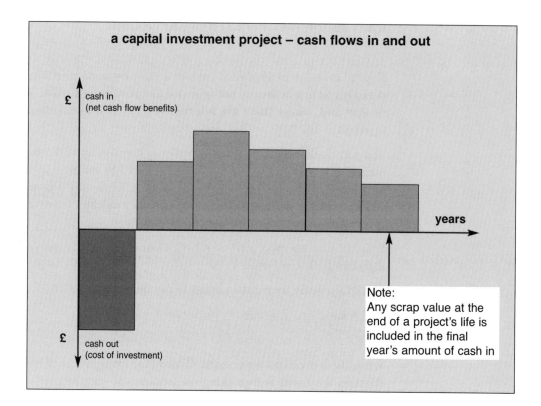

Here, the cost of the investment, or capital expenditure, is being spent at the start – either at the very beginning of the project (often stated as 'year 0'), or during the first year. The difference between these two is illustrated by the following:

- bought a new photocopier is a cash outflow at the beginning of the project
- the installation of a new production line may well incur cash outflows during the first year

The cost of the investment brings benefits (or reduced costs) in future years for as long as the project lasts. Businesses and organisations need to apply capital investment appraisal methods to ensure that the long-term decisions they make are the correct choices.

INVESTMENT APPRAISAL IN CONTEXT

As well as the cash flows in and out for a capital investment project, a number of other factors need to be considered before a long-term decision is made. These factors include:

- *Source of finance*. Where is the money coming from to finance the project? Is it from a cash surplus, an existing or new bank overdraft, loans? A limited company may decide on a share or debenture (loan) issue to raise the finance for a large project. Assets such as machinery, equipment and vehicles are often financed using hire purchase and leasing.

- *Cost of capital*. All finance has a cost – invariably expressed as a rate of return. The rate of return will be different for each source of finance – from the interest foregone on cash surpluses, to that which must be paid on bank overdrafts and loans. With ordinary shares, the cost of capital is the dividend that shareholders expect to receive. Hire purchase and leasing payments include the interest cost. Note that, with variable interest rates, cost of capital may well vary during the life of a project.

- *Total estimated cost of project*. It is important to forecast accurately the total capital expenditure cost of projects. Historically, the cost of large-scale projects has often been under-estimated and the final actual cost has been much higher than anticipated, leading to financial difficulties.

- *Taxation implications*. A project will usually include both tax allowances and payments. The allowances occur when new assets – such as machinery, equipment and vehicles – are purchased; called writing down allowances, these reduce the amount of tax to be paid. However, the cost savings or increasing profits of the investment project will increase overall profitability of the business and will lead to more tax being paid.

- *Working capital requirements*. Most projects will also require an investment in working capital – inventories, receivables and payables. Thus an amount of working capital is needed at the start, and throughout the project's life. It will only be recovered at the end of the project.

- *Audit of project*. It is important to keep a regular check on costs to ensure that they are in line with the estimates. There are three separate phases that should be audited:

  – costs of bringing the project into commission

  – operational costs

  – decommissioning costs

- *Other considerations*

  Economic climate – recession or period of growth.

  Political implications – a possible change of government may affect investment decisions.

  Commissioning – the length of time that it will take for the project to be up and running.

  Training – the costs and implications of staff training.

Location – where the project is to be located, and subsequent effects on the culture of the organisation.

Capacity – effect on overall output of the organisation.

Product life cycle – the implications on the project of the stage of the company's output in the product life cycle.

AYE OR BEE: WHICH PROJECT?
MAKING THE DECISION

situation

A business is investing in a new project and has to make the choice between Project Aye and Project Bee. The initial cost and the net cash flow (income, less expenses but not depreciation) to the business have been calculated over five years for each project as follows:

	PROJECT AYE	PROJECT BEE
Initial cost at the beginning of the project	£20,000	£28,000
Net cash inflow:		
Year 1	£8,000	£10,000
Year 2	£12,000	£10,000
Year 3	£5,000	£8,000
Year 4	£4,000	£9,000
Year 5	£2,000	£9,000

- At the end of year 5, both projects will have a scrap value of £1,000; this amount is already included in the year 5 cash inflows.
- Only one project can be undertaken.
- The business requires an annual rate of return of 10 per cent on new projects.

Which project should be chosen?

solution

The two methods commonly used to appraise a capital investment project such as this are:

- payback period
- discounted cash flow

These methods will be considered in this chapter in order to help the business to make its decision. At the end of the chapter we will also look at how the internal rate of return (or discounted cash flow yield) is used in order to make a direct comparison between projects which have different amounts of capital investment at the start.

PAYBACK PERIOD

Payback is the period of time it takes for the initial cost of capital investment to be repaid from net cash inflows.

From the Case Study of Projects Aye and Bee, the cash flows and the cumulative cash flows (ie net cash flows to date) are shown in the table below. From this information it can be seen that project Aye costs £20,000 (paid out at the beginning of the project) and it is expected that the net cash flow over the first two years will equal the cost. The payback period for Project Aye is, therefore, two years, while that for Project Bee is three years. So, using payback, Project Aye is preferable because it has the shorter payback period.

Year	PROJECT AYE Cash Flow £	PROJECT AYE Cumulative Cash Flow £	PROJECT BEE Cash Flow £	PROJECT BEE Cumulative Cash Flow £
0	(20,000)	(20,000)	(28,000)	(28,000)
1	8,000	(12,000)	10,000	(18,000)
2	12,000	–	10,000	(8,000)
3	5,000	5,000	8,000	–
4	4,000	9,000	9,000	9,000
5	2,000	11,000	9,000	18,000

The payback period is indicated by the shading

Although these payback periods work out to exact years, they rarely do so in practice – be prepared to calculate part years in Assessments. For example, if Project Aye had an initial cost of £22,000, the payback would require £2,000 of the £5,000 cash flow in year 3. The payback period would then be 2 years + (£2,000/£5,000 x 12 months) = 2 years and 5 months (taken to the nearest month). Note that, in calculating part years, we are making the assumption that cash flows occur at an even rate throughout the year – this may not be the case for all projects – revenues (and costs) may be higher at certain times: for example, retailers are likely to have high revenues in the pre-Christmas shopping period.

The shorter the payback period the better, particularly where high technology or fashion projects are concerned – they may be out-of-date before they reach the end of their useful lives. Earlier cash flows are likely to prove more accurate estimates than later cash flows. Thus, if two projects have the same payback, the one with the greater cash flow in the early years is preferred. For example, consider two projects with a payback period of two years from the following cash flows:

	Wye	Zed
Year 1	£8,000	£12,000
Year 2	£12,000	£8,000

While both projects have the same payback period of two years, Zed is the preferred project under the payback method because of earlier cash flows.

advantages of payback

- it is easy to calculate

- it is easy to understand

- it places emphasis on the earlier cash flows, which are more likely to be accurate than later cash flows

- an ideal capital investment appraisal method for high technology projects

disadvantages of payback

- all cash flows after the payback period are ignored

- within the payback period it fails to take into account the timing of net cash flows, eg Project Aye would still have had a payback of two years even if the cash flows for years one and two had been reversed (as noted above, greater cash flows in earlier years are to be preferred)

- the effects of inflation are ignored

- the time value of money is ignored, unlike the discounted cash flow method

- the life of the asset is not considered

- the estimates of cash flows may be inaccurate

DISCOUNTED CASH FLOW

Discounted cash flow (DCF) is a method of capital investment appraisal which recognises that money has a time value – it compares net cash flows, at their present values, with the initial cost of the capital investment to give a net present value of the capital project.

A quick example of a discounted cash flow decision is where a friend asks you to lend her £1 and offers to repay you either tomorrow, or in one year's time, which will you choose? The answer is clear: you would want the money back sooner rather than later because, if you don't intend to spend it, you can always save it in a bank where it will earn interest. Thus the rate of interest represents the time value of money.

Using £1 as an example, if it is invested with a bank at an interest rate of 10 per cent per year, it will increase as follows:

original investment	£1.00
interest at 10% on £1	£0.10
value at end of first year	£1.10
interest at 10% on £1.10	£0.11
value at end of second year	£1.21

This uses the technique of compound interest. So, with interest rates of 10 per cent per year, we can say that the future value of £1 will be £1.10 at the end of year one, £1.21 at the end of year two, and so on; thus £1 set aside now will gain in value so that, at some time in the future, we will have access to a larger sum of money. However, supposing that we were to receive £1 at the end of year one, what is it worth to us now? To find the answer to this, we need to carry out the following calculation:

$$\text{£1} \quad \times \quad \frac{100}{110^*} \quad = \quad \text{£0.91}$$

* 100 per cent, plus the rate of interest (in this example, 10 per cent).

Therefore, if we had £0.91 now and invested it at 10 per cent per year, we would have £1 at the end of year one. We can say that the *present value* of £1 receivable in one year's time is £0.91. In the same way, £1 receivable in two years' time is £0.83, calculated as follows:

$$\text{£1} \quad \times \quad \frac{100}{110} \quad \times \quad \frac{100}{110} \quad = \quad \text{£0.83}$$

We can build up a *table of present value (PV) factors* (for 10 per cent interest rate) as shown below:

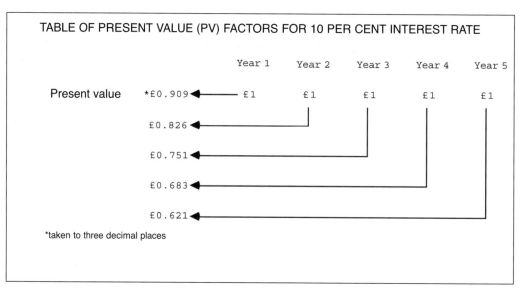

TABLE OF PRESENT VALUE (PV) FACTORS FOR 10 PER CENT INTEREST RATE

	Year 1	Year 2	Year 3	Year 4	Year 5
Present value	*£0.909 ◄——— £1	£1	£1	£1	£1
	£0.826 ◄				
	£0.751 ◄				
	£0.683 ◄				
	£0.621 ◄				

*taken to three decimal places

Note that there is no need to learn how to calculate present value factors – the correct factors will always be given to you in Assessments; the table above shows factors to three decimal places – some AAT Assessments use four decimal places for greater accuracy.

The table of factors reminds us of the basic principle that *money has a time value* and, from this, the further into the future that we expect to receive money, then the lower is its *present value*. Thus the present value (or discount) factors relate to interest rates which represent the cost of capital (ie the rate of return that the business or organisation expects on its money, or the rate of interest it has to pay when borrowing).

Let us now return to the problem of the business which has to choose between Projects Aye and Bee. We will look at this assuming, firstly, a cost of capital – or rate of return – of 10 per cent. For each project, the expected net cash flows are multiplied by the relevant factor to give the *discounted cash flow*; the difference between total discounted cash flow and the initial cost is the *net present value* of the project.

DISCOUNTED CASH FLOW CALCULATIONS

Project Aye

	Cash Flow		Discount Factor		Discounted Cash Flow
	£				£
Year 0*	(20,000)	x	1.000	=	(20,000)
Year 1	8,000	x	0.909	=	7,272
Year 2	12,000	x	0.826	=	9,912
Year 3	5,000	x	0.751	=	3,755
Year 4	4,000	x	0.683	=	2,732
Year 5	2,000	x	0.621	=	1,242
	Net Present Value (NPV)			=	4,913

* Year 0 is the beginning of the project when the initial cost is paid. Some projects such as the installation of a new production line – may well incur cash outflows during the first year.

Notes:

- The initial cost is shown in brackets because it is a cost, whereas the net cash inflows are positive amounts. Net Present Value (NPV) is the net sum of all the discounted cash inflows and outflows.

- When using discount factors, the assumption is made that cash flows occur at the end of each year – apart, that is, from the Year 0 initial cash flow.

Project Bee

	Cash Flow		Discount Factor		Discounted Cash Flow
	£				£
Year 0	(28,000)	x	1.000	=	(28,000)
Year 1	10,000	x	0.909	=	9,090
Year 2	10,000	x	0.826	=	8,260
Year 3	8,000	x	0.751	=	6,008
Year 4	9,000	x	0.683	=	6,147
Year 5	9,000	x	0.621	=	5,589
	Net Present Value (NPV)			=	7,094

Here, with a cost of capital – or rate of return – of 10 per cent, Project Bee is better, producing a considerably higher net present value than Aye. Note that both projects give a positive net present value at 10 per cent: this means that either project will be of benefit to the organisation but Bee is preferable; a negative NPV would indicate that a project should not go ahead.

Thus, using a discounted cash flow method, future cash flows are brought to their value now; this means that, the further on in time that cash flows are receivable, the lower is the net present value.

advantages of discounted cash flow

- all cash flows are used
- the time value of money is used
- the timing of cash flows is taken into account
- although more complex to calculate than payback, when using a table of factors the calculations are easy to make

disadvantages of discounted cash flow:

- the cost of capital rate – or rate of return – is, in practice, difficult to ascertain and may also vary over the life of the project
- the meaning of net present value is not always clear to users of the information
- when comparing two projects, the one with the higher net present value does not always represent the better project for the business or organisation – other factors need to be considered, eg quality of output, compatibility with existing equipment and systems
- the estimates of cash flows may be inaccurate

CAPITAL INVESTMENT APPRAISAL: COMPARISON

It is unlikely that a business will rely on one investment appraisal method only; instead both methods might need to be satisfied before a capital project is given the go-ahead. Supposing, for example, that the organisation, having to choose between Projects Aye and Bee, applied the following criteria: "projects must have a maximum payback period of two-and-a-half years, and must have a positive net present value at a 10 per cent rate of return." How do the two projects compare?

	Project Aye	Project Bee
Payback period	2 years	3 years
NPV at 10 per cent	£4,913	£7,094

Under the criteria that the organisation has laid down, Aye would be chosen. However, Bee seems a better project on the net present value basis and is only rejected because it does not meet the payback period requirement. However, the capital expenditure required for Bee is £8,000 greater than Aye – £28,000 compared with £20,000; this is something which NPV does not take fully into account. To obtain a better analysis, we need to use the method of *internal rate of return* – see next page.

THE USE OF NET PRESENT COST IN DISCOUNTED CASH FLOW

Net present cost uses discounted cash flow methods to compare cash outflows in order to minimise costs.

In this chapter we have used discounted cash flow to appraise capital investment projects, ie capital expenditure at the start of the project with cash inflows over the life of the project – generally resulting in a net present value, a positive figure. A further use of discounted cash flow is to minimise costs – eg making a choice between alternative electricity or telephone suppliers – with the aims of cost effectiveness or cost reduction. The same principles are applied as with capital investment projects but, because we are looking at costs, the preferred choice will be the one with the lower net present cost. This is shown by the following:

- Estimated annual electricity costs from two suppliers, based on a three-year contract:

	POWER UK	MERCIAN ENERGY
Year 1	£2,000	£1,500
Year 2	£2,000	£2,000
Year 3	£2,000	£2,500

- At a cost of capital of 10 per cent, with factors of 0.909, 0.826 and 0.751 for years 1, 2 and 3 respectively, the net present costs of the two suppliers are:

	POWER UK			MERCIAN ENERGY		
		£	£		£	£
Year 1	(2,000) x 0.909	=	(1,818)	(1,500) x 0.909	=	(1,364)
Year 2	(2,000) x 0.826	=	(1,652)	(2,000) x 0.826	=	(1,652)
Year 3	(2,000) x 0.751	=	(1,502)	(2,500) x 0.751	=	(1,878)
Net Present Cost			(4,972)			(4,894)

The preferred supplier – based solely on the calculations – is Mercian Energy, because it is the one with the lower net present cost.

Net present cost can be used in a number of circumstances – both in business and personally – such as:

– choosing a utility supplier

– making finance cost comparisons when buying a car, etc

– comparing loan/mortgage deals from banks

– comparing purchase price and running costs for vehicles and machines

INTERNAL RATE OF RETURN

> Tutorial note: For AAT Assessments you will need to be aware of the meaning of internal rate of return but tasks requiring calculations will not be set.

The principles of discounted cash flow can be developed further in order to calculate the capital investment appraisal method of *internal rate of return* (IRR) – this method is also known as *DCF (Discounted Cash Flow) yield*.

The internal rate of return is the rate of cost of capital at which the present value of the cash inflows exactly balances the initial investment.

In other words, it shows the cost of capital, or rate of return, percentage at which the investment 'breaks-even', ie income equals expenditure, but still applying discounted cash flow principles.

The table, below, is an illustration of how IRR can be found.

We start with a cost of capital which gives a positive net present value – using the example of Projects Aye and Bee we saw earlier on page 283, a 10 per cent cost of capital for Project Aye gives a NPV of £4,913. We increase the cost of capital by one or two percentage points each time, and repeat the NPV calculation (workings not shown here) until, eventually, it becomes negative. This is shown as follows (note that net present value is calculated from column A minus column B):

	PROJECT AYE		
Cost of Capital*	Present Value of Cash Flow	Capital Investment	Net Present Value
	£	£	£
	A	B	A – B
10%	24,913	(20,000)	4,913
12%	23,946	(20,000)	3,946
14%	23,025	(20,000)	3,025
16%	22,177	(20,000)	2,177
18%	21,375	(20,000)	1,375
20%	20,619	(20,000)	619
22%	19,915	(20,000)	(85)
24%	19,242	(20,000)	(758)

* or rate of return

The net present value that balances the present value of cash flow with the initial investment lies between 20% and 22% – closer to 22% than 20%, so we can call it approximately 22% (an answer to the nearest one or two percentage points is acceptable for most long-term decisions).

commenting on internal rate of return

Returning to the two projects, Aye and Bee, the table shows that the IRR for Aye is approximately 22%. Although not shown here, the calculations for Bee are found to be approximately 20%. Thus, Aye gives a higher IRR – this is the preferred capital investment. The reason for this is that Aye requires a lower capital expenditure than Bee, and the timing of its cash flows is weighted towards the earlier years.

The decision-making criteria when using IRR is to:

- accept the higher IRR, where there is a choice between different capital investments
- accept projects with an IRR greater than either the cost of borrowing (the cost of capital), or the rate of return specified by the business or organisation

Thus, while IRR can be compared between two (or more) different capital investments, it can also be applied to cost of capital. In the example we have followed in this chapter, the cost of capital is 10%. The business could have gone ahead with either investment. However, if the cost of capital had been 20%, project Bee would have been rejected and Project Aye accepted – although the 2% margin above the cost of capital is very tight.

advantages of internal rate of return

- all cash flows are used
- the time value of money is used
- the timing of cash flows is taken into account
- it identifies the percentage cost of capital at which projects break-even
- it indicates
  - a margin of safety where IRR is higher than cost of capital
  - a shortfall where IRR is lower than cost of capital

disadvantages of internal rate of return

- it is more complex to calculate and identify
- the meaning of IRR is not always clear to users of the information
- it may not indicate the better project where capital sums invested differ greatly, eg a project with capital invested of £10,000, and giving a slightly higher IRR, may be accepted instead of a £1m project which could bring much greater profits to the business

OTHER CONSIDERATIONS

As well as the numerical techniques that can be used for capital investment appraisal, an organisation must consider a number of other factors before making the final decision. These include:

- *Total implications*. The effect of the project on the organisation as a whole will include implications for
  - sales, with possible increases in output
  - output, with changes in techniques, eg a switch from labour-intensive to machine-intensive output
  - staff, with possible redundancies, training needs, pay structure
  - working capital required for the project
  - needs, such as premises, transport, materials

- *Cost of finance*. Possible changes in the cost of capital will have a direct effect on the viability of the project. For example, an increase in the general level of interest rates will reduce the project's overall profitability. Projects are often financed through fixed interest rate loans, or through hire purchase and leasing, thus establishing some part of the finance at fixed rates; however, invariably working capital is financed by a bank overdraft at variable rates.

- *Taxation considerations*. The project will include the implications of both tax allowances and charges. However, a change in the level of taxation will affect the viability of the project.

- *Forecasting techniques*. These can be used to answer 'what if?' questions: for example, "what if sales increase by 25 per cent?" or "what if materials costs fall by 5 per cent?" In this way, a business or organisation can see how the project is affected by changes to any of the data used in the appraisal.

- *Size of the investment*. A major project can be destabilising for a small business if cash inflows prove to be lower than expected.

REPORTING DECISIONS

Capital investment appraisal decisions often have to be reported to managers, or other appropriate people, in a clear and concise way. The information should include recommendations which are supported by well-presented reasoning.

To conclude, we include a written report addressed to the General Manager on Projects Aye and Bee, which we have looked at in this chapter. The company has the following criteria: "projects must have a payback period not exceeding two-and-a-half years, and must have a positive net present value at a 10 per cent rate of return."

REPORT

To:	General Manager
From:	Accounts Assistant
Date:	Today

Projects Aye and Bee

Introduction

- This report applies capital investment appraisal methods to these two projects.

- In this appraisal, the cash inflows and outflows used are those that have been given.

Report

- Please refer to the calculation sheet *(tutorial note: see page 279 and pages 283)*.

- Both projects are acceptable from a financial viewpoint because they each return a positive net present value (NPV) at a discount rate of 10%, as follows: Project Aye £4,913; Project B £7,094. These calculations assume that net cash inflows occur at the end of each year.

- The payback periods are: Project Aye, 2 years; Project B, 3 years.

- The internal rates of return (IRR) for the projects are: Project Aye, 22%; Project B, 20%. Both of these are well above the required rate of return of 10 per cent.

Conclusion

- Project A meets both the company requirements of payback within two-and-a-half years, and a positive NPV at a 10 per cent rate of return. It also has a higher IRR than Project B.

- Project B does not meet the payback requirement, but does have a positive NPV at a 10 per cent rate of return. It has a lower IRR than Project A.

- Project A has a lower NPV than Project B. While A's initial cost is lower, so is the total discounted cash inflow – the combination of these gives a lower NPV for Project A. This imbalance of NPVs is neutralised by the IRR calculation, which shows Project A to be superior.

- On balance, Project A is recommended:
    - lower initial cost
    - high cash inflows in the first two years
    - quick payback
    - positive NPV
    - higher IRR in relation to the company's required rate of return

<table>
<tr><td rowspan="2" style="background:#333;color:#fff">Case Study</td><td rowspan="2"># PREPARING FOR ASSESSMENT: CAPITAL INVESTMENT APPRAISAL</td></tr>
</table>

PREPARING FOR ASSESSMENT: CAPITAL INVESTMENT APPRAISAL

situation

You are an accounts assistant at Wyvern Limited, a company which manufactures kitchenware such as baking trays, saucepans, etc.

One of the machines in the cutting department is nearing the end of its useful life and Wyvern Ltd is considering purchasing a replacement machine.

Estimates have been made for the initial capital cost, sales revenue and operating costs of the replacement machine, which is expected to have a useful life of three years, at the end of which it will be sold for £10,000.

	Year 0 £000	Year 1 £000	Year 2 £000	Year 3 £000
Capital expenditure	50			
Disposal				10
Other cash flows:				
Sales revenue		45	65	50
Operating costs		25	30	30

The company appraises capital investment projects using a 10% cost of capital.

You have been asked to:

- complete the table below (shown in the solution) and to calculate the net present value of the proposed replacement machine (to the nearest £000).
- state whether the net present value is positive or negative.
- calculate the payback period of the proposed replacement machine to the nearest whole month.

solution

You complete the table as follows (your figures shown in italics):

	Year 0 £000	Year 1 £000	Year 2 £000	Year 3 £000
Capital expenditure	*(50)*			
Disposal				*10*
Sales revenue		*45*	*65*	*50*
Operating costs		*(25)*	*(30)*	*(30)*
Net cash flows	*(50)*	*20*	*35*	*30*
PV factors	1.0000	0.9091	0.8264	0.7513
Discounted cash flows	*(50)*	*18*	*29*	*23*
Net present value	*20*			

Tutorial note: AAT Assessments may give the PV (present value) factors to four decimal places for greater accuracy.

The net present value is positive.

The payback is 1 year and 10 months

ie year 1 £20,000 + (year 2 £30,000/£35,000 x 12), using net cash flows

Chapter Summary

- Capital investment appraisal uses a number of methods to help in management decision-making.

- The main methods are payback period and discounted cash flow.

- Businesses often use a combination of appraisal methods before making long-term decisions about major projects.

- Internal rate of return (also known as DCF yield) is used to rank projects, while still applying the principles of discounted cash flow.

- Before authorising a capital project, other considerations include:
  - total implications for the organisation
  - cost of finance, and effect of changes
  - taxation
  - forecasting techniques to answer 'what if?' questions
  - size of the investment relative to the size of the business

Key Terms

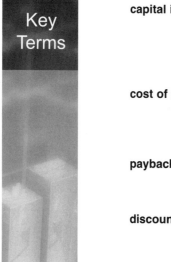

capital investment appraisal   enables a business or organisation to make decisions as to whether or not to invest in a particular capital investment project and, where there are alternatives, to help to assist in deciding in which to invest

cost of capital   the percentage cost of financing an investment – either the rate of return that the business expects on its money, or the rate of interest it has to pay when borrowing

payback period   period of time it takes for the initial cost of the capital investment to be repaid from net cash inflows

discounted cash flow   capital investment appraisal method that uses cash flows and recognises the time value of money

net present value (NPV)	the value of cash outflows and inflows for a project discounted to present-day amounts
net present cost	uses discounted cash flow methods to compare cash outflows in order to minimise costs
internal rate of return (IRR)	the rate of return at which the net present value of cash inflows equals the cost of the initial investment

Activities

TABLE OF DISCOUNTED CASH FLOW FACTORS (to three decimal places)								
Cost of capital/ rate of return	10%	12%	14%	16%	18%	20%	22%	24%
Year 1	0.909	0.893	0.877	0.862	0.847	0.833	0.820	0.806
Year 2	0.826	0.797	0.769	0.743	0.718	0.694	0.672	0.650
Year 3	0.751	0.712	0.675	0.641	0.609	0.579	0.551	0.524
Year 4	0.683	0.636	0.592	0.552	0.516	0.482	0.451	0.423
Year 5	0.621	0.567	0.519	0.476	0.437	0.402	0.370	0.341
Year 6	0.564	0.507	0.456	0.410	0.370	0.335	0.303	0.275

Tutorial note: In Assessments you will always be given the appropriate factors.

10.1 Robert Smith is considering two major capital investment projects for his business. Only one project can be chosen and the following information is available:

	Project Exe £	Project Wye £
Initial cost at the beginning of the project	80,000	100,000
Net cash inflows, year: 1	40,000	20,000
2	40,000	30,000
3	20,000	50,000
4	10,000	50,000
5	10,000	40,000

The initial cost occurs at the beginning of the project and you may assume that the net cash inflows will arise at the end of each year. Smith requires an annual rate of return of 12 per cent. Neither project will have any residual value at the end of five years.

To help Robert Smith make his decision, as accounts assistant you are to:

• produce numerical assessments of the two projects based on the following capital investment appraisal methods:

   (a)   the payback period

   (b)   the net present value

• write a report to Robert Smith on the relative merits of the project appraisal methods, and advise him which capital investment, if either, should be undertaken.

10.2   Sesame Shoes Limited manufactures shoes at its factory in Wyvern. The company requires an annual rate of return of 10% on any new project. The Managing Director has asked you to appraise the financial effects of developing a new range of shoes. You are given the following information relating to this project.

	Year 0 £000	Year 1 £000	Year 2 £000	Year 3 £000	Year 4 £000	Year 5 £000
Design costs	–	95	–	–	–	–
Sales revenue	–	–	60	80	100	50
Variable costs	–	–	30	40	50	25
10% Present value factor	1.000	0.909	0.826	0.751	0.683	0.621

Task 1

Calculate for the new project:

(a)   the payback period

(b)   the net present value

Task 2

A few days after submitting your calculations to the Managing Director, she says to you:

"I have calculated the internal rate of return on the new project to be almost 20 per cent. What I don't understand is whether this is good or bad in relation to the 10 per cent return we require on new projects."

Explain the significance of the internal rate of return in relation to the return required on new projects. (There is no need to show how IRR is calculated.)

10.3 You are an accounts assistant at Durning Foods Limited. The company produces ready meals which are sold in supermarkets and convenience stores. You have just received the following email from the general manager:

EMAIL

From   General Manager

To   Accounts Assistant

Subject   Purchase of new vehicles

Date   10 November 20-4

We are considering the purchase and operation of our own fleet of delivery vehicles at the end of this year.

The distribution manager tells me that we will be able to cancel our current delivery contract and, as a result, there will be cash savings of £28,300 each year from 20-5 onwards, after taking account of the vehicle operating costs.

The vehicles will cost us £80,000 and will have a resale value of £10,000 when they are sold at the end of 20-8.

Please appraise this proposal from a financial viewpoint. I need to know the payback period and the net present value. As you know, the maximum required payback period is three years and, for net present value, we require a return of 12 per cent.

Task 1

Use the working paper on the next page to calculate the net present value and the payback period of the proposed investment. Ignore inflation and calculate all money amounts to the nearest £.

Task 2

Write a report, dated 12 November 20-4, to the General Manager evaluating the proposal from a financial viewpoint. State any assumptions you have made in your analysis. (Use a copy of the report form in the Appendix.)

DURNING FOODS LIMITED

Working paper for the financial appraisal of purchase of delivery vehicles

DISCOUNTED CASH FLOW

Year	Cash Flow	Discount Factor at 12%	Discounted Cash Flow
	£		£
20-4	_____	1.000	_____
20-5	_____	0.893	_____
20-6	_____	0.797	_____
20-7	_____	0.712	_____
20-8	_____	0.636	_____

Net Present Value (NPV)   ▬▬▬▬▬▬▬

PAYBACK PERIOD

Year	Cash Flow	Cumulative Cash Flow
	£	£
20-4	_____	_____
20-5	_____	_____
20-6	_____	_____
20-7	_____	_____
20-8	_____	_____

Payback period = _____

10.4 The Wyvern Bike Company is planning to introduce a new range of bikes in addition to its existing range. The company requires an annual rate of return of 12 per cent on any new project. The Managing Director has asked you, the accounts assistant, to appraise the financial effects of introducing the new range. You are given the following information relating to this project (see next page).

	Year 0 £000	Year 1 £000	Year 2 £000	Year 3 £000	Year 4 £000	Year 5 £000
Development costs	40	60	–	–	–	–
Sales revenue	–	–	75	90	150	100
Variable costs	–	–	30	36	60	40
12% Present value factor	1.000	0.893	0.797	0.712	0.636	0.567

Task 1

Calculate for the new project:

(a)   the payback period

(b)   the net present value

Task 2

Use the data from Task 1 to prepare a report to the Managing Director on the new bike project. Your report should be based on the format shown in this chapter and will:

(a)   identify *two* additional items of information relevant to appraising this project

(b)   make a recommendation to accept or reject the project based on its net present value

10.5   Printpront Limited is a printing company. It needs to replace a printing press that is nearing the end of its working life.

Estimates have been made for the initial capital cost, sales income and operating costs of the replacement printing press, which is expected to have a useful life of three years, at the end of which it will be sold for £20,000.

	Year 0 £000	Year 1 £000	Year 2 £000	Year 3 £000
Capital expenditure	90			
Disposal				20
Other cash flows:				
Sales revenue		55	70	60
Operating costs		12	15	19

The company appraises capital investment projects using a 15% cost of capital.

(a)   Complete the table below and calculate the net present value of the proposed replacement printing press (to the nearest £000).

	Year 0 £000	Year 1 £000	Year 2 £000	Year 3 £000
Capital expenditure				
Disposal				
Sales revenue				
Operating costs				
Net cash flows				
PV factors	1.0000	0.8696	0.7561	0.6575
Discounted cash flows				
Net present value				

Tick to show if the net present value is

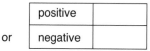

positive	
or | negative | |

(b)   Calculate the payback period of the proposed replacement printing press to the nearest whole month.

The payback period is ———— year(s) and ———— months.

10.6   You are an accounts assistant at Laceby Limited. You have been given the task of investigating the cost the company pays for electricity and gas, with a view to reducing costs. You have contacted two different suppliers for both electricity and gas and, over a contract period of three years, you have estimated the annual costs. You have applied the principles of discounted cash flow to these costs and have calculated the following net present costs for each potential supplier over the three year period:

Electricity	Wyvern Energy	net present cost	£8,550
	Power Plus	net present cost	£7,950
Gas	WestGas	net present cost	£10,700
	Thermogas	net present cost	£11,250

On the basis of cost, which suppliers will you recommend to the management of Laceby Limited?

(a)   electricity: Wyvern Energy; gas: WestGas

(b)   electricity: Wyvern Energy; gas: Thermogas

(c)   electricity: Power Plus; gas WestGas

(d)   electricity: Power Plus; gas Thermogas

Answer (a) or (b) or (c) or (d)

Answers to activities

CHAPTER 1: AN INTRODUCTION TO COST ACCOUNTING

1.1   (a)   •   The principle behind this Activity is the identification of relevant costs
•   Whilst the type of organisation selected may well not fit with the exact layout for a manufacturing business, as shown on page 13, the Activity should generate thought and discussion of costs involved
•   As an example, an outline of the costs incurred by a school or college is as follows:

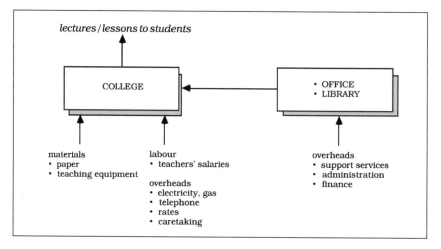

   (b)   •   What are the units of output of the organisation to which costs can be charged?
•   The main sections of the organisation should be identified. Does the costing system in use charge costs to these sections, whether or not they are formally called cost centres?
•   In the school/college described above, the example cost unit is student hours, and cost centres examples are teaching departments, learning resources, administration.

   (c)   •   Responsibility centres are sections of a business or organisation for which a manager is accountable.
•   Examples of responsibility centres are:
   –   cost centres
   –   profit centres
   –   investment centres

1.2   (a)   •   cost centres – section of a business to which costs can be charged
•   profit centre – section of a business to which costs can be charged, revenue can be identified, and profit can be calculated
•   investment centre – section of a business where profit can be compared with the amount of money invested in the centre

   (b)   •   school or college – teaching departments, eg languages, science; also administrative departments, eg human resources, educational technology
•   manufacturing business – by product, eg product A, product B, or by factory, eg Birmingham, Coventry

1.3

REPORT

To: Finance Director
From: Accounts Assistant
Date: today

Costs and income for last year
I report on the details of the costs and income for last year of each section of the business.
Details are as follows:

	Newspapers and magazines	Books	Stationery
Cost Centre	£000	£000	£000
• materials	155	246	122
• labour	65	93	58
• expenses	27	35	25
• total	247	374	205
Profit Centre			
Revenue	352	544	230
less Costs (see above)	247	374	205
Profit	105	170	25
Investment Centre			
Profit (see above)	105	170	25
Investment	420	850	250
Expressed as a percentage	25%	20%	10%

1.4 (a) See text, pages 13-17

(b) • raw materials: variable
• factory rent: fixed
• telephone: semi-variable
• direct labour: variable
• indirect labour: fixed
• commission to sales staff: variable

Classifying costs by behaviour identifies them as being fixed, or semi-variable, or variable. This helps with decision making – the business might be able to alter the balance between fixed and variable costs in order to increase profits.For example, a furniture manufacturing business will have to make decisions on whether to use direct labour (variable cost) or machinery (fixed cost) for many of the production processes. The decision will be based very much on the expected level of sales, ie for lower sales it is likely to make greater use of direct labour, while for higher sales a more machine-intensive method of production might be used.

1.5

tubular steel	direct materials
factory supervisor's salary	indirect labour
wages of employee operating moulding machine	direct labour
works canteen assistant's wages	indirect labour
rates of factory	indirect expenses
power to operate machines	indirect expenses*
factory heating and lighting	indirect expenses
plastic for making chair seats	direct materials
hire of special machinery for one particular order	direct expenses
cost of grease for the moulding machine	indirect materials
depreciation of factory machinery	indirect expenses
depreciation of office equipment	indirect expenses

* Note: the cost of power to operate machines has been classified above as an indirect expense. This is often the case because it is not worthwhile analysing the cost of power for each unit of production. An industry that uses a lot of power will often have meters fitted to each machine so that costs may be identified and allocated to production as a direct expense. Other, lesser users of power, are unlikely to calculate the separate cost and will consider power to be an indirect expense. Whichever treatment is used, it is important that it is applied consistently.

1.6

COST ITEM	CLASSIFICATION (write your answer)
Dressings	direct materials
Disposable scalpels	direct materials
Surgeon's salary	direct labour
Floor cleaning materials	indirect materials
Laundry	indirect expenses*
Depreciation of staff drinks machine	indirect expenses*
Theatre heat and light	indirect expenses*
Porter's wages	indirect labour
Anaesthetic gas	direct materials
Depreciation of theatre equipment	indirect expenses
Maintenance of theatre equipment	indirect expenses
Cost of CDs for music in theatre	indirect expenses
Anaesthetist's salary	direct labour

* These items have been classified as indirect expenses – this is the most likely classification. If the money amount of any item was large, it would be worthwhile looking at the costing system to see if the item could be identified as a direct expense.

1.7

Cost item	Total cost £	Prime cost £	Production overheads £	Admin costs £	Selling and distribution costs £
Wages of employees working on the bottling line	6,025	6,025			
Wages of employees in the stores department	2,750		2,750		
Cost of bottles	4,050	4,050			
Safety goggles for bottling line employees	240		240		
Advertisement for new employees	125			125	
Depreciation of bottling machinery	500		500		
Depreciation of sales staff's cars	1,000				1,000
Royalty paid to local farmer	750	750			
Cost of trade exhibition	1,500				1,500
Computer stationery	210			210	
Sales staff salaries	4,095				4,095
TOTALS	21,245	10,825	3,490	335	6,595

1.8   (a)

Hughes Limited
Total cost statement for the year ended 31 December 20-4

	£	£
Direct materials		118,830
Direct labour		117,315
PRIME COST		236,145
Production overheads		
Rent and rates	16,460	
Factory power	3,825	
Factory heat and light	1,185	
Factory expenses and maintenance	4,095	
Depreciation of factory plant and machinery	3,725	
		29,290
PRODUCTION COST		265,435

Non-production overheads

Selling and distribution costs:

Advertising	11,085

Administration costs:

Salaries of office staff	69,350	
Office expenses	3,930	
		73,280
TOTAL COST		349,800

Note: It has been assumed in the cost statement that:
- all of the raw materials used in the factory are direct materials
- all of the factory wages are direct labour – with additional information, it would be possible to split the cost between direct and indirect labour

(b)

Hughes Limited
Income statement for the year ended 31 December 20-4

		£
	Revenue	426,350
less	Total cost	349,800
	PROFIT	76,550

1.9 (b)

1.10 (d)

1.11 (a)

MANLEY MANUFACTURING LIMITED
Total cost statement for the year ended 31 December 20-8

	£	£
Direct materials		75,280
Direct labour		69,180
Direct expenses		15,110
PRIME COST		159,570
Production overheads		
Salaries of maintenance staff	30,950	
Depreciation of factory plant and machinery	5,000	
Electricity	4,160	
Rent and rates	10,290	
Factory expenses	3,020	
		53,420
PRODUCTION COST		212,990
Non-production overheads		
Administration costs:		
Salaries of office staff	38,450	
Depreciation of office equipment	2,400	
Office expenses	1,590	
		42,440
TOTAL COST		255,430

Note: it has been assumed in the cost statement that:
- all the raw materials used in the factory are direct materials
- maintenance staff spend all of their time in the factory, and none in the office
- all the electricity and rent and rates have been incurred by the factory

With additional information, it would be possible to split these costs:
- raw materials between direct and indirect materials
- salaries of maintenance staff between production overheads and non-production overheads
- electricity and rent and rates between production overheads and non-production overheads

(b)

MANLEY MANUFACTURING LIMITED
Income statement for the year ended 31 December 20-8

	£
Revenue	315,840
less Total cost	255,430
PROFIT	60,410

CHAPTER 2: MATERIALS COSTS

2.1   *Stock item D*

- maximum space = 350 units; maximum usage = 95 days x 3 units per day = 285 units; therefore maximum inventory is 285 units

- minimum inventory = 10 days x 3 units per day = 30 units

- re-order level = 30 units + (7 days x 3 units per day) = 51 units

- re-order quantity = 285 units – 30 units = 255 units

Stock item E

- maximum space = 350 units; maximum usage = 95 days x 4 units per day = 380; therefore maximum inventory is 350 units

- minimum inventory = 10 days x 4 units per day = 40 units

- re-order level = 40 units + (7 days x 4 units per day) = 68 units

- re-order quantity = 350 units – 40 units = 310 units

2.2 $$\text{Economic Order Quantity (EOQ)} = \sqrt{\frac{2 \times 56{,}250 \text{ kg} \times £10}{£2}}$$

$$= \sqrt{\frac{1{,}125{,}000}{£2}}$$

$$= \sqrt{562{,}500}$$

$$= \underline{750 \text{ kg}}$$

2.3   (a)   inventory record

(b)   inventory list

(c)   inventory reconciliation

(d)   cost and net realisable value

2.4 FIFO

INVENTORY RECORD

Date	Receipts			Issues			Balance		
	Quantity (units)	Cost per unit	Total Cost	Quantity (units)	Cost per unit	Total Cost	Quantity (units)	Cost per unit	Total Cost
		£	£		£	£		£	£
20-4 January	20	3.00	60.00				20	3.00	60.00
February	10	3.60	36.00				20	3.00	60.00
							10	3.60	36.00
							30		96.00
March				8	3.00	24.00	12	3.00	36.00
							10	3.60	36.00
							22		72.00
April	10	4.00	40.00				12	3.00	36.00
							10	3.60	36.00
							10	4.00	40.00
							32		112.00
May				12	3.00	36.00			
				4	3.60	14.40	6	3.60	21.60
				16		50.40	10	4.00	40.00
							16		61.60

LIFO

INVENTORY RECORD

Date	Receipts			Issues			Balance		
	Quantity (units)	Cost per unit	Total Cost	Quantity (units)	Cost per unit	Total Cost	Quantity (units)	Cost per unit	Total Cost
		£	£		£	£		£	£
20-4 January	20	3.00	60.00				20	3.00	60.00
February	10	3.60	36.00				20	3.00	60.00
							10	3.60	36.00
							30		96.00
March				8	3.60	28.80	20	3.00	60.00
							2	3.60	7.20
							22		67.20
April	10	4.00	40.00				20	3.00	60.00
							2	3.60	7.20
							10	4.00	40.00
							32		107.20
May				10	4.00	40.00			
				2	3.60	7.20			
				4	3.00	12.00			
				16		59.20	16	3.00	48.00

AVCO

INVENTORY RECORD

Date	Receipts			Issues			Balance		
	Quantity (units)	Cost per unit	Total Cost	Quantity (units)	Cost per unit	Total Cost	Quantity (units)	Cost per unit	Total Cost
20-4		£	£		£	£		£	£
January	20	3.00	60.00				20	3.00	60.00
February	10	3.60	36.00				20	3.00	60.00
							10	3.60	36.00
							30	3.20	96.00
March				8	3.20	25.60	22	3.20	70.40
April	10	4.00	40.00				22	3.20	70.40
							10	4.00	40.00
							32	3.45	110.40
May				16	3.45	55.20	16	3.45	55.20

2.5

FIFO

INVENTORY RECORD: TYPE X

Date	Receipts			Issues			Balance		
	Quantity (units)	Cost per unit	Total Cost	Quantity (units)	Cost per unit	Total Cost	Quantity (units)	Cost per unit	Total Cost
20-4		£	£		£	£		£	£
January	100	4.00	400.00				100	4.00	400.00
February				80	4.00	320.00	20	4.00	80.00
March	140	4.20	588.00				20	4.00	80.00
							140	4.20	588.00
							160		668.00
April	100	3.80	380.00				20	4.00	80.00
							140	4.20	588.00
							100	3.80	380.00
							260		1,048.00
May				20	4.00	80.00			
				120	4.20	504.00	20	4.20	84.00
				140		584.00	100	3.80	380.00
							120		464.00
June	80	4.50	360.00				20	4.20	84.00
							100	3.80	380.00
							80	4.50	360.00
							200		824.00

LIFO

INVENTORY RECORD: TYPE X

Date	Receipts			Issues			Balance		
	Quantity (units)	Cost per unit	Total Cost	Quantity (units)	Cost per unit	Total Cost	Quantity (units)	Cost per unit	Total Cost
20-4		£	£		£	£		£	£
January	100	4.00	400.00				100	4.00	400.00
February				80	4.00	320.00	20	4.00	80.00
March	140	4.20	588.00				20	4.00	80.00
							140	4.20	588.00
							160		668.00
April	100	3.80	380.00				20	4.00	80.00
							140	4.20	588.00
							100	3.80	380.00
							260		1,048.00
May				100	3.80	380.00	20	4.00	80.00
				40	4.20	168.00	100	4.20	420.00
				140		548.00	120		500.00
June	80	4.50	360.00				20	4.00	80.00
							100	4.20	420.00
							80	4.50	360.00
							200		860.00

AVCO

INVENTORY RECORD: TYPE X

Date	Receipts			Issues			Balance		
	Quantity (units)	Cost per unit	Total Cost	Quantity (units)	Cost per unit	Total Cost	Quantity (units)	Cost per unit	Total Cost
20-4		£	£		£	£		£	£
January	100	4.00	400.00				100	4.00	400.00
February				80	4.00	320.00	20	4.00	80.00
March	140	4.20	588.00				20	4.00	80.00
							140	4.20	588.00
							160	4.17	668.00
April	100	3.80	380.00				160	4.17	668.00
							100	3.80	380.00
							260	4.03	1,048.00
May				140	4.03	564.20	120	4.03	483.80
June	80	4.50	360.00				120	4.03	483.80
							80	4.50	360.00
							200	4.22	843.80

Note: some figures have been rounded to the nearest penny

FIFO INVENTORY RECORD: TYPE Y

Date	Receipts			Issues			Balance		
	Quantity (units)	Cost per unit	Total Cost	Quantity (units)	Cost per unit	Total Cost	Quantity (units)	Cost per unit	Total Cost
20-4		£	£		£	£		£	£
January	200	10.00	2,000.00				200	10.00	2,000.00
February	100	9.50	950.00				200	10.00	2,000.00
							100	9.50	950.00
							300		2,950.00
March				200	10.00	2,000.00			
				40	9.50	380.00			
				240		2,380.00	60	9.50	570.00
April	100	10.50	1,050.00				60	9.50	570.00
							100	10.50	1,050.00
							160		1,620.00
May	140	10.00	1,400.00				60	9.50	570.00
							100	10.50	1,050.00
							140	10.00	1,400.00
							300		3,020.00
June				60	9.50	570.00			
				40	10.50	420.00	60	10.50	630.00
				100		990.00	140	10.00	1,400.00
							200		2,030.00

LIFO INVENTORY RECORD: TYPE Y

Date	Receipts			Issues			Balance		
	Quantity (units)	Cost per unit	Total Cost	Quantity (units)	Cost per unit	Total Cost	Quantity (units)	Cost per unit	Total Cost
20-4		£	£		£	£		£	£
January	200	10.00	2,000.00				200	10.00	2,000.00
February	100	9.50	950.00				200	10.00	2,000.00
							100	9.50	950.00
							300		2,950.00
March				100	9.50	950.00			
				140	10.00	1,400.00	60	10.00	600.00
				240		2,350.00			
April	100	10.50	1,050.00				60	10.00	600.00
							100	10.50	1,050.00
							160		1,650.00
May	140	10.00	1,400.00				60	10.00	600.00
							100	10.50	1,050.00
							140	10.00	1,400.00
							300		3,050.00
June				100	10.00	1,000.00	60	10.00	600.00
							100	10.50	1,050.00
							40	10.00	400.00
							200		2,050.00

AVCO

INVENTORY RECORD: TYPE Y

Date	Receipts			Issues			Balance		
	Quantity (units)	Cost per unit	Total Cost	Quantity (units)	Cost per unit	Total Cost	Quantity (units)	Cost per unit	Total Cost
20-4		£	£		£	£		£	£
January	200	10.00	2,000.00				200	10.00	2,000.00
February	100	9.50	950.00				200	10.00	2,000.00
							100	9.50	950.00
							300	9.83	2,950.00
March				240	9.83	2,360.00	60	9.83	590.00
April	100	10.50	1,050.00				60	9.83	590.00
							100	10.50	1,050.00
							160	10.25	1,640.00
May	140	10.00	1,400.00				160	10.25	1,640.00
							140	10.00	1,400.00
							300	10.13	3,040.00
June				100	10.13	1,013.00	200	10.13	2,027.00

Note: some figures have been rounded to the nearest penny

Valuation at 30 June 20-4:

	£	
Type X	824.00	(cost price, using FIFO)
Type Y	1,950.00	(net realisable value)
	2,774.00	

2.6 Task 1

INVENTORY RECORD

Product: Wholewheat flour

Date	Receipts			Issues			Balance	
	Quantity (kgs)	Cost per kg	Total Cost	Quantity (kgs)	Cost per kg	Total Cost	Quantity (kgs)	Total Cost
20-4 Balance at 1 May		£	£		£	£	10,000	£ 2,500
6 May	20,000	0.30	6,000				30,000	8,500
10 May				10,000 10,000 20,000	0.25 0.30	2,500 3,000 5,500	10,000	3,000
17 May	10,000	0.35	3,500				10,000 10,000 20,000	3,000 3,500 6,500
20 May				10,000 5,000 15,000	0.30 0.35	3,000 1,750 4,750	5,000	1,750

Task 2

20-4	Code number	Debit £	Credit £
6 May	3000	£6,000	
6 May	5000		£6,000
10 May	3000		£5,500*
10 May	3300	£5,500	
17 May	3000	£3,500	
17 May	5000		£3,500
20 May	3000		£4,750**
20 May	3300	£4,750	

* £2,500 + £3,000   ** £3,000 + £1,750

2.7 (a)

$$\text{Economic Order Quantity (EOQ)} = \sqrt{\frac{2 \times 57{,}600 \text{ kg} \times £25}{£2}}$$

$$= \sqrt{\frac{2{,}880{,}000}{£2}}$$

$$= \sqrt{1{,}440{,}000}$$

$$= \underline{1{,}200 \text{ kg}}$$

(b) and (c)

Inventory record for plastic grade P5

Date	Receipts			Issues			Balance	
	Quantity (kg)	Cost per kg	Total Cost	Quantity (kg)	Cost per kg	Total Cost	Quantity (kg)	Total Cost
		£	£		£	£		£
Balance as at 22 June							4,400	10,560
23 June	1,200	2.634	3,161				5,600	13,721
25 June				1,000	2.450	2,450	4,600	11,271
26 June	1,200	2.745	3,294				5,800	14,565
29 June				1,500	2.511	3,767	4,300	10,798

2.8

	Transaction	Account debited	Account credited
1.	Receipt of materials into inventory, paying on credit	Inventory	Trade payables control
2.	Issue of materials from inventory to production	Production	Inventory
3.	Receipt of materials into inventory, paying immediately by BACS	Inventory	Bank
4.	Return of materials from production to inventory	Inventory	Production

CHAPTER 3: LABOUR COSTS

3.1

N Ball:	35 hours x £11.00 per hour = £385.00 (no bonus)
T Smith:	37 hours x £9.00 per hour = £333.00 + bonus £9.00 = £342.00
L Lewis:	38 hours x £10.00 per hour = £380.00 + bonus £15.00 = £395.00
M Wilson:	36 hours x £12.00 per hour = £432.00 + bonus £12.00 = £444.00

3.2

REPORT

To:	Office Manager
From:	Accounts Assistant
Date:	Today

Labour payment methods for production-line workers

I have been asked to produce a report on labour payment methods for production-line workers.

At present the company pays these workers on a time-rate basis. The main advantages of such a system from the viewpoint of both employer and employees are as follows:

- it is easy to calculate and understand
- there is no requirement to establish time allowances and piecework rates
- employees receive a regular wage, which is unaffected by fluctuations in output
- the system can be applied to all direct labour employees
- the quality of finished output does not suffer as a result of hurried work

The disadvantages of time rate are that:

- all production-line employees are paid the same, whether they work efficiently or inefficiently
- no incentive is given to employees to work harder
- the company needs to employ supervisors to ensure that output is maintained
- slow working by employees does not affect the basic wage, but could lead to the company having to pay overtime rates to ensure that output is completed.

Employee representatives have approached the company management with a request that other labour payment methods be considered. In particular piecework systems, or a time rate with a production bonus system have been suggested.

A *piecework system* is where payment is based on the quantity of output.

The main advantages of this are that:

- payment of wages is linked directly to output
- more efficient workers earn more than those who are less efficient
- work is done quicker and less time is wasted

The main disadvantages are that:

- the system is not suitable for all direct labour employees
- there may be difficulty in agreeing piecework rates between employer and employees
- the quality of the finished product may be low and more inspections may be needed
- control system will be needed to check the amount produced by each worker
- from the employer's point of view, the quality of the finished product may be low
- pay calculations will be more complex and the employer cannot plan ahead for wages costs

Employees need to be aware that pay is reduced if there are production problems, eg machine breakdown, or shortage of materials. A way around this is to use a piecework system with a guaranteed time rate. A further disadvantage is that there may be difficulties in agreeing piecework rates.

A time rate with a production bonus is a method used to encourage employees to be more efficient where work is not so repetitive. There are a number of variations of bonus including increased bonuses for higher levels of output, and group bonuses paid to groups of employees.

The main advantages of bonus systems are that:

- wages are linked to output, but a minimum wage – the time rate – is guaranteed each week
- work is done quicker and less time is wasted
- the more efficient workers earn more
- a bonus system can often be applied to the entire workforce

The disadvantages are that:

- from the employee's point of view, the bonus is not paid if circumstances such as machine breakdown, or shortage of materials occur
- from the employer's point of view, the quality of the finished product may be low and more inspections will be needed
- there may be difficulty in agreeing bonus rates with employees
- control procedures are needed, and pay calculations will be more complex

Conclusion

Each of the three labour payment methods of remuneration has advantages and disadvantages. In selecting a suitable system both employer and employee must consider that:

- reward should be related to effort and fair to all staff
- the system should be easy to manage and administer, and be cheap and efficient to run
- it should be easy for employees to understand how pay is calculated
- payment should be made at regular intervals and soon after the event
- the principles of the scheme should remain constant, but there should be flexibility to deal with changes in production techniques

3.3 (a) • L Fry: £400.00 (time rate)
   • R Williams: £450.00 (piecework rate)
   • P Grant: £362.50 (piecework rate)

(b) • not suitable for all direct labour employees
   • employees' pay is reduced if there are production problems
   • quality of the finished product may be low, so not suitable where quality is more important than quantity
   • more inspections may be needed
   • control systems needed to check the amount produced by each worker
   • more complex pay calculations
   • may be difficulty in agreeing piecework rates with employees
   • the employer cannot plan ahead for wages costs, as they may be for irregular amounts

3.4 Gross wages

		£
• Steve Kurtin:	35 hours at £10.50 per hour =	367.50
	4 hours overtime at £14.00 per hour =	56.00
	production bonus 45 x 50p =	22.50
		446.00
• Pete Singh:	35 hours at £12.00 per hour =	420.00
	3 hours overtime at £16.00 per hour =	48.00
	4 hours overtime at £18.00 per hour =	72.00
	production bonus 57 x 50p =	28.50
		568.50

Piecework rate for Steve Kurtin
£446.00 ÷ 45 = £9.91 per 1,000 copies printed

3.5

	MOULDING	FINISHING
• Time saved	–	500
• Bonus (£)	–	2,525*
• Total labour cost (£)	41,160	47,975

   * £45,450 ÷ 4,500 hours = £10.10 x 500 hours = £5,050 ÷ 2 = £2,525

3.6 (a) Week 1: 400 hours at £10.20 per hour = £4,080
      50 hours at 1.5 x £10.20 = 50 x £15.30 = £765
      Total gross earnings for Week 1 = £4,080 + £765 = £4,845

   Week 2: 400 hours at £10.20 per hour = £4,080 = Total gross earnings

(b) Week 1: Normally treated as indirect labour cost would be overtime premium on 50 hours, ie 50 x 0.5 x £10.20 = £255

   Week 2: Normally treated as indirect labour cost would be 20 hours of non-production work at basic pay, ie 20 x £10.20 = £204

3.7   **Employee's weekly time sheet for week ending 15 April 20-6**

Employee:	T Mantle			Profit Centre: Finishing			
Employee number: 170				Basic pay per hour: £14.00			
	Hours spent on production	Hours worked on indirect work	Notes	Basic pay £	Overtime premium £	Total pay £
Monday	6	0		84	0	84
Tuesday	5	2	8am-10am maintenance	98	7	105
Wednesday	7	0		98	7	105
Thursday	6	3	9am-12 noon training	126	21	147
Friday	8	0		112	14	126
Saturday	5	0		70	28	98
Sunday	0	0		0	0	0
Total	37	5		588	77	665

3.8   **Task 1**

Dr   **Wages Control Account**   Cr

	£		£
Cash/bank (net wages)	7,500	Production (direct labour)	6,500
HM Rev. & Customs (income tax & NIC)	1,450	Production overheads (indirect labour)	2,700
Pension contributions	750	Non-production overheads (administration)	500
	9,700		9,700

Task 2

20-4	Code number	Debit £	Credit £
26 March	3300	£6,500	
26 March	5200		£6,500
26 March	3500	£2,700	
26 March	5200		£2,700
26 March	3700	£500	
26 March	5200		£500

3.9 Total cost of direct labour for October:

			£
14,400 hours	x £10 per hour	=	144,000
1,600 hours	x £15 (£10 + £5) per hour	=	24,000
16,000 hours			168,000

Cost book-keeping entries:

	Debit	Credit
	£	£
• production – 'Mulligan' clubs (1500)	168,000	
• wages control (5000)		168,000

CHAPTER 4: EXPENSES

4.1 (a) *Capital expenditure:* expenditure incurred on the purchase, alteration or improvement of non-current assets. Examples: purchase of premises, vehicles, machinery; legal costs of buying property; installation and setting up of a machine.

(b) *Revenue expenditure:* expenditure incurred on running costs. Examples: fuel for vehicles; repairs to premises; labour costs of running the business.

4.2 (a) *Direct expenses:* those expenses that can be identified directly with units of output. Examples: royalties payable to the designer of a product; special items bought in for a particular product or job; power costs metered to output; depreciation methods linked directly to output (eg units of output method).

(b) *Indirect expenses:* other expenses which cannot be identified directly with specific units of output. Examples: rent and rates, heating and lighting, depreciation methods not linked directly to output (eg straight-line and reducing balance methods).

4.3 Fred Jarvis' wages will be shown in wages control account as:

– *debit* cash/bank

– *credit* property

Thus the cost of his labour is debited to the non-current asset account of property (rather than production, as would be the usual case for production-line employees). As he is building an extension to the warehouse, his wages (and also the cost of the materials he uses) are treated as capital expenditure because he is adding to the value of a non-current asset.

4.4 **Graph A**

• shows a *fixed cost,* which remains constant over a range of output levels

• as output increases, the *cost per unit* falls

• at an output beyond the limit of the graph, the fixed cost will increase as another factory needs to be rented; the behaviour of such a cost is known as a *stepped fixed cost.*

Graph B

• shows a *variable cost,* which alters directly with changes in output levels

• as output increases then the cost increases, ie the cost per unit remains the same

4.5

	capital expenditure	revenue expenditure
(a) purchase of vehicles	✓	
(b) depreciation of vehicles		✓
(c) payment of office rent		✓
(d) salaries of office staff		✓
(e) legal fees relating to the purchase of property	✓	
(f) re-decoration of office		✓
(g) installation of air-conditioning in office	✓	
(h) wages of own employees used to build extension to the stockroom	✓	
(i) installation and setting up of a new machine	✓	

4.6

	direct expenses	indirect expenses	either*
(a) hire of machinery for a particular job	✓		
(b) office rent		✓	
(c) cleaning materials		✓	
(d) power costs			✓
(e) royalty paid to designer for each unit of output	✓		
(f) sales staff car expenses		✓	
(g) depreciation of production machinery			✓
(h) consultant's fees relating to a particular job	✓		
(i) heating and lighting		✓	

(d) Power costs are direct expenses where machinery is separately metered and used for a particular product or job; otherwise, they are indirect expenses.

(g) Depreciation of production machinery is a direct expense when the depreciation method is linked directly to output (eg units of output method); it is an indirect expense when the depreciation method is not linked directly to output (eg straight-line and reducing balance methods).

4.7

	fixed	semi-fixed	variable
(a) rates of business premises	✓		
(b) royalty paid to designer for each unit of output			✓
(c) car hire with fixed rental and charge per mile		✓	
(d) employees paid on piecework basis			✓
(e) straight-line depreciation	✓		
(f) units of output depreciation			✓
(g) direct materials			✓
(h) telephone bill with fixed rental and charge for each call made		✓	
(i) office salaries	✓		

4.8 (a) cleaning materials for the machines: indirect materials

(b) wages of factory supervisor: indirect labour

(c) clay from which pots are made: direct materials

(d) royalty paid to designer: direct expenses

(e) salary of office assistant: indirect expenses*

(f) electricity used to heat the kilns: indirect expense (or possibly a direct expense – see note to question 4.6(d) above)

(g) rates of factory: indirect expense

(h) depreciation of office equipment: indirect expense

(i) wages of production line workers: direct labour

(j) salesperson's salary: indirect expenses*

(k) interest charged on bank overdraft: indirect expenses

* Note: Both the salary of the office assistant and the salesperson's salary have been classified as indirect expenses, rather than indirect labour. This is because neither of them work in the factory and so the cost cannot be identified directly with production. By contrast, the wages of the factory supervisor are classified as indirect labour – here the employee does work in the factory, and the cost is more closely linked to production.

- *production overheads:* (a), (b), (f), (g)
- *selling and distribution overheads:* (j)
- *administration overheads:* (e), (h)
- *finance overheads:* (k)

4.9   Task 1

Dr		General Expenses Account (5150)		Cr

20-2		£	20-2		£
30 June	Balance b/d	28,250	30 June	Production: treadmill	5,450
			30 June	Production: exercise cycles	3,170
			30 June	Production overheads	12,950
			30 June	Non-production overheads:	
				selling and distribution	3,860
			30 June	Non-production overheads:	
				administration	2,820
		28,250			28,250

Task 2

20-2	Code number	Debit £	Credit £
30 June	2100	£5,450	
30 June	5150		£5,450
30 June	2200	£3,170	
30 June	5150		£3,170
30 June	3500	£12,950	
30 June	5150		£12,950
30 June	4200	£3,860	
30 June	5150		£3,860
30 June	4400	£2,820	
30 June	5150		£2,820

4.10 ·

	high output	15,000 units	£65,000
less	low output	10,000 units	£50,000
equals	difference	5,000 units	£15,000

· amount of variable cost per unit:

$$\frac{£15,000}{5,000} = £3 \text{ variable cost per unit}$$

· at 10,000 units of output the cost structure is:

	total cost	£50,000
less	variable costs (10,000 units x £3 per unit)	£30,000
equals	fixed costs	£20,000

· check at 15,000 units of output when the cost structure is:

	variable costs (15,000 units x £3 per unit)	£45,000
add	fixed costs (as above)	£20,000
equals	total costs	£65,000

· therefore fixed costs, at these levels of output, are £20,000

4.11

20-8 FORECAST REVENUE AND COSTS			
UNITS PRODUCED AND SOLD	250,000	300,000	350,000
	£	£	£
Sales revenue	1,000,000	1,200,000	1,400,000
Variable costs			
Materials	400,000	480,000	560,000
Labour	325,000	390,000	455,000
Expenses	100,000	120,000	140,000
	825,000	990,000	1,155,000
Fixed costs			
Labour	96,500	96,500	96,500
Overheads	67,500	67,500	67,500
	164,000	164,000	164,000
Total cost	989,000	1,154,000	1,319,000
Total profit	11,000	46,000	81,000
Cost per unit (to 2 decimal places)	3.96	3.85	3.77
Profit per unit (to 2 decimal places)	0.04	0.15	0.23

Tutorial notes

- Sales revenue per unit is calculated at £4.00 (ie £1,000,000 ÷ 250,000 units)
- Variable costs per unit are:
    - materials, £1.60 (ie £400,000 ÷ 250,000 units)
    - labour, £1.30
    - expenses, £0.40
- Fixed costs remain fixed at the higher levels of output
- The costs at higher levels of output are on the basis that
    - there is a linear relationship for variable costs
    - there are no stepped fixed costs
- The fall in cost per unit as output increases occurs because the fixed costs are being spread over a greater number of units, ie the fixed cost per unit falls
- As cost per unit falls, so profit per unit increases (always provided that the selling price per unit can be maintained)

4.12

Batches produced and sold	1,000	1,200	2,000
	£	£	£
Sales revenue	35,000	42,000	70,000
Variable costs:			
• Direct materials	7,500	9,000	15,000
• Direct labour	10,500	12,600	21,000
• Overheads	6,000	7,200	12,000
Semi-variable costs:	4,500		
• Variable element		1,800	3,000
• Fixed element		3,000	3,000
Total cost	28,500	33,600	54,000
Total profit	6,500	8,400	16,000
Profit per batch (to 2 decimal places)	6.50	7.00	8.00

CHAPTER 5: OVERHEADS

5.1
- allocation of overheads – the charging to a cost centre of those overheads that have been directly incurred by that cost centre
- apportionment of overheads – the charging to a cost centre of a proportion of overheads

5.2 (a)

OVERHEAD ANALYSIS SHEET		
	MOULDING	FINISHING
Budgeted total overheads (£)	9,338	3,298
Budgeted machine hours	1,450	680
Budgeted overhead absorption rate (£)	6.44*	4.85**

*   £9,338 ÷ 1,450 hours
**   £3,298 ÷ 680 hours

(b)

JOB OVERHEAD ANALYSIS SHEET		
	MOULDING	FINISHING
Job machine hours	412	154
Budgeted overhead absorption rate (£)	6.44	4.85
Overhead absorbed by job (£)	2,653.28*	746.90**

*   412 hours x £6.44 per hour
**   154 hours x £4.85 per hour

(c) Direct labour hour

- With this method, production overhead is absorbed on the basis of the number of direct labour hours worked.

- While this is a commonly-used method, it is inappropriate where some output is worked on by hand while other output passes quickly through a machinery process and requires little direct labour time.

- This method may be appropriate for Wyvern Fabrication; however, much depends on the balance between direct labour hours and machine hours in the two production departments.

5.3 (a)

cost	basis of apportionment	total	dept A	dept B	dept C
		£	£	£	£
Rent and rates	Floor area	7,210	3,090	1,545	2,575
Depn. of machinery	Value of machinery	10,800	5,400	3,240	2,160
Supervisor's salary	Production-line				
	employees	12,750	6,800	3,400	2,550
Machinery insurance	Value of machinery	750	375	225	150
		31,510	15,665	8,410	7,435

(b) 37 hours x 48 weeks = 1,776 direct labour hours per employee

    Dept A: 8 employees = 14,208 hours = £1.10 per direct labour hour

    Dept B: 4 employees = 7,104 hours = £1.18 per direct labour hour

    Dept C: 3 employees = 5,328 hours = £1.40 per direct labour hour

5.4 (a) and (b)

cost	basis of apportionment	total	machining	finishing	maintenance
		£	£	£	£
Rent and rates	Floor area	5,520	2,760	1,840	920
Buildings insurance	Floor area	1,320	660	440	220
Machinery insurance	Value of machinery	1,650	1,200	450	–
Lighting and heating	Floor area	3,720	1,860	1,240	620
Depn of machinery	Value of machinery	11,000	8,000	3,000	–
Supervisory salaries	No. of employees	30,000	18,000	9,000	3,000
Maintenance dept					
salary	Allocation	16,000	–	–	16,000
Factory cleaning	Floor area	4,800	2,400	1,600	800
		74,010	34,880	17,570	21,560
Re-apportionment of maintenance dept	Value of machinery	–	15,680	5,880	(21,560)
		74,010	50,560	23,450	–

(c)   35 hours x 47 weeks = 1,645 direct labour hours per employee
Machining Dept: 6 employees = 9,870 hours = £5.12 per direct labour hour
Finishing Dept: 3 employees = 4,935 hours = £4.75 per direct labour hour

(d)   Depending on the method and type of production, the company is most likely to use overhead absorption rates based on:
  •   direct labour hour, or
  •   machine hour
These are discussed in the text (pages 136-137). Alternative methods could be based on a percentage of certain costs, eg direct materials, direct labour, prime cost.

5.5

	total	business studies	general studies	administration	technical support
		£	£	£	£
Overheads	81,600	40,000	20,000	9,600	12,000
Technical support	–	6,000	3,000	3,000	(12,000)
				12,600	–
Administration	–	8,400	4,200	(12,600)	–
	81,600	54,400	27,200	–	–

5.6   (a) $\dfrac{\text{total overheads}}{\text{total hours}}$ = $\dfrac{£59,900}{3,290}$ =   £18.21 per partner hour

(b) $\dfrac{£59,900 + £60,000}{3,290}$ =   £36.44 per partner hour

(c)   2 hours x 47 weeks x £18.21   =   £1,711.74 per partner
(ie £3,423.48 in total)

5.7   (a)   Direct labour hour: (3 hours x 80 seats) + (3.5 hours x 40 seats)
= 380 direct labour hours per month = £2.63 per hour.

Machine hour: (1 hour x 80 seats) + (2.5 hours x 40 seats)
= 180 machine hours per month = £5.56 per hour.

Alternative methods could be based on a percentage of certain costs, eg direct labour.

(b)   *Direct labour hour*

'Standard'	£36.50 + £7.89	=	£44.39
'De Luxe'	£55.00 + £9.21	=	£64.21

Machine hour

'Standard'	£36.50 + £5.56	=	£42.06
'De Luxe'	£55.00 + £13.89	=	£68.89

Note: some figures have been rounded to the nearest penny

(c)   See text. The machine hour rate charges most to 'de luxe' model. On balance, direct labour hours may be the best method to use because the products are more labour-intensive than machine-intensive.

5.8 Task 1

Fixed overheads for November 20-1	Basis	Total £	Warehouse £	Manufacturing £	Sales £	Administration £
Depreciation	Net book value*	9,150	1,830	6,100	305	915
Rent	Floor space	11,000	1,650	6,600	1,100	1,650
Other property overheads	Floor space	6,200	930	3,720	620	930
Administration overheads	Allocated	13,450				13,450
Staff costs	Allocated	27,370	3,600	9,180	8,650	5,940
		67,170	8,010	25,600	10,675	22,885

* carrying amount

Task 2

Budgeted fixed overhead absorption rate for the manufacturing department:

£25,600 ÷ 10,000 hours = £2.56 per machine hour

5.9   Task 1

Fixed overheads for August 20-3	Basis	Total £	Accommodation £	Restaurant £	Bar £	Kitchen £	Administration £
Bedroom repairs	Allocated	3,200	3,200				
Electricity	Metered	1,700	550	250	150	700	50
Rent	Floor space	9,000	5,850	1,350	900	450	450
Kitchen repairs	Allocated	1,025				1,025	
Staff costs	Allocated	23,595	4,550	6,740	3,045	2,310	6,950
Other property overheads	Floor space	4,000	2,600	600	400	200	200
		42,520	16,750	8,940	4,495	4,685	7,650
Administration			4,590	1,530	765	765	(7,650)
		42,520	21,340	10,470	5,260	5,450	–

Task 2

Budgeted fixed overhead absorption rate for the kitchen:

£5,450 ÷ 1,000 hours = £5.45 per labour hour

5.10

	Basis of apportionment	Moulding £	Finishing £	Maintenance £	Stores £	Admin £	Totals £
Depreciation of equipment	NBV* of equipment	1,200	750				1,950
Power for production machinery	Power usage	1,736	868				2,604
Rent and rates	Floor space			1,140	1,425	1,710	4,275
Light and heat	Floor space			780	975	1,170	2,925
Indirect labour	Allocated			32,200	17,150	28,450	77,800
Totals		2,936	1,618	34,120	19,550	31,330	89,554
Reapportion Maintenance		25,590	8,530	(34,120)			
Reapportion Stores		11,730	7,820		(19,550)		
Reapportion Administration		15,665	15,665			(31,330)	
Total overheads to production centres		55,921	33,633				89,554

* carrying amount

5.11 1. (d)

   2. (a)

   3. (b)

5.12

Dr	**Production Overheads Account: Moulding Department**		Cr
	£		£
Bank (overheads incurred)	5,000	Production	4,800
		Income statement (under-absorption)	200
	5,000		5,000

Dr	**Production Overheads Account: Finishing Department**		Cr
	£		£
Bank (overheads incurred)	7,000	Production	7,500
Income statement (over-absorption)	500		
	7,500		7,500

20-6	Code number	Debit £	Credit £
26 May	3000	£4,800	
26 May	3400		£4,800
26 May	3000	£7,500	
26 May	3500		£7,500
26 May	6000	£200	
26 May	3400		£200
26 May	3500	£500	
26 May	6000		£500

CHAPTER 6: METHODS OF COSTING

6.1 The method of costing for each business should be justified; however, the following are the most likely methods:

- *accountant* – job costing, because each job will take a different length of time and is likely to involve a number of staff, each with different skill levels

- *bus company* – service costing, where the object is to find the cost per unit of service, eg passenger mile; job costing used for 'one-offs', eg quoting for the transport for a trip to the seaside for an old people's home

- *baker* – batch costing, where identical units are produced in batches, eg loaves; job costing could be used for 'one-off' items, eg a wedding cake

- *sports centre* – service costing, or job costing for 'one-off', eg hire of the main sports hall for an exhibition

- *hotel* – different methods of costing are likely to be used, eg service costing for the rooms, batch costing in the restaurant, and job costing for special events

6.2

		£	£
Direct materials:	100m x £7.50	750.00	
	75m x £4.00	300.00	
			1,050.00
Direct labour:	35 hours x £10.00		350.00
Overheads:	35 hours x £8.50		297.50
(a) TOTAL COST			1,697.50
Profit (20% of total cost)			339.50
(b) SELLING PRICE			2,037.00

6.3

JOB COST SHEET **Replacement Cylinder Head**		
		£
Direct Materials		
100 kg of high-strength steel at £10 per kg		1,000.00
Direct Labour		
Foundry:	10 hours at £10.00 per hour	100.00
Finishing:	15 hours at £12.00 per hour	180.00
Overheads		
Foundry:	80% of direct labour cost	80.00
Finishing:	12 machine hours x £20 per hour	240.00
TOTAL COST		1,600.00
Profit (25% of total cost)		400.00
SELLING PRICE		2,000.00

6.4 *Total costs:*

	£
Depreciation of diesel trains £60,000* x 6 trains	360,000
Leasing charges for track	1,000,000
Maintenance charges for trains	910,000
Fuel for trains	210,000
Wages of drivers and conductors	480,000
Administration	520,000
	3,480,000

* (£1,300,000 – £100,000) ÷ 20 years = £60,000 per train per year

Cost per passenger mile:

$$\frac{£3,480,000}{2.5m \text{ journeys x 5 miles}} = £0.28 \text{ per passenger mile}$$

6.5

Cost element	Costs	Completed Units	Work-in-progress			Total Equivalent Units	Cost per Unit	WIP valuation
			Units	% complete	Equivalent Units			
	A	B	C	D	E	F	G	H
					C x D	B + E	A ÷ F	E x G
	£						£	£
Direct materials	11,500	20,000	5,000	100	5,000	25,000	0.46	2,300
Direct labour	9,000	20,000	5,000	50	2,500	22,500	0.40	1,000
Production overheads	18,000	20,000	5,000	50	2,500	22,500	0.80	2,000
Total	38,500						1.66	5,300

- Cost per toy is £1.66 each
- Work-in-progress valuation is £5,300

6.6

Dr **Process Account** Cr

	Quantity (litres)	Unit cost £	Total cost £		Quantity (litres)	Unit cost £	Total cost £
Materials	22,000	0.25	5,500	Normal loss	2,000	0.20	400
Labour		0.15	3,300	Finished goods	20,000	0.53	10,600
Overheads		0.10	2,200				
	22,000		11,000		22,000		11,000

Dr **Normal Loss Account** Cr

	£		£
Process account	400	Bank/receivables	400

Tutorial note:

The cost per unit of the expected output is:

$$\frac{£11,000 - £400}{20,000 \text{ litres}} = £0.53 \text{ per litre}$$

6.7

Dr   **Process Account**   Cr

	Quantity (kg)	Unit cost £	Total cost £		Quantity (kg)	Unit cost £	Total cost £
Materials	42,000	0.25	10,500	Normal loss	2,000	0.20	400
Labour		0.10	4,200	Finished goods	39,500	0.41	16,195
Overheads		0.05	2,100	Abnormal loss	500	0.41	205
	42,000		16,800		42,000		16,800

Dr   **Normal Loss Account**   Cr

	£		£
Process account	400	Bank/receivables	400

Dr   **Abnormal Loss Account**   Cr

	£		£
Process account	205	Bank/debtors (500 kg x 20p)	100

Tutorial note:

The cost per unit of the expected output is:

$$\frac{£16,800 - £400}{40,000 \text{ kilos}} = £0.41 \text{ per kg}$$

6.8

Dr   **Process 1 Account**   Cr

	Quantity (litres)	Unit cost £	Total cost £		Quantity (litres)	Unit cost £	Total cost £
Materials	10,000	0.50	5,000	Normal loss (10%)	1,000	0.40	400
Labour		0.40	4,000	Transfer to			
Overheads		0.20	2,000	process 2	9,000	1.18	10,600
	10,000		11,000		10,000		11,000

Dr   **Process 2 Account**   Cr

	Quantity (litres)	Unit cost £	Total cost £		Quantity (litres)	Unit cost £	Total cost £
Transfer from				Normal loss (5%)	450	0.50	225
process 1	9,000	1.18	10,600	Finished goods	8,300	1.58	13,130
Labour		0.20	1,800	Abnormal loss	250	1.58	395
Overheads		0.15	1,350				
	9,000		13,750		9,000		13,750

Dr   **Normal Loss Account**   Cr

	£		£
Process 1 account	400	Bank/receivables	400
Process 2 account	225	Bank/receivables	225
	625		625

Dr   **Abnormal Loss Account**   Cr

	£		£
Process 2 account	395	Bank/receivables (250 litres x 50p)	125

Tutorial notes:

- In process 1, the cost per unit of the expected output is:

$$\frac{£11,000 - £400}{9,000 \text{ litres}} = £1.18 \text{ per litre}$$

- In process 2, the cost per unit of the expected output is:

$$\frac{£13,750 - £225}{8,550 \text{ litres}} = £1.58 \text{ per litre}$$

6.9

Dr   **Process Account**   Cr

	Quantity (litres)	Unit cost £	Total cost £		Quantity (litres)	Unit cost £	Total cost £
Materials	11,000	0.50	5,500	Normal loss	1,000	0.30	300
Labour		0.35	3,850	Finished goods	10,200	1.18	12,036
Overheads		0.25	2,750				
			12,100				
Abnormal gain	200	1.18	236				
	11,200		12,336		11,200		12,336

Dr		Abnormal Gain Account		Cr
	£			£
Normal loss account	*60	Process account		236

Dr		Normal Loss Account		Cr
	£			£
Process account	300	Bank/receivables		240
		Abnormal gain account		*60
	300			300

* 200 litres at 30p per litre

Tutorial note:

The cost per unit of the expected output is:

$$\frac{£12,100 - £300}{10,000 \text{ litres}} = £1.18 \text{ per litre}$$

6.10

Description	kg	Unit cost £	Total cost £	Description	kg	Unit cost £	Total cost £
Material AB4	500	1.50	750	Normal loss	100	0.80	80
Material AC5	200	2.20	440	Output	900	16.60	14,940
Material AD6	300	4.10	1,230				
Labour			4,200				
Overheads			8,400				
	1,000		15,020		1,000		15,020

	Debit ✓	Credit ✓
Abnormal loss		✓
Abnormal gain	✓	

CHAPTER 7: MARGINAL AND ABSORPTION COSTING

7.1   (a)   *Marginal cost per coffee machine* £

	£
Direct materials	25.00
Direct labour	20.00
MARGINAL COST	45.00

(b)   *Absorption cost per coffee machine*

	£
Direct materials	25.00
Direct labour	20.00
Fixed production overheads £270,000 ÷ 15,000 machines	18.00
ABSORPTION COST	63.00

(c)

COFFEEWORKS LIMITED
INCOME STATEMENT: 15,000 COFFEE MACHINES

	£	£
Sales revenue (15,000 x £80)		1,200,000
Direct materials (15,000 x £25)	375,000	
Direct labour (15,000 x £20)	300,000	
Fixed production overheads	270,000	
TOTAL COST		945,000
PROFIT		255,000

7.2   (a)   *Marginal cost per barbecue*

	£
Direct materials	30.00
Direct labour	25.00
MARGINAL COST	55.00

(b)   *Absorption cost per barbecue*

	£
Direct materials	30.00
Direct labour	25.00
Fixed production overheads 150,000 ÷ 10,000 barbecues	15.00
ABSORPTION COST	70.00

(c)

COOK-IT LIMITED
INCOME STATEMENT: 10,000 BARBECUES

	£	£
Sales revenue (10,000 x £90)		900,000
Direct materials (10,000 x £30)	300,000	
Direct labour (10,000 x £25)	250,000	
Fixed production overheads	150,000	
TOTAL COST		700,000
PROFIT		200,000

7.3

MAXXA LIMITED
INCOME STATEMENT FOR THE MONTH ENDED 31 JANUARY 20-7

	MARGINAL COSTING		ABSORPTION COSTING	
	£	£	£	£
Sales revenue 3,000 units at £8 each		24,000		24,000
Variable costs				
Direct materials at £1.25 each	5,000		5,000	
Direct labour at £2.25 each	9,000		9,000	
	14,000			
Less Closing inventory (marginal cost*)				
1,000 units at £3.50 each	3,500			
	10,500			
Fixed production overheads	6,000		6,000	
			20,000	
Less Closing inventory (absorption cost*)				
1,000 units at £5 each			5,000	
Less Cost of sales		16,500		15,000
PROFIT		7,500		9,000

* Closing inventory is calculated on the basis of this year's costs:

marginal costing, variable costs only, ie £1.25 + £2.25 = £3.50 per unit

absorption costing, variable and fixed costs, ie £20,000 ÷ 4,000 units = £5 per unit

The difference in the profit is caused only by the closing inventory figures: £3,500 under marginal costing, and £5,000 under absorption costing. With marginal costing, the full amount of the fixed production overheads has been charged in this year's income statement; by contrast, with absorption costing, part of the fixed production overheads (here £6,000 x 25%* = £1,500) has been carried forward in the inventory valuation.

* 1,000 units in stock out of 4,000 units manufactured

7.4   (a)   **ACTIVTOYS LIMITED**
INCOME STATEMENT FOR THE YEAR ENDED 31 DECEMBER 20-1

	MARGINAL COSTING		ABSORPTION COSTING	
	£	£	£	£
Sales revenue at £125 each		162,500		162,500
Variable costs				
Direct materials at £25 each	37,500		37,500	
Direct labour at £30 each	45,000		45,000	
	82,500			
Less Closing inventory (marginal cost*)				
200 frames at £55 each	11,000			
	71,500			
Fixed production overheads	82,500		82,500	
			165,000	
Less Closing inventory (absorption cost*)				
200 frames at £110 each			22,000	
Less Cost of sales		154,000		143,000
PROFIT		8,500		19,500

* Closing inventory is calculated on the basis of this year's costs:

marginal costing, variable costs only, ie £25 + £30 = £55 per frame x 200 frames = £11,000

absorption costing, variable and fixed costs,
ie £165,000 ÷ 1,500 frames = £110 per frame x 200 frames = £22,000

(b)   Reasons for different profit figures:

- The difference in the profit figures is caused by the closing inventory figures: £11,000 under marginal costing and £22,000 under absorption costing – the same costs have been used, but fixed production overheads have been treated differently.

- Only fixed production overheads are dealt with differently using the techniques of marginal and absorption costing – both methods charge non-production overheads in full to the income statement in the year to which they relate.

- With marginal costing, the full amount of the fixed production overheads has been charged in this year's income statement; by contrast, with absorption costing, part of the fixed production overheads (here, £11,000) has been carried forward to next year in the inventory valuation.

Comment on the directors' statement:

- A higher profit does not mean more money in the bank.

- The two costing methods simply treat fixed production overheads differently and, in a year when there is no closing inventory, total profits to date are exactly the same – but they occur differently over the years.

- For financial statements, Activtoys Limited must use the absorption cost inventory valuation of £22,000 in order to comply with IAS 2, *Inventories*.

7.5 (a)

DURNING LIMITED

INCOME STATEMENT FOR THE MONTH ENDED 30 APRIL 20-4

	MARGINAL COSTING		ABSORPTION COSTING	
	£	£	£	£
Sales revenue 8,000 units at £4 each		32,000		32,000
Variable costs				
Direct materials at £0.80 each	8,000		8,000	
Direct labour at £1.60 each	16,000		16,000	
	24,000			
Less Closing inventory (marginal cost*)				
2,000 units at £2.40 each	4,800			
	19,200			
Fixed production overheads	10,000		10,000	
			34,000	
Less Closing inventory (absorption cost*)				
2,000 units at £3.40 each			6,800	
Less Cost of sales		29,200		27,200
PROFIT		2,800		4,800

* Closing inventory is calculated on the basis of this year's costs:

marginal costing, variable costs only, ie £0.80 + £1.60 = £2.40 per unit x 2,000 units = £4,800

absorption costing, variable and fixed costs,
ie £34,000 ÷ 10,000 units = £3.40 per unit x 2,000 units = £6,800

(b)   The difference in the profit figures is caused only by the closing inventory figures: £4,800 under marginal costing, and £6,800 under absorption costing. With marginal costing, the full amount of the fixed production overheads has been charged in this year's income statement; by contrast, under absorption costing, part of the fixed production overheads (here £10,000 x 20%* = £2,000) has been carried forward in the inventory valuation.

   * 2,000 units of closing inventory out of 10,000 units manufactured

7.6 (c)

7.7 (d)

7.8

		Manufacturing account	Income statement
(a)	factory rent	✓	
(b)	production supervisors' wages	✓	
(c)	insurance of factory buildings	✓	
(d)	depreciation of office equipment		✓
(e)	sales commission		✓
(f)	direct materials purchased	✓	
(g)	advertising		✓

7.9

CROWN HEATH MANUFACTURING COMPANY
MANUFACTURING ACCOUNT AND INCOME STATEMENT
for the year ended 31 December 20-6

	£	£
Opening inventory of direct materials		10,500
Add Purchases of direct materials		27,200
		37,700
Less Closing inventory of direct materials		10,200
DIRECT MATERIALS USED		27,500
Direct labour		12,600
PRIME COST		40,100
Add Production (factory) overheads:		
Indirect labour	3,900	
Rent and rates	1,200	
Power	2,000	
Depreciation of factory machinery	900	
Repairs to factory buildings	300	
Sundry factory expenses	900	
		9,200
PRODUCTION (FACTORY) COST OF GOODS MANUFACTURED		49,300
Sales revenue		60,400
Opening inventory of finished goods	4,300	
Production (factory) cost of goods manufactured	49,300	
	53,600	
Less Closing inventory of finished goods	3,200	
COST OF SALES		50,400
Gross profit		10,000
Less Non-production overheads		6,500
Profit for the year		3,500

7.10

<table>
<tr><td colspan="3" align="center">**BARBARA FRANCIS**</td></tr>
<tr><td colspan="3" align="center">**MANUFACTURING ACCOUNT AND INCOME STATEMENT**</td></tr>
<tr><td colspan="3" align="center">**for the year ended 31 December 20-7**</td></tr>
<tr><td></td><td align="center">£</td><td align="center">£</td></tr>
<tr><td>Opening inventory of direct materials</td><td></td><td>31,860</td></tr>
<tr><td>Add Purchases of direct materials</td><td></td><td>237,660</td></tr>
<tr><td></td><td></td><td>269,520</td></tr>
<tr><td>Less Closing inventory of direct materials</td><td></td><td>44,790</td></tr>
<tr><td>DIRECT MATERIALS USED</td><td></td><td>224,730</td></tr>
<tr><td>Direct labour</td><td></td><td>234,630</td></tr>
<tr><td>PRIME COST</td><td></td><td>459,360</td></tr>
<tr><td>Add Production (factory) overheads:</td><td></td><td></td></tr>
<tr><td>Rent and rates</td><td>24,690</td><td></td></tr>
<tr><td>Power</td><td>7,650</td><td></td></tr>
<tr><td>Heat and light</td><td>2,370</td><td></td></tr>
<tr><td>Sundry expenses and maintenance</td><td>8,190</td><td></td></tr>
<tr><td>Depreciation of plant and machinery</td><td>7,450</td><td></td></tr>
<tr><td></td><td></td><td>50,350</td></tr>
<tr><td>PRODUCTION (FACTORY) COST OF GOODS MANUFACTURED</td><td></td><td>509,710</td></tr>
<tr><td>Sales revenue</td><td></td><td>796,950</td></tr>
<tr><td>Opening inventory of finished goods</td><td>42,640</td><td></td></tr>
<tr><td>Production (factory) cost of goods manufactured</td><td>509,710</td><td></td></tr>
<tr><td></td><td>552,350</td><td></td></tr>
<tr><td>Less Closing inventory of finished goods</td><td>96,510</td><td></td></tr>
<tr><td>COST OF SALES</td><td></td><td>455,840</td></tr>
<tr><td>**Gross profit**</td><td></td><td>341,110</td></tr>
<tr><td>Less Non-production overheads:</td><td></td><td></td></tr>
<tr><td>Rent and rates</td><td>8,230</td><td></td></tr>
<tr><td>Salaries</td><td>138,700</td><td></td></tr>
<tr><td>Advertising</td><td>22,170</td><td></td></tr>
<tr><td>Office expenses</td><td>7,860</td><td></td></tr>
<tr><td></td><td></td><td>176,960</td></tr>
<tr><td>**Profit for the year**</td><td></td><td>164,150</td></tr>
</table>

7.11

RYEDALE LIMITED
MANUFACTURING ACCOUNT AND INCOME STATEMENT
for the year ended 31 October 20-4

	£	£
Opening inventory of direct materials		41,210
Add Purchases of direct materials		311,050
		352,260
Less Closing inventory of direct materials		46,380
DIRECT MATERIALS USED		305,880
Direct labour		180,860
PRIME COST		486,740
Add Production (factory) overheads:		
Indirect labour	45,170	
Rent and rates	26,730	
Power	12,040	
Heat and light	5,030	
Sundry expenses and maintenance	10,390	
Depreciation of plant and machinery	12,500	
		111,860
		598,600
Add Opening inventory of work-in-progress		7,200
		605,800
Less Closing inventory of work-in-progress		8,450
PRODUCTION (FACTORY) COST OF GOODS MANUFACTURED		597,350
Sales revenue		874,360
Opening inventory of finished goods	29,470	
Production (factory) cost of goods manufactured	597,350	
	626,820	
Less Closing inventory of finished goods	38,290	
COST OF SALES		588,530
Gross profit		285,830
Less Non-production overheads:		
Rent and rates	8,910	
Administration salaries	154,610	
Advertising	30,780	
Office expenses	10,390	
Depreciation of office equipment	2,500	
		207,190
Profit for the year		78,640

CHAPTER 8: ASPECTS OF BUDGETING

8.1   (c)

8.2   (d)

8.3   (a)

8.4

Flexed budget	True	False
Fixed overheads are shown in the flexed budget at a cost of £24,240		✓
Fixed overheads are shown in the flexed budget at a cost of £21,000		✓
Fixed overheads are shown in the flexed budget at a cost of £20,200	✓	
There is a fixed overheads variance of £800 adverse	✓	
There is a fixed overheads variance of £2,040 adverse		✓
There is no fixed overheads variance		✓

8.5

Cause of variance	Adverse	Favourable
increase in cost of direct materials	✓	
fewer materials are wasted		✓
cheaper direct materials are used		✓
theft of direct materials	✓	
direct labour receives a pay rise	✓	
the supervisor organises the direct labour more efficiently to improve output		✓
overtime is paid to direct labour	✓	
inflation increases the cost of fixed overheads	✓	
a cheaper electricity supplier is used for the fixed overhead		✓
selling prices are increased		✓
there is an increase in the volume of output sold		✓

8.6

BUDGET REPORT				
	Fixed budget	**Actual**	**Variance**	**Favourable (F) or Adverse (A)**
Output level	100%			
	£	£	£	
Direct materials	85,000	83,000	2,000	F
Direct labour	62,000	65,000	3,000	A
Fixed overheads	54,000	59,000	5,000	A
TOTAL	201,000	207,000	6,000	A

8.7

BUDGET REPORT				
	Flexed budget	**Actual**	**Variance**	**Favourable (F) or Adverse (A)**
Output level	90%			
	£	£	£	
Direct materials	4,230	5,200	970	A
Direct labour	9,720	8,900	820	F
Fixed overheads	4,100	4,500	400	A
TOTAL	18,050	18,600	550	A

8.8

	Flexed budget	Actual	Variance	Favourable (F) or Adverse (A)
Volume sold	33,000	33,000		
	£000	£000	£000	
Sales revenue	1,980	1,950	30	A
Less costs:				
Direct materials	605	610	5	A
Direct labour	374	365	9	F
Overheads	650	710	60	A
Operating profit	351	265	86	A

8.9

	Flexed budget	Actual	Variance	Favourable (F) or Adverse (A)
Volume sold	27,500	27,500		
	£000	£000	£000	
Sales revenue	1,750	1,675	75	A
Less costs:				
Direct materials	375	360	15	F
Direct labour	625	645	20	A
Overheads	420	480	60	A
Operating profit	330	190	140	A

CHAPTER 9: SHORT-TERM DECISIONS

9.1

units of output	fixed costs	variable costs	total cost	sales revenue	profit/(loss)*
	£	£	£	£	£
0	7,500	0	7,500	0	(7,500)
500	7,500	2,500	10,000	5,000	(5,000)
1,000	7,500	5,000	12,500	10,000	(2,500)
1,500	7,500	7,500	15,000	15,000	nil
2,000	7,500	10,000	17,500	20,000	2,500
2,500	7,500	12,500	20,000	25,000	5,000
3,000	7,500	15,000	22,500	30,000	7,500

* brackets indicate a loss

9.2 **(a)** **table method**

units of output	fixed costs	variable costs	total cost	sales revenue	profit/(loss)*
	£	£	£	£	£
100	12,000	2,000	14,000	3,500	(10,500)
200	12,000	4,000	16,000	7,000	(9,000)
300	12,000	6,000	18,000	10,500	(7,500)
400	12,000	8,000	20,000	14,000	(6,000)
500	12,000	10,000	22,000	17,500	(4,500)
600	12,000	12,000	24,000	21,000	(3,000)
700	12,000	14,000	26,000	24,500	(1,500)
800	12,000	16,000	28,000	28,000	nil
900	12,000	18,000	30,000	31,500	1,500
1,000	12,000	20,000	32,000	35,000	3,000
1,100	12,000	22,000	34,000	38,500	4,500
1,200	12,000	24,000	36,000	42,000	6,000

* brackets indicate a loss

(b) **graph method**

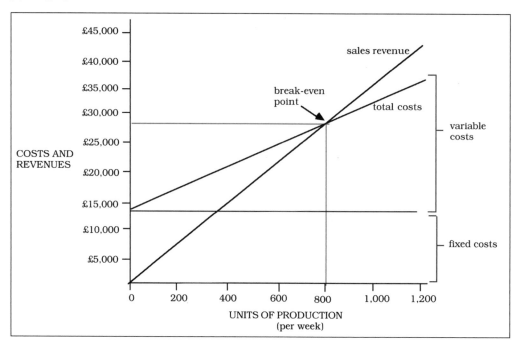

(c) **calculation method**

Fixed costs of £12,000 ÷ contribution of £15 per bat = 800 bats to break-even.

(d) **profit/(loss)**

·   200 bats

	£
Sales (£35 per bat)	7,000
Less variable costs (£20 per bat)	4,000
Contribution	3,000
Less fixed costs	12,000
Loss for month	(9,000)

·   1,200 bats

	£
Sales (£35 per bat)	42,000
Less variable costs (£20 per bat)	24,000
Contribution	18,000
Less fixed costs	12,000
Profit for month	6,000

(e) **margin of safety**

$$\frac{\text{current output} - \text{break-even output}}{\text{current output}} \times \frac{100}{1} = \frac{1,000 - 800}{1,000}$$

= 20 per cent, or 200 units

9.3   (a)   2,000 units

(b)   £56,000

(c)

Units of WV5 sold	2,500	4,000
Margin of safety (units)	500	2,000
Margin of safety percentage	20%	50%

(d)   3,500 units

(e)   D

9.4   **Task 1**

• contribution sales (CS) ratio

$$\frac{\text{contribution (£)}}{\text{selling price (£)}} = \frac{£15^*}{£25} = 0.6 \text{ or } 60\%$$

* selling price £25 – variable cost £10

• break-even point in units

$$\frac{\text{fixed costs (£)}}{\text{contribution per unit (£)}} = \frac{£300,000}{£15} = 20,000 \text{ units}$$

• break-even point in sales revenue

$$\frac{\text{fixed costs (£)}}{\text{CS ratio}} = \frac{£300,000}{0.6} = £500,000$$

check: 20,000 units x selling price £25 per unit = £500,000

• margin of safety at output of 30,000 units

$$\frac{\text{current output} - \text{break-even output}}{\text{current output}} = \frac{30,000 - 20,000}{30,000} \times \frac{100}{1}$$

= 33.3%, or 10,000 units, or £250,000 of sales revenue

• number of units to generate a target profit of £100,000

$$\frac{\text{fixed costs (£)} + \text{target profit (£)}}{\text{contribution per unit (£)}} = \frac{£300,000 + £100,000}{£15} = 26,667 \text{ units}$$

Task 2

		forecast output (30,000 units)	maximum output (40,000 units)
		£	£
	sales revenue (at £25 each)	750,000	1,000,000
less	variable costs (at £10 each)	300,000	400,000
equals	contribution (to fixed costs and profit)	450,000	600,000
less	monthly fixed costs	300,000	300,000
equals	forecast profit for month	150,000	300,000

Task 3

- contribution sales (CS) ratio

$$\frac{£10^*}{£20} \quad = \quad 0.5 \text{ or } 50\%$$

  * selling price £20 – variable cost £10

- break-even point in units

$$\frac{£300,000}{£10} \quad = \quad 30,000 \text{ units}$$

- break-even point in sales revenue

$$\frac{£300,000}{0.5} \quad = \quad £600,000$$

  check: 30,000 units x selling price £20 per unit = £600,000

- margin of safety at maximum output of 40,000 units

$$\frac{40,000 - 30,000}{40,000} \times \frac{100}{1} \quad = 25\%, \text{ or } 10,000 \text{ units, or } £200,000 \text{ of sales revenue}$$

- forecast profit at sales of 40,000 units

		£
	sales revenue (at £20 each)	800,000
less	variable costs (at £10 each)	400,000
equals	contribution (to fixed costs and profit)	400,000
less	monthly fixed costs	300,000
equals	forecast profit for month	100,000

REPORT
To: General Manager
From: Accounts Assistant
Date: Today

Proposal to reduce selling price

Introduction

- You asked me to report on the suggestion from one of the managers that the selling price for our product should be reduced from £25 per unit to £20.

- The manager has suggested that the effect of this reduction would be to increase output from the forecast of 30,000 units per month to our maximum output of 40,000 units per month.

Report

- As can be seen from the workings at current levels of output of 30,000 units per month:
    - contribution sales ratio is 60%
    - break-even point is 20,000 units
    - margin of safety is 33.3%
    - forecast profit is £150,000 per month
- If the manager's suggestion is adopted sales will increase to our maximum output of 40,000 units per month; this will give us:
    - contribution sales ratio of 50%
    - break-even point of 30,000 units
    - margin of safety of 25%
    - forecast profit of £100,000 per month

Conclusion

- From the data summarised above it can be seen that the manager's suggestion would reduce our contribution sales ratio, increase the break-even point, and reduce the margin of safety. All of these are all movements in the wrong direction.

- The main point to note is that forecast profit will fall by £50,000 per month to £100,000 per month, and the volume of output will need to be higher.

- Although we would be working at maximum output if the suggestion is adopted, this does mean that there is no scope to increase output and sales in the future without major changes to our cost structure. We would not be able to meet requests for additional sales from our existing customers, and this could cause them to seek all of their supplies from our competitors.

- For these reasons, I would recommend that the manager's suggestion is not undertaken.

9.5   **Task 1**

Product	'Madrid' £	'Paris' £	'Rome' £
Selling price per unit	30	40	60
Less: Unit variable costs			
Direct materials	10	15	20
Direct labour	5	8	12
Variable overheads	2	3	2.50
Contribution per unit	13	14	25.50

Task 2

Break-even point for the 'Madrid' range is:

$$\frac{\text{fixed costs (£)}}{\text{contribution per unit (£)}} = \frac{£72,800}{£13} = \underline{5,600 \text{ units}}$$

Task 3

Product	'Madrid'	'Paris'	'Rome'
Contribution per unit	£13	£14	£25.50
Machine hours per unit	0.5	0.4	0.75
Contribution per machine hour	£26	£35	£34

Task 4

- Machine hours are the limiting factor here, with only 3,000 hours available.

- To maximise profits, the company should maximise the contribution from each machine hour.

- The preferred order is 'Paris' (at £35 contribution per machine hour), 'Rome' (at £34), and 'Madrid' (at £26).

- The company's production plan will be:

'Paris', 3,000 units x 0.4 hours per unit   = 1,200 hours

'Rome', 500 units x 0.75 hours per unit   =   375 hours

'Madrid', 2,850 units x 0.5 hours per unit   = 1,425 balance of hours available
                                                                    3,000 hours

Note that this production plan does not allow for full production of the 'Madrid' range.

9.6

REPORT

To:	Production Manager
From:	Accounts Assistant
Date:	Today

Production of products A and B

Introduction

- You asked for my recommendations for next week's production.

- Materials used in the production of both products are in short supply and we are currently only able to obtain 500 kgs each week. We therefore need to use these materials to the best advantage of the company.

Report

- With insufficient direct materials we have a limiting factor (or a scarce resource). To make best use of this limiting factor to produce profits for the company, we must maximise the contribution (selling price – variable costs) from each kg of direct material.

- The contribution from producing each unit of A is £30. As this product requires two kgs of material, the contribution per kg is £30 ÷ 2 kgs = £15.

- The contribution from producing each unit of B is £50. As this product requires four kgs of material, the contribution per kg is £50 ÷ 4 kgs = £12.50.

- To make best use of the limiting factor of direct material, the company should produce all of product A that can be sold, ie 200 per week. This will take 400 kgs of materials (200 units x 2 kgs each) and will leave 100 kgs available to produce 25 of product B (25 units x 4 kgs each).

- Please note that, if this production plan is followed, insufficient of product B will be produced to meet demand. This may make it difficult to re-establish it in the market when full production of this product can be resumed once the shortage of direct materials has been resolved.

Conclusion

- Based on the concept of maximising the contribution from each kg of material (the limiting factor), I recommend that the production for next week should be:

    200 units of product A

    25 units of product B

- This will give a forecast income statement for next week as follows:

		product A £	product B £	total £
	Sales revenue:			
	200 product A at £150 per unit	30,000		30,000
	25 product B at £200 per unit		5,000	5,000
		30,000	5,000	35,000
less	Variable costs:			
	200 product A at £120 per unit	24,000		24,000
	25 product B at £150 per unit		3,750	3,750
equals	Contribution	6,000	1,250	7,250
less	Fixed overheads			4,000
equals	Profit			3,250

9.7   Task 1

DURNING FOODS LIMITED: Production line for Indian meals

Planned results for November 20-8

Number of meals to be sold	36,000
	£
Direct materials at 75p per meal	27,000
Direct labour at 45p per meal	16,200
Direct expenses at 20p per meal	7,200
Overheads for Indian meals production line	
at £7,500 + 15p per meal	12,900
Other production overheads	4,000
Total cost	67,300
Sales revenue at £2.00 per meal	72,000
Profit	4,700

Workings (using figures for July):

-     direct materials per meal   = £25,125 ÷ 33,500 meals = £0.75
-     direct labour per meal   = £15,075 ÷ 33,500 meals = £0.45
-     direct expenses per meal   = £6,700 ÷ 33,500 meals = £0.20
-     overheads for Indian meals production line

	meals	*£*
high	34,700	12,705
low	31,000	12,150
difference	3,700	555

    variable cost per meal   = £555 ÷ 3,700 meals   = £0.15

    fixed cost   = £12,525 – (£0.15 x 33,500 meals) = £7,500

-     other production overheads: fixed cost = £4,000 per month
-     sales revenue per meal = £67,000 ÷ 33,500 meals = £2.00

Task 2

DURNING FOODS LIMITED: Production line for Indian meals

Planned results for November 20-8: increased activity

	£
Number of meals to be sold	40,000
Direct materials at 75p – 20% = 60p per meal	24,000
Direct labour at 45p per meal	18,000
Direct expenses at 20p per meal	8,000
Overheads for Indian meals production line at £7,500 + 15p per meal	13,500
Other production overheads	4,000
Total cost	67,500
Sales revenue at £2.00 per meal	80,000
Profit	12,500

Break-even point

		£	£
Contribution per meal:			
	selling price		2.00
less	variable costs:		
	direct materials	0.60	
	direct labour	0.45	
	direct expenses	0.20	
	production line overheads	0.15	
			1.40
equals	contribution per meal		0.60
Fixed costs:			
	production line overheads		7,500
	other production overheads		4,000
			11,500

Break-even point:

$$\frac{£11,500}{£0.60} = 19,167 \text{ meals}$$

Margin of safety

$$\frac{40,000 - 19,167}{40,000} \times \frac{100}{1} = 52\%$$

9.8 The marginal cost per unit of Exe is £5 (direct materials £3 + direct labour £2), and so any contribution, ie selling price less marginal cost, will be profit:

• *200 units at £6 each*

The offer price of £6 is above the marginal cost of £5 and increases profit by the amount of the £1 extra contribution, ie (£6 – £5) x 200 units = £200 extra profit.

• *500 units at £4 each*

This offer price is below the marginal cost of £5; therefore there will be a fall in profit if this order is undertaken of (£4 – £5) x 500 units = £500 reduced profit.

WESTFIELD LIMITED
monthly income statements

	Existing production of 2,000 units	Existing production + 200 units @ £6 each	Existing production + 500 units @ £4 each
	£	£	£
Sales revenue (per month):			
2,000 units at £12 each	24,000	24,000	24,000
200 units at £6 each	–	1,200	–
500 units at £4 each	–	–	2,000
	24,000	25,200	26,000
Less production costs:			
Direct materials (£3 per unit)	6,000	6,600	7,500
Direct labour (£2 per unit)	4,000	4,400	5,000
Production overheads (fixed)	8,000	8,000	8,000
PROFIT	6,000	6,200	5,500

The conclusion is that the first special order should be accepted, and the second declined.

9.9

POPCAN LIMITED
monthly income statements

	Existing production of 150,000 cans	Existing production + 50,000 cans at 18p each
	£	£
Sales revenue (per month):		
150,000 cans at 25p each	37,500	37,500
50,000 cans at 18p each	–	9,000
	37,500	46,500
Less production costs:		
Direct materials (5p per can)	7,500	10,000
Direct labour (5p per can)	7,500	10,000
Production overheads – variable (4p per can)	6,000	8,000
– fixed*	9,000	9,000
PROFIT	7,500	9,500

* 6p x 150,000 cans = £9,000

The offer from the supermarket chain should be accepted because:

- the marginal cost of producing each can is 14p (direct materials 5p, direct labour 5p, variable production overheads 4p)

- the offer price is 18p per can, which is above marginal cost, and gives a contribution of 4p

- profits increase by the amount of the extra contribution, ie (18p – 14p) x 50,000 cans = £2,000 extra profit

CHAPTER 10: LONG-TERM DECISIONS

10.1 (a) payback period

	PROJECT EXE		PROJECT WYE	
Year	Cash Flow	Cumulative Cash Flow	Cash Flow	Cumulative Cash Flow
	£000	£000	£000	£000
0	(80)	(80)	(100)	(100)
1	40	(40)	20	(80)
2	40	–	30	(50)
3	20	20	50	–
4	10	30	50	50
5	10	40	40	90

As can be seen from the above table:
- Project Exe pays back after two years
- Project Wye pays back after three years

(b) net present value

		PROJECT EXE		PROJECT WYE	
Year	Discount Factor	Cash Flow £000	Discounted Cash Flow £000	Cash Flow £000	Discounted Cash Flow £000
0	1.000	(80)	(80)	(100)	(100)
1	0.893	40	35.72	20	17.86
2	0.797	40	31.88	30	23.91
3	0.712	20	14.24	50	35.60
4	0.636	10	6.36	50	31.80
5	0.567	10	5.67	40	22.68
Net Present Value (NPV)			13.87		31.85

REPORT

To:	Robert Smith
From:	Accounts Assistant
Date:	Today

Capital investment projects: Exe and Wye

I have carried out an appraisal of these two projects, based on the information provided. I have used two techniques:

- payback

- net present value

The first of these, payback, sees how long it takes for the initial outlay of the project to be repaid by the net cash flow coming in. For Project Exe, the payback period is two years; for Project Wye, it is three years. Using this technique, Project Exe is more favourable.

Payback is an easy technique both to calculate and understand. However, it does have the disadvantage of ignoring all cash flows after the payback period. With these two projects, Wye has strong cash inflows in years 4 and 5, after the payback period (however, these could be a disadvantage if the project is likely to go out-of-date soon).

The net present value (NPV) technique relies on discounting relevant cash flows at an appropriate rate of return, which is 12 per cent for these projects. Net present value is a more sophisticated technique than payback in that it uses all cash flows and takes the timing of cash flows into account. However, the meaning of NPV is not always clear, and the rate of return required on the projects may vary over their life.

Project Wye has a higher NPV (but also a higher initial cost) at £31,850, when compared with Exe at £13,870. The fact that both figures are positive means that either project will be worthwhile. However, in view of the differing initial costs, it would be appropriate to calculate the internal rate of return, so that a comparison can be made directly between the two projects.

10.2   Task 1

The net cash flows are:

	£000
year 1	(95)
year 2	30
year 3	40
year 4	50
year 5	25

(a)   payback period

Year	Cash Flow	Cumulative Cash Flow	
	£000	£000	
1	(95)	(95)	
2	30	(65)	
3	40	(25)	
4	50	25	∴ £25,000 required
5	25	50	

The design costs are recovered half-way through year 4: £30,000 + £40,000 + (£25,000/£50,000 x 12 months). Thus the payback period is 3 years and 6 months from the start of the project; in terms of revenue, the payback period is 2 years and 6 months. Note that these assume even cash flows during the year.

(b)   net present value

Year	Cash Flow		Discount Factor	Discounted Cash Flow
	£000			£000
1	(95)	x	0.909	(86.36)
2	30	x	0.826	24.78
3	40	x	0.751	30.04
4	50	x	0.683	34.15
5	25	x	0.621	15.53
			Net Present Value (NPV)	18.14

Task 2

• For this new project IRR, at almost 20 per cent, is much higher than the 10% return required on new projects.

• This means that, in financial terms, the new project is acceptable – the wider the margin of IRR above the return required, the better.

10.3 Task 1

DURNING FOODS LIMITED

Working paper for the financial appraisal of purchase of delivery vehicles

DISCOUNTED CASH FLOW

Year	Cash Flow	Discount Factor at 12%	Discounted Cash Flow
	£		£
20-4	(80,000)	1.000	(80,000)
20-5	28,300	0.893	25,272
20-6	28,300	0.797	22,555
20-7	28,300	0.712	20,150
20-8	*38,300	0.636	24,359
Net Present Value (NPV)			12,336

* £28,300 + £10,000 resale value

PAYBACK PERIOD

Year	Cash Flow	Cumulative Cash Flow	
	£	£	
20-4	(80,000)	(80,000)	
20-5	28,300	(51,700)	
20-6	28,300	(23,400)	
20-7	28,300	4,900	£23,400* required
20-8	38,300	43,200	

* £28,300 − £4,900

Payback period =   2 years + (£23,400/£28,300) = 2.8 years, ie 2 years and 10 months

Task 2

	REPORT

To: General Manager

From: Accounts Assistant

Date: 12 November 20-4

Purchase of delivery vehicles

The proposal to purchase delivery vehicles is acceptable from a financial viewpoint because it returns a positive net present value of £12,336 at a discount rate of 12 per cent. This calculation assumes that all cash flows occur at the end of each year.

The payback period is during 20-7. If we assume even cash flows during the year, the payback period can be calculated as 2.8 years (or 2 years and 10 months) from the start. This is acceptable since it is shorter than the company requirement of a maximum of three years, although there is not a great deal of room for error in the cash flow calculations.

10.4   Task 1

The net cash flows are:

	£000
year 0	(40)
year 1	(60)
year 2	45
year 3	54
year 4	90
year 5	60

(a)   payback period

Year	Cash Flow £000	Cumulative Cash Flow £000	
0	(40)	(40)	
1	(60)	(100)	
2	45	(55)	
3	54	(1)	
4	90	89	∴ £1,000 required
5	60	149	

The development costs are recovered in the very early part of year 4: £45,000 + £54,000 + (£1,000/£90,000 x 12 months). Thus the payback period is 3 years and 0.13 months (ie less than one week into the next year) from the start of the project; in terms of revenue, the payback period is 2 years and 0.13 months. Note that these assume even cash flows during the year.

(b)   net present value

Year	Cash Flow		Discount Factor	Discounted Cash Flow
	£000			£000
0	(40)	X	1.000	(40)
1	(60)	X	0.893	(53.58)
2	45	X	0.797	35.86
3	54	X	0.712	38.45
4	90	X	0.636	57.24
5	60	X	0.567	34.02
			Net Present Value (NPV)	71.99

Task 2

REPORT

To: Managing Director

From: Accounts Assistant

Date: Today

Introduction of a new range of bikes

I have carried out an appraisal on the project, based on the information provided.

The net present value technique relies on discounting relevant cash flows at an appropriate rate of return. It would be helpful to know:

1.   whether there are any additional cash flows beyond year 5

2.   whether the introduction of a new range of bikes will affect sales of our existing bikes

On the basis of the information provided, the project has a positive net present value of £71,990 and should be carried out.

10.5 (a)

	Year 0 £000	Year 1 £000	Year 2 £000	Year 3 £000
Capital expenditure	(90)			
Disposal				20
Sales income		55	70	60
Operating costs		(12)	(15)	(19)
Net cash flows	(90)	43	55	61
PV factors	1.0000	0.8696	0.7561	0.6575
Discounted cash flows	(90)	37	42	40
Net present value	29			

or

positive	✓
negative	

(b) The payback period is 1 year and 10 months

ie 43 + (47/55 x 12 months), using net cash flows

10.6 (c)

Appendix

photocopiable documents

INVENTORY RECORD

Date	Receipts			Issues			Balance		
	Quantity (units)	Cost per unit	Total Cost	Quantity (units)	Cost per unit	Total Cost	Quantity (units)	Cost per unit	Total Cost
		£	£		£	£		£	£

EMPLOYEE'S WEEKLY TIME SHEET

	Hours spent on production	Hours worked on indirect work	Notes	Basic pay £	Overtime premium £	Total pay £
Employee:			Cost/Profit/Investment Centre:			
Employee number:			Basic pay per hour:			
Monday						
Tuesday						
Wednesday						
Thursday						
Friday						
Saturday						
Sunday						
Total						

WORK-IN-PROGRESS CALCULATION

Cost element	Costs	Completed Units	Work-in-progress			Total Equivalent Units	Cost per Unit	WIP value
			Units	% complete	Equivalent Units			
	A	B	C	D	E	F	G	H
					C x D	B + E	A ÷ F	E x G
	£						£	£

PROCESS COSTING ACCOUNTS

Dr				Process Account				Cr
	Quantity	Unit cost £	Total cost £		Quantity	Unit cost £	Total cost £

Dr	Abnormal Gain/Loss* Account	Cr
	£	£

* delete as required

Dr	Normal Loss Account	Cr
	£	£

MANUFACTURING ACCOUNT AND INCOME STATEMENT

MANUFACTURING ACCOUNT AND INCOME STATEMENT
for the year ended

	£	£
Opening inventory of direct materials		
Add Purchases of direct materials		
	___	
Less Closing inventory of direct materials		
DIRECT MATERIALS USED	___	
Direct labour		
Direct expenses		
PRIME COST	___	
Add Production (factory) overheads:		
	___	
		___
Add Opening inventory of work-in-progress		___
Less Closing inventory of work-in-progress		
PRODUCTION (FACTORY) COST OF GOODS MANUFACTURED		___
		▬▬
Sales revenue		
Opening inventory of finished goods		
Production (factory) cost of goods manufactured	___	
Less Closing inventory of finished goods	___	
COST OF SALES	___	
Gross profit	___	
Less Non-production overheads:		
	___	
Profit for the year	___	
	▬▬	

BUDGET REPORT

	Flexed budget	**Actual**	**Variance**	**Favourable (F) or Adverse (A)**
Volume sold				
	£000	£000	£000	
Sales revenue				
Less costs:				
Direct materials				
Direct labour				
Overheads				
Operating profit				

REPORT
To:
From:
Date:

Index

for your notes

for your notes

for your notes

for your notes

for your notes

for your notes

for your notes